CH

Lost Legacy

D1603476

Lost Legacy

The Mormon Office of Presiding Patriarch

Second Edition

Irene M. Bates and
E. Gary Smith

UNIVERSITY OF ILLINOIS PRESS
Urbana, Chicago, and Springfield

Library of Congress Cataloging-in-Publication Data

Names: Bates, Irene M., 1921–2015, author. | Smith, E. Gary, 1938– author.

Title: Lost legacy : the Mormon office of Presiding Patriarch / Irene M. Bates and E. Gary Smith.

Description: Second edition. | [Urbana, Illinois] : [University of Illinois Press], [2017] | Includes bibliographical references and index. | Identifiers: LCCN 2017024250 (print) | LCCN 2017025294 (ebook) | ISBN 9780252050138 (ebook) | ISBN 9780252071157 | ISBN 9780252071157 (hardcover : alk. paper) | ISBN 9780252083099 (pbk. : alk. paper)

Subjects: LCSH: Patriarchs (Mormon theology)—History of doctrines. | Smith, Joseph, Sr., 1771–1840. | Smith, Hyrum, 1800–1844. | Smith, William, 1811–1893. | Smith, John, 1781-1854. | Smith, John, 1832–1911. | Smith, Hyrum Gibbs, 1879–1932. | Smith, Joseph F. (Joseph Fielding), 1899–1964. | Smith, Eldred G. (Eldred Gee), 1907–2013. | Mormon Church—United States—Biography. | Church of Jesus Christ of Latter-day Saints—Biography. | LCGFT: Biographies.

Classification: LCC BX8643.P36 (ebook) | LCC BX8643.P36 B37 2017 (print) | DDC 262/.13—dc23

LC record available at https://lccn.loc.gov/2017024250

Contents

Preface to the Second Edition

Lost Legacy: The Mormon Office of Presiding Patriarch was first published in 1996 by the University of Illinois Press.[1] At that time the last patriarch to hold the position of Patriarch to the Church was only eighty-nine years old. "Only," because Eldred Gee Smith lived another seventeen years, to the age of 106. Thus, the final chapter of this interesting office in the Mormon ecclesiastical hierarchy was still unwritten at that time. The story of those final years is now included in this new edition.[2]

Those emeritus years were different from the way Eldred would have spent them as an active General Authority, but they were also different from those of other emeritus General Authority Seventies. Those years involved a unique emeritus status—one that included significant active General Authority dimensions, but with an invisibility that resulted in a sometimes complex and uncomfortable situation for Patriarch Smith. This revised edition inserts a new chapter to tell this story; it also contains a few corrections and footnote additions in other parts of the book. This preface has been expanded to include personal comments from the author of this new edition.

Eldred G. "Gee" Smith was called to be Patriarch to the Church in 1947. His eldest son, E. (Eldred) Gary Smith, was then nine years old. Eldred was the eighth person to hold the hereditary office that had descended from father to eldest son through the lineage of Joseph Smith Sr. Gary remembers that shortly after his father had been made Patriarch to the Church, several men in his ward asked him at different times if he was the eldest son in the family. They then congratulated him, told him he had a great heritage to live up to, and assured him that someday he would follow his father as the Patriarch to the Church. Gary has no recollection of discussing any of this with his father until well after he was an adult. However, soon after the encounters with the men in the ward he recalls going to his mother[3] to ask what this was all about. She confirmed that there was a tradition of this office going from eldest son to eldest son, starting with Joseph Smith Sr. and Hyrum Smith. However, she was adamant: "It may never happen. Never plan on it. Don't make decisions based on it. Always live so that if it occurs you will be worthy of it."

As Gary later learned from his parents and other family members, this was not the message that Eldred received from *his* mother, Martha Electa Gee Smith.[4] Martha was anxious for her son to follow in the steps of her husband. Shortly before Hyrum G. Smith's death at age fifty-two he asked Martha to bring Eldred so that he could ordain him as successor to the office of Presiding Patriarch, similar to the way Joseph Smith Sr. shortly before his death, had bestowed the office on Hyrum Smith. Martha assured Hyrum that he was not going to die at such a young age, and so no ordination took place.[5] But he did die, and after that Martha wanted very much for her son to succeed her husband in the patriarchal office.[6]

As discussed in chapter 8, Eldred waited ten years after the death of his father before he learned that the decision had been made to call someone else to the position. George Albert Smith, when referring to this decision in his journal, said he was disappointed, and added, "I am sure that Martha and Eldred will feel bad about it."[7] It is telling that George Albert Smith was concerned not just that Eldred would feel bad, but Martha also. He knew that Martha saw the office as her son's birthright. This feeling of birthright entitlement was inculcated into Eldred's vision of his life's purpose.

During Gary's mission to the British Isles from 1958 to 1960, Selvoy J. Boyer, the first president of the London Temple, shared with him stories about the history of the office of Church Patriarch. Gary had not known that there were controversial aspects to the history. After completing law school and settling down to his profession Gary began collecting information and documents with the intent of someday writing a history of the office. In the late 1970s Gary received encouragement from Leonard Arrington (then Church Historian), Valleen Tippets Avery, and Linda Newell to begin writing the book. At the 1980 Mormon History Association annual meeting he received further encouragement from Jan Shipps, Lavina Fielding Anderson, and others.

Gary then asked long-time friend Irene Bates if she would work with him on the project. She agreed. The research was not easy. D. Michael Quinn, an accomplished historian of the Mormon hierarchy even at that time, said in an early letter to Gary, "There is no single source or set of sources that provide the evidence for the kind of study that you desire." He noted, too, the sketchiness of the diaries of Hyrum Smith (1800–1844), Uncle John Smith (1781–1854), young John Smith (1832–1911), and Hyrum Gibbs Smith (1879–1932)—all important persons in the contemplated history. Quinn concluded his letter by pointing out, "The only way one could do the kind of study you want is for them to read virtually every possible document of interest in Mormon History for the purpose of collecting those many needles in thousands of haystacks that would make such a study of the patriarchal office possible."

Gary and Irene began searching haystacks for needles, and along the way each of them published several articles on their subject. They accessed archives from coast to coast and scoured both primary and secondary sources. During a hiatus in Gary's available time Irene returned to UCLA, where she had been valedictorian of her class a few years before, and obtained her master's degree. She then received her doctorate in history in 1991, having drawn on the research from the book project for her dissertation.

Then the writing of this book began in earnest. Throughout, Irene and Gary enjoyed the unique benefits of friendship with others in the field of Mormon history. Many knowledgeable scholars, as well as Smith family members, shared freely their sources and information. Among those in this category are Valeen Tippetts Avery, Ian Barber, Maureen Ursenbach Beecher, Gary Bergera, Bunny and Verona Clark, Lyndon Cook, Joseph Geisner, B. Carmon Hardy, Cleone Isom, William Knecht, Linda King Newell, Greg Prince, D. Michael Quinn, Ralph and Geneva Smith, Brian Stuy, and Buddy Youngreen.

The authors are grateful for the courtesy and professional assistance of the librarians and staff of the Beinecke Rare Books and Manuscripts Library, Yale University, Coe Collection, New Haven, Connecticut; Harold B. Lee Library, Brigham Young University, Provo, Utah; Henry E. Huntington Library and Art Gallery, San Marino, California; Historical Department of the Church of Jesus Christ of Latter-day Saints, Salt Lake City, Utah; RLDS Library-Archives, Independence, Missouri; University of Utah Marriott Library, Salt Lake City, Utah; State Historical Society of Wisconsin, Madison, Wisconsin; and the Utah State Historical Society, Salt Lake City, Utah.

It would be impossible to name all those who gave advice and encouragement, but among them are Lavina Fielding Anderson, Leonard Arrington, Lowell L. Bennion, Ruth Bloch, Daniel Walker Howe, Jeffrey Johnson, Stanley Kimball, David Shibley, and Jan Shipps.

The Church of Jesus Christ of Latter-day Saints has not reviewed or approved any edition of this book, and the authors, and the authors alone, take full responsibility for what is written. The permission of Patriarch Eldred G. Smith to use his personal papers as a resource for this book is especially appreciated. His cooperation was extended from the beginning of the project, and he provided written permission for the use of his papers on October 5, 1990. It must be made clear, however, that this book was not approved by Patriarch Smith, nor is it in any way his product. He did not participate in the research or writing. During a visit with Gary in California, Gary shared with his father the chapter dealing with Eldred's incumbency and summarized the book in general. Eldred replied, "This is a story that needs to be told." Although he later requested that the efforts on the book be discontinued, in subsequent conversations it appeared that Eldred's only objection was to the conclusion in the book that the retirement of the office was inevitable, appropriate, and necessary.

The authors also express their deep-felt thanks to their families for their patience, encouragement, and assistance. Elizabeth Shaw Smith donated her professional editing talent in preliminary revisions of both the original and this new edition of the book. She also contributed to the narrative, both substantively and technically. William Bates gave unfailing support throughout, and he "held down the fort" during times when Irene was busy with this project. The writing of the book has been a labor of love—and fueled the mutual respect that always existed between the authors.

When Gary moved back to Utah in 2008 after practicing law in California for over forty years, Eldred was one hundred years old. For six years Gary spent a great amount of time with his father. They became best friends. The conversations were in-depth and enlightening. Eldred was a man without guile, and sometimes this got him into trouble, but there was no trace of the chameleon in him. What you saw, virtues and flaws alike, was what you got. It was a refreshing characteristic. Eldred gave more than eighteen thousand patriarchal blessings. Countless people have told him and Gary how those blessings benefited their lives. May the man and his office rest in peace.

Notes

1. The first paperback edition was published in 2003, also by the University of Illinois Press.

2. Co-author, Irene M. Bates, passed away on August 10, 2015.

3. Jeanne Audrey Ness Smith (1908–1977).

4. Martha was a direct descendant of Asael Smith, brother of Joseph Smith Sr.

5. See p. 165, chap. 7.

6. During a 1971 meeting of the Twelve while discussing the office of Patriarch, the minutes say that "others mentioned that his [Patriarch Smith's] mother may have influenced him unduly in the years that he was not called to serve as Patriarch to the Church." Later Patriarchal Blessings of the Church of Jesus Christ of Latter-day Saints, compiled by H. Michael Marquardt, Smith-Pettit Foundation, Salt Lake City, 2012, p. xlvi—quoting minutes of the regular meeting of the Quorum of the Twelve Apostles, April 22, 1971.

7. See chap. 8, n36.

Lost Legacy

Prologue

Eldred G. Smith, the Patriarch of the Church of Jesus Christ of Latter-day Saints, had no premonition of what would follow when he was summoned to the office of Spencer W. Kimball, president of the Mormon church, in early October 1979. Certainly the general membership of the church did not anticipate that the prestigious office of Patriarch to the Church, part of the hierarchy from the very beginning, would be eliminated. It was an office the Prophet Joseph Smith himself had bestowed by revelation upon his family and their descendants.

President Kimball sat at his desk, and on either side were his counselors, N. Eldon Tanner and Marion G. Romney. The president began by telling Eldred how much his services had been appreciated over the years, and then he said that Eldred would be designated an "emeritus" general authority at the upcoming October General Conference of the church. Eldred would retain his living allowance, as had been the case with the other general authorities who had been made emeritus. The official work heretofore accomplished by the Patriarch to the Church would now be carried on by the stake (local) patriarchs.

Eldred was stunned. Sensing that this explanation might mean the elimination of the office of Church Patriarch altogether, not simply his own retirement, he asked about the effect this would have on the local patriarchs. President Kimball replied that Eldred did not preside over the local patriarchs. Eldred expressed additional concerns about eliminating an office established by revelation. President Kimball, after conferring privately with President Romney, said, "You agree that we can make changes, don't you?" Eldred replied that he would abide by the decision of the president of the church, since the president had the authority and responsibility for such matters.

There was some additional brief discussion, during which President Tanner did the speaking to ease the stress on President Kimball's ailing voice. Eldred was assured that he was not being released from the opportunity to give patriarchal blessings and that he would continue to be provided office space for that purpose. President Kimball then said that the Brethren thought he would feel good about this. Eldred replied that he would accept the decision because he did not have any choice but that he did not feel good about it.

This decision finally eliminated the tension, existing since Hyrum Smith's death in 1844, between holders of the lineal office of Presiding Patriarch and members of the Quorum of the Twelve Apostles. This tension, which Max Weber maintains is inevitable during the transformation of charismatic movements, was between those holding office by virtue of an inherited "familial charisma" and those claiming "office charisma," that is, through appointment to office by the laying on of hands by existing officers. The Mormon church's solution was to do away with the problematic office of Church Patriarch.

On October 6, 1979, during the sustaining of officers at the semiannual General Conference of the church, President N. Eldon Tanner read a statement that announced the designation of Eldred G. Smith as Patriarch Emeritus because "of the large increase in the number of stake patriarchs and the availability of patriarchal service throughout the world." This was later reported in the November *Ensign* magazine. There was no further comment. The only other announcement from the church came in the October 13 edition of the *Church News* (a weekly insert to the *Deseret News,* a church-owned daily in Salt Lake City). It had a small item at the bottom of page 24 entitled "New Leaders Named." After listing some reassignments of auxiliary leaders, it stated at the end, "ANOTHER PERSONNEL CHANGE among the General Authorities was the announcement that Elder Eldred G. Smith, patriarch to the church, is now appointed patriarch emeritus to the church. He is released honorably from the patriarchal duties since in most parts of the world stakes now have their own patriarchs who provide the necessary blessings."

By contrast, the *Salt Lake Tribune* (the rival daily newspaper in Salt Lake City, which is not controlled by the church) ran an article on October 9 noting that no successor had been named to the position vacated by Patriarch Smith and adding that "there has been speculation among the church members that the position of Patriarch to the Church is being abolished or that Patriarch Smith and his position are being 'placed on the shelf.' Mr. [Charles] Gibbs [of Church Public Communications] said he could neither deny nor confirm the speculation, but said the reasons for the change and the future of the position will be brought up Wednesday during an early morning meeting with President [N. Eldon] Tanner [of the First Presidency]."

Nothing further was reported by the *Tribune,* and the meeting with President Tanner to which Gibbs referred might well have been an occasion when Gibbs was simply receiving instructions on what he was to say when asked about the ambiguous announcement at the conference and in the *Deseret News*. The answer was most certainly, "Say nothing." Indeed, nothing has been said since.

If the announcement was not clear to the public, it was not clear to Eldred either. Several days after the announcement, Eldred encountered a senior apostle and asked if the Brethren were going to call someone to replace him. The apostle replied that no one was going to be called to replace him, that the intent was to retire the office.

Indeed, it was through the announcement of Eldred's emeritus status that the office was retired. No official announcement of the abolition of the office was ever made. Ironically, since Eldred's responsibilities immediately before the announcement had already been diminished to only giving blessings, and since he was fully authorized to continue to do so, Eldred personally was not retired at all. So why the change in official status? Answers to that question can only be found within the complex history of this initially very important, primal office.

Introduction

Also there is provided a presiding patriarch over all the patriarchs of the church, and he is known as the presiding patriarch of the church, holding the keys of the patriarchal blessings upon the heads of the Lord's people . . . and he presides over, instructs and directs the labors of all the patriarchs of the church.

—B. H. Roberts, *A Comprehensive History of the Church of Jesus Christ of Latter-day Saints*

The office of Presiding Patriarch, or Church Patriarch, was long an important calling in the organization of the LDS priesthood. When the founding prophet, Joseph Smith, Jr., ordained his father as Church Patriarch on December 18, 1833, he said that Joseph Smith, Sr., would hold "the keys of the patriarchal priesthood over the kingdom of God on earth, even the Church of the Latter-day Saints."[1] The office was the second unit of the church hierarchy to be established, more than twelve months before even the twelve apostles were called.

Then, almost 146 years later, at the October 1979 General Conference of the church, the incumbent patriarch, Eldred G. Smith, was declared "emeritus," an action that eliminated the hierarchical office of Church Patriarch.[2] This was particularly surprising in light of past pronouncements by Mormon officials that the office would always exist. The Prophet Joseph Smith said in 1839 that "whenever the Church of Christ is established in the earth, there should be a Patriarch for the benefit of the posterity of the Saints."[3] On December 27, 1847, Brigham Young, president of the Quorum of the Twelve, declared that "it was necessary to keep up a full organization of the Church through all time as far as could be. At least the three first Presidency, quorum of the Twelve, Seventies, and Patriarch over the whole Church &c so that the devil could take no Advantage of us."[4]

From Old Testament times there has been a general acceptance of the idea of patriarchal authority and order. The hereditary office of Patriarch in the LDS Church had historical roots in the Old Testament. As part of the Mormon "restoration of all things," this literal manifestation of the return to "first times" was consistent with the primitivism celebrated by the new nation during the first half of the nineteenth century. Mormonism's primitivism, however, reaches beyond the early Christian church to the beginning of time itself and embraces patriarchy as a divine, eternal order.[5] The Mormon patriarch was initially told he was accorded all the rights, dignity, and authority enjoyed by the Ancients. Insofar as his place in the ecclesiastical structure is concerned, however, only during a relatively short period of time did the Mormon patriarch share executive authority with the Prophet, although at times he did have jurisdiction over local patriarchs.

While the office of Mormon patriarch existed, it differed significantly from patriarchal offices familiar for centuries in other religious orders. It had little in common with patriarchs in early Christian and Greek Orthodox churches. When Christianity was recognized as the Roman state religion in A.D. 313, the church adapted its ecclesiastical organization to mirror that of the state, and patriarchs became chief executive officers. Bishops of the larger towns were given jurisdiction over dioceses, and the title of archbishop, exarch, or patriarch, was bestowed on them. The root of *patriarch* is *patri,* meaning "father"; it evoked not only the respect accorded Old Testament patriarchs but also the homage due God the Father. The pope of Rome, after the fifth century and following much disputation over succession and jurisdiction, became the "Holy Father of the Catholic Church." Like the word *patriarch, pope* means "father"; Catholic bishops, too, are addressed as "father."

The title "patriarch" carried even greater weight in the East. Patriarchates were of equal authority at first and were independent of Rome, and over time each developed its own hierarchical organization, rituals, and dogma. Although the office included spiritual power, the patriarchate was also an administrative calling. In Alexandria, local bishops were placed directly under the patriarch; by the fourth century the patriarch headed more than one hundred dioceses. About A.D. 500 the patriarch of Constantinople received the title "ecumenical"; that is, he became the patriarch standing at the head of the whole Eastern Empire. In the early Gregorian, or Armenian church, there were twelve hereditary patriarchs, appointed by Gregory from converted pagan priestly families. (Gregory himself, of royal blood, was in supreme command as "Catholicus.") During later centuries some of these Eastern groups joined with Rome, adjusting their rites and liturgies to conform with Roman orthodoxy. These patriarchs would then function as an archbishop does in the Western Catholic church, responsible to the central authority in Rome.

Despite the historical honor and power associated with the title, the Mormon Patriarchate, unlike the early Christian patriarchs, for the most part had only an honorary, not an executive, role in the ecclesiastical organization. The purpose of this study is to provide a history of the office of the Presiding Patriarch of (or Patriarch to) the Church of Jesus Christ of Latter-day Saints from the office's inception in 1833 to its demise in 1979. The authors have found sociologist Max Weber's pioneering work on the development of religious institutions to be especially helpful to their study. Drawing a general framework from Weber's analysis, this study focuses on the following questions: What was the history and context of the origin of the office? What was the definition and authority of the office during its existence? What were the dynamics of the office, including the responsibilities of the office and the personalities of the incumbents as they related to the other members of the hierarchy? What was the Patriarch's relationship with local patriarchs? What factors contributed to the decline and eventual demise of this significant office? Finally, what lessons can be learned as we reflect on the birth, troubled life, and elimination of this ecclesiastical position?

The history of the office of Church Patriarch has received little attention from scholars. Brief sketches of particular patriarchs have appeared in Mormon church publications, and a biography of Hyrum Smith was published in 1963.[6] There are unpublished biographies of two church patriarchs, Joseph Smith, Sr., and William Smith, in the form of master's theses.[7] Several essays in unofficial Mormon journals have addressed specific time periods or particular aspects of the calling, but there has not been any overall treatment of the office itself.[8] Yet for 146 years the Patriarch to the Church was an important and honorable office with significant historical continuity.

The calling of Presiding Patriarch was, in practice, the only hereditary office in the church. When Joseph Smith, Sr., was ordained Patriarch in 1833, it was stated that this calling would be his "and his seed after him to the uttermost."[9] According to the former official church historian Apostle Joseph Fielding Smith, "The Lord foreshadowed the coming of this priesthood as it would descend upon the head of Hyrum Smith [elder brother of the Prophet Joseph, and Church Patriarch from 1841–44]."[10] In a revelation given at Manchester, New York, in April 1830, Hyrum was told, "Thy duty is unto the church forever, and this because of thy family."[11] On March 28, 1835, a revelation was recorded stating that "the order of this priesthood was confirmed to be handed down from father to son and rightly belongs to the literal descendants of the chosen seed, to whom the promises were made."[12] These words echo the promise made to Abraham and later to Isaac and Jacob.[13] When Hyrum succeeded his father in 1841, the office was "appointed unto him by his father by blessing and also by right."[14] Between 1833 and 1979 there have been eight incumbents, all descendants of Joseph Smith, Sr., with the exception of his brother, "Uncle John," who replaced William Smith (Uncle John's nephew and the brother of the Prophet) after William was excommunicated.[15]

The function of the Patriarch was to bless the church and its people, according to the ancient order as described in the Old Testament book of Genesis. Mormon scripture said of Hyrum, "From henceforth he shall hold the keys of the patriarchal blessings upon the heads of all my people. That whoever he blesses shall be blessed, and whoever he curses shall be cursed; that whatsoever he shall bind on earth shall be bound in heaven; and whatsoever he shall loose on earth shall be loosed in heaven."[16] Hyrum would "hold the sealing blessings of my church, even the Holy Spirit of promise, whereby ye are sealed up unto the day of redemption."[17]

Patriarchal blessings represent personal revelations from God to all who request one and who are deemed worthy. Following a short interview that may provide some knowledge of the recipient's background and personality, the Patriarch lays his hands on the head of the person seeking a blessing and pronounces blessings as he is inspired to do. Traditionally, the blessings contain an inspired and prophetic statement of the life mission of the recipient, together with such blessings, cautions, and admonitions that the Patriarch may be prompted to give for the accomplishment of such life's mission. It is always clear that the realization of all promised blessings are conditioned upon faithfulness to the gospel.[18]

In bestowing a blessing, the Patriarch, if so inspired, may declare the specific tribe of Israel through which blessings will come. Mormons believe that it is "through the lineage of Abraham alone that the mighty blessings of the Lord for His children on earth are to be consummated."[19] This is directly related to the promise made to Abraham in Genesis 22:18 that "in thy seed shall all the nations of the earth be blessed; because thou hast obeyed my voice." Although some early leaders believed the declaration of lineage was a statement of actual blood descendancy, it also has been taught that it does not matter whether this lineage is of blood or adoption.[20] As Patriarch Eldred G. Smith explained, "Many of us are mixtures of several tribes of Israel, and so it is the right of the patriarch to declare that line through which the blessings of Israel shall come."[21]

Administrative duties associated with the office of Patriarch included presiding over local patriarchs. Until 1932 the Church Patriarch had, by definition, the right to preside over stake patriarchs. An official history of the church, published in 1930, states, "Also there is provided a presiding patriarch over all the patriarchs of the church . . . and he presides over, instructs, and directs the labors of all the [local] patriarchs of the church."[22] Generally, however, the Presiding Patriarch was perceived as the spiritual father of the entire church. He was the honorary father to the church rather than an actual authority figure. By 1979, when the office was eliminated, the Church Patriarch was no longer presiding over local patriarchs. He functioned simply as a bestower of blessings, a role that remained undisturbed by the announcement that he was now "emeritus." Despite previous authoritative statements that the office must always exist in the church hierarchy, the once significant hereditary office of Church Patriarch was deemed redundant and was itself retired.

The official explanation would be that there were now sufficient local patriarchs to carry on the work. Closer historical scrutiny, however, reveals other reasons for the institutional change. This study, besides chronicling a history of the office and its incumbents, outlines the reasons behind the decline and eventual abolition of the patriarchate.

Chapter 1 establishes the theoretical framework for this study, namely, Max Weber's "ideal types" of authority in an institution. The chapter examines the evolution of a religious movement, dominated by a charismatic individual, into a rationalized social and religious institution. Chapter 2 recounts the emergence of the office of Presiding Patriarch when Joseph Smith, Sr., is ordained as the first patriarch. Chapter 3 highlights the zenith of the office of Patriarch during the tenure of Hyrum Smith, eldest son of the first patriarch. It ends with the assassination of Patriarch Hyrum Smith and his brother, the Prophet Joseph Smith, Jr., in June 1844.

Chapter 4 deals with the pivotal succession crisis that followed the death of the martyrs. This period was a watershed in the history of the patriarchal office, as well as for the church itself. The third patriarch, William Smith, played a significant role, whose echoes have since affected the way in which the office has been regarded.

Chapter 5 discusses the tenure of the fourth patriarch, "Uncle" John Smith, brother of Joseph Smith, Sr. Chapter 6 covers the fifty-year incumbency of the fifth patriarch, young John Smith (Hyrum's son). Chapter 7 traces the evolution of the office toward its second major crisis. Hyrum G. Smith, John's grandson and the sixth patriarch, represents perhaps the most effective incumbent since his great-grandfather, Hyrum. Yet his very effectiveness also served to highlight the continuing dilemma the office created for the church hierarchy.

After the death of Hyrum G. Smith in 1932, the basic difficulties inherent in the office of Church Patriarch were made manifest in a ten-year hiatus, discussed in chapter 8. It was not until 1942 that the president of the church and the Quorum of the Twelve were able to reconcile their differences about a successor to the office. The compromise involved calling Joseph F. Smith II instead of the legitimate heir, Eldred G. Smith.[23] The troubling resignation of Joseph F. Smith II four years later resulted in Eldred G. Smith's assuming his long-delayed rightful position.

Chapter 9 deals with the active General Authority period of Eldred Gee Smith, which continued the debate over the relevancy and scope of the office. Adjustments were made in the functions formerly performed by the Presiding Patriarch, culminating in moving the man and the office into an emeritus status in 1979. Chapter 10 in this new edition explains the unique emeritus status that Patriarch Smith lived with for the next thirty-five years, and why it was a different emeritus status than any other emeritus General Authority, including the issue of how a "prophet, seer, and revelator" should or could be emeritized. The last chapter draws some conclusions about the history of his office, a calling that had claimed legitimacy through "familial charisma" (to use Weberian terminology for hereditary leadership) within a church that had chosen "office charisma" as more compatible with the worldwide institution.

Notes

1. Manuscript History of the Church, December 18, 1833, Oliver Cowdery, clerk and recorder, Archives of the Church of Jesus Christ of Latter-day Saints, Salt Lake City, quoted in Joseph Fielding Smith, comp., *Teachings of the Prophet Joseph Smith* (1938; reprint, Salt Lake City: Deseret Book, 1969), 38–40.

2. It is ironic that the office of Church Patriarch, an important symbol of the patriarchal order, was retired at the very time when the church—in response to growing feminist criticism—was actively engaged in *reasserting* the patriarchal nature of the priesthood.

3. As quoted by Franklin D. Richards and James A. Little, *A Compendium of the Doctrines of the Gospel* (1882; reprint, Salt Lake City: Deseret News, 1925), 73. In this text, Apostle Franklin D. Richards commented, "As the singular number is here used, exclusively, doubtless the Prophet Joseph, in the above passage, speaks of the Patriarch of the whole Church."

4. Scott G. Kenney, ed., *Wilford Woodruff's Journal, 1833–1898*, 3 vols. (Midvale, Utah: Signature Books, 1983–85), 3:301.

5. The pervasive myth of a restoration of "first times" has been explored by Richard T. Hughes and C. Leonard Allen in *Illusions of Innocence: Protestant Primitivism in America, 1630–1875* (Chicago: University of Chicago Press, 1988), 133–52.

6. H. Pearson Corbett, *Hyrum Smith, Patriarch* (Salt Lake City: Deseret Book, 1963).

7. Earnest M. Skinner, "Joseph Smith, Sr.: First Patriarch to the Church" (M.S. thesis, Brigham Young University, 1958); Calvin Rudd, "William Smith, Brother of the Prophet Joseph Smith" (M.A. thesis, Brigham Young University, 1973).

8. *Dialogue: A Journal of Mormon Thought* has published several essays on the subject: Irene M. Bates, "William Smith, 1811–1893: Problematic Patriarch," 16 (Summer 1983): 11–23; E. Gary Smith, "The Patriarchal Crisis of 1845,"

16 (Summer 1983): 24–35; Paul M. Edwards, "William B. Smith: The Persistent Pretender," 18 (Summer 1985): 128–39; Irene M. Bates, "Uncle John Smith, 1781–1854: Patriarchal Bridge," 20 (Fall 1987): 79–89. See also E. Gary Smith, "The Office of Presiding Patriarch: The Primacy Problem," *Journal of Mormon History* 14 (1988): 35–47.

9. Quoted in Joseph Fielding Smith, comp., *Teachings of the Prophet*, 39.

10. Joseph Fielding Smith, *Doctrines of Salvation*, 3 vols., comp. Bruce R. McConkie (Salt Lake City: Bookcraft, 1954–56), 3:164.

11. *Doctrine and Covenants of the Church of Jesus Christ of Latter-day Saints* (Salt Lake City: Deseret Book, 1955), 23:3.

12. *Doctrine and Covenants* 107:40.

13. Genesis 22:18, 26:4, and 28:4.

14. *Doctrine and Covenants* 124:91.

15. William Smith was called to be the Patriarch when the heir-apparent to the office, young John Smith—Hyrum's son—was only twelve years of age. Details of the excommunication of William are discussed in chapter 4.

16. *Doctrine and Covenants* 124:92–93. This echoes the words of Christ to Peter, "And I will give unto thee the keys of the kingdom of heaven: and whatsoever thou shalt bind on earth shall be bound in heaven; and whatsoever thou shalt loose on earth shall be loosed in heaven." Matthew 16:19.

17. *Doctrine and Covenants* 124:123–24. David John Buerger, "The Fulness of the Priesthood: The Second Anointing in Latter-day Saint Theology and Practice," *Dialogue: A Journal of Mormon Thought* 16 (Spring 1983): 14, explains the changes involved in sealing ordinances in the church. In 1831, for example, high priests were allowed to "seal [persons] up unto eternal life."

18. *The Handbook for Stake Patriarchs* (after 1963), cited in R. Clayton Brough and Thomas W. Grassley, *Understanding Patriarchal Blessings* (Bountiful, Utah: Horizon, 1984), 35.

19. John A. Widtsoe, "What Is the Meaning of Patriarchal Blessings?" *Improvement Era* 45 (January 1942), cited in Brough and Grassley, *Understanding Patriarchal Blessings*, 35.

20. Apostle James L. Faust, in a speech given as recently as March 30, 1980, at Brigham Young University, offered comfort to those "who are not of the blood lineage of a specific tribe of Jacob." He said that "no one need assume he or she will be denied blessings by reason of not being of the blood lineage of Israel." He also spoke of being "spiritually begotten" through faith and quoted Joseph Smith as teaching that the Holy Ghost would "purge out the old blood," making one actually of the seed of Abraham. James L. Faust, "Patriarchal Blessings," in *Devotional Speeches* (Provo, Utah: Brigham Young University Press, 1981), 53–57.

21. Eldred G. Smith, "Lectures on Theology: Last Message Series," Address given at the Salt Lake Institute of Religion, April 30, 1971, 2, Eldred G. Smith Personal Records, Salt Lake City. Many Mormons, both leaders and rank and file, still believe there is a direct blood relationship.

22. B. H. Roberts, *A Comprehensive History of the Church of Jesus Christ of Latter-day Saints: Century I*, 6 vols. (Salt Lake City: Deseret News Press,

1930), 1:387. This was an official, church-authorized compilation.

23. Joseph F. Smith II was descended from Hyrum Smith's *second* wife, Mary Fielding. Eldred was the eldest son of the previous incumbent, who was the eldest grandson of Patriarch John Smith, who was the eldest son of the Patriarch Hyrum Smith and his *first* wife, Jerusha Barden. Primogeniture was the prescribed pattern from the beginning, though departures were necessary when the rightful heir was too young.

1

Charisma and Authority

The Crucible for the Office of Patriarch

It is the fate of charisma . . . to recede with the development of
permanent institutional structures.

—Max Weber, *Economy and Society*

Over the past 160 years the Mormon church has grown from a small,
charismatic religious movement into a worldwide centralized bureaucracy.
It is misleading, however, to view the growth of any institution as simply
an increase in the size of the membership. The sociologist Max Weber
has suggested that the internal dynamics of all institutions go through
somewhat predictable metamorphoses. These phenomena, as applied to
the growth of the Mormon church, help explain much of the birth, troubled life, and demise of the office of Presiding Patriarch.

Weberian dynamics at play in this history are discussed here so later
chapters can be more easily understood. We do not assume that historical or sociological theories or paradigms are ever exact in their application, but we do find the Weberian theories particularly useful for explaining the conflict between the lineal office of Patriarch and the other offices
of authority in the Mormon church following the martyrdom of the
prophet Joseph Smith and his patriarch brother, Hyrum Smith.

The concept of authority is central to any study of institutional development. Without a structure for authority, there simply cannot be an institution. Whenever two or more people purport to act together toward
a common purpose, whether it be a business, a religion, a political movement, or any other group, there must be some authority to determine
what the parameters of the group are, or the group does not become an
institution. Who mediates disputes and what rules govern? How are the
rules defined and changed, and who gets to be involved in the process?
Anarchy is the antithesis of institutional stability.

A classic theoretical framework proposed by Max Weber as an aid for studying change in institutions suggests "ideal types" of authority or "domination," which provide structural models that help to define types of religious authority (see table 1). These three types of influence or order are (1) "charismatic," (2) "traditional," and (3) "legal/rational." We refer to these categories in the chapters that follow. These models help reveal the uniqueness of a particular expression of authority and at the same time illuminate the process by which change in leadership takes place and the consequences of such change.

Weber describes *charismatic authority* as that which "knows no abstract laws and regulations and no formal adjudication. Its 'objective law' flows from the highly personal experience of divine grace and god-like heroic strength and rejects all external order solely for the sake of glorifying genuine prophetic and heroic ethos." Weber defines charisma itself as "the specifically creative revolutionary force of history."[1]

Traditional authority is described as depersonalized or routinized charisma, in the sense that it can be transferable through "familial charisma" (hereditary blood lines) or through "office charisma," which is attained by a "magical" transference of authority by the laying on of hands by members of an inner group of disciples, as in apostolic succession.[2] According to Reinhard Bendix, "Familial charisma depends upon kinship ties, and institutional [or office] charisma requires a separation from such ties."[3] In other words, traditional authority can function either through a hereditary scheme or through an orderly transference of office but not both. Where both are present, one *must* essentially give way to the other.

Table 1. Weberian Types of Authority

---

1. *Charismatic Authority:* Creative, innovative, personal experience of divine grace. Joseph Smith, Jr., gave birth to Mormonism using this authority.
2. *Traditional Authority:* Depersonalized or routinized charisma. It transforms the originating charisma of the founding experience into a system to perpetuate the benefits of the original experience.
   A. *Familial Charisma:* Depends on kinship ties. The office of Patriarch fell within this category and passed lineally to the oldest son.
   B. *Office Charisma:* Divinely sanctioned transference of authority by the laying on of hands. The Council of the Twelve Apostles and, by extension, the First Presidency fall within this category.
3. *Legal/Rational Authority:* Authority by rules requiring hierarchical subordination. The rule of presidential succession out of the Council of the Twelve is now in this category.

Legal/rational authority represents the formal rationalization of an organization, with strict discipline according to instrumental rules and regulations, and it requires hierarchical subordination to an authority also bound by rules, regardless of who occupies the office, in the interest of institutional efficiency.[4] An example of this type of authority is the U.S. Constitution. Individuals and offices are subordinated to the principles set out in the Constitution. Such legal/rational authority need not be written, however, and can often exist by way of formalized tradition or historical precedent.

Joseph Smith's mystical experiences and prophetic leadership in giving birth to Mormonism provide a classic example of Weberian charismatic authority. The beginnings of Mormonism did not presage an institution at all. Joseph Smith acted individually, with the support of his family, in proclaiming his message of a restoration of ancient powers. It was only after several years of visionary experiences, the publication of the Book of Mormon, and the commitment of a number of adherents to Joseph Smith as a prophet that institutional requirements were finally acknowledged. The concept of a restoration of primitive Christianity, rather than a reformation, came naturally from the revelatory experiences of Joseph Smith, who demonstrated biblical power in the present. Innovative charisma thus gave form to an institution based on a unique concept of primitivism.[5] This beginning experience is a classic example of the Weberian "ideal type" of charismatic leadership.

The story of Joseph Smith's visionary experiences, resulting in the organization of the Mormon church, can be found in most historical studies relating to Mormonism.[6] Briefly, in the spring of 1820, when Joseph Smith, Jr., was in his fifteenth year and confused by the conflicting claims of the various religious movements in the vicinity, he went to pray in the woods near his home in Palmyra, New York. God and Christ appeared to Joseph, and he was told to join no church—that all the churches were wrong.[7] Later, this personal, sacred event began to assume such an importance in the church that leaders have repeatedly emphasized it as fundamental to a belief in Mormonism itself.[8] Accounts of other visitations by heavenly messengers tell how Joseph Smith was led to recover gold plates declared to be a history of earlier inhabitants of the American continents. The subsequent translation and publication of this history by the Smith family resulted in the new scripture, the Book of Mormon. According to church history, during the course of translation and in answer to inquiries in 1829 about authority and ordinances, there was a restoration of priesthood authority by divine visitation when keys were given to Joseph Smith, Jr., for the performance of basic religious ordinances, such as baptism.[9] Whether Smith had intended to found a church before 1830, once the translation of the Book of Mormon was completed and published, he organized the church at Fayette, New York. All of Smith's immediate family were involved as well as a few early converts, such as Oliver Cowdery and Peter and David Whitmer (at whose home the organization of the church took place).

From these charismatic beginnings, the church as an institution began to evolve. According to Thomas O'Dea, "The recognition of prophetic leadership implies the development of a hierarchical church structure with authority flowing from top to bottom. . . . The original relationship between the prophet and his disciples evolved into a relationship between the prophet and an oligarchy of leading elders, which merged into and exercised ascendancy over the rank and file of the membership."[10]

That this hierarchical organization was evolutionary can be seen in an early description of presiding authorities as "a conference of high priests," a term that was changed in a later edition of the Doctrine and Covenants to "the First Presidency of the Church."[11] There is no contemporary record of the restoration of the higher Melchizedek Priesthood, merely later references to its restoration. Coupled with other evidence, this suggests that the early church did not make the distinctions currently made concerning priesthood. The introduction of high priests in June 1831 brought new internal strains to Mormonism. Until then, every worthy adult male member of the church held the office of elder as part of a lay priesthood. The selection of certain men for higher office was seen by some members as a move toward a hierarchical priesthood.[12] Paul Edwards, a descendant of Joseph Smith and a scholar of the Mormon past, suggests that by that time Joseph's views of his mission had changed: "After 1830 they appear more and more reflective of the needs of an institution than they were expressions of the divine." Mormonism, according to Edwards, "is the theological and philosophical ism that emerged in explanation of the singular mystical experience of Joseph Smith."[13] It is clear that some routinization of the charismatic movement was under way even at the formal organization of the church.

It should be noted, however, that Joseph Smith's role as a prophet did not take place in a vacuum. The times were ripe for acceptance of his type of mystic leadership. Gordon Wood notes the religious and social chaos that produced the popular evangelicalism of the early nineteenth century: "The disintegration of older structures of authority [after the Revolution] released torrents of popular religiosity into public life. Visions, dreams, prophesyings, and new emotion-soaked religious seekings acquired a validity they had not earlier possessed. . . . Thousands upon thousands became seekers looking for signs and prophets and for new explanations for the bewildering experiences of their lives."[14] In addition,

Wood argues, ordinary people "found in evangelicalism a counter-culture that condemned the conventional society and offered them alternative measures of self-esteem."[15]

During the 1820s and 1830s, along with Joseph Smith, there were Charles G. Finney, Robert Matthews, Alexander Campbell, and the Shakers, each launching particular appeals to the religious yearnings of the time. Campbell's Disciples of Christ, like the Mormon church, held central religious ideas similar to those of the Methodists, Baptists, Presbyterians, and Universalists.[16] Some suggest that the Mormon convert Sidney Rigdon, a former Campbellite preacher, had at least some influence on Joseph Smith.[17]

Although some LDS doctrines and practices emerged after Rigdon joined the church, much of what Mormonism taught and practiced, which continues to be a part of the faith, was in the Book of Mormon or was included in the early revelations of the Prophet. Basic to Mormonism before the Saints left New York were the concepts of faith, repentance, baptism by immersion for the remission of sins, bestowal of the Holy Ghost by the laying on of hands, free agency, the fall of man, the doctrine of the atonement of Christ, and millennialism. Many doctrines and practices, however, were taught by the Prophet later on—for example, the idea of a preexistence, the three degrees of glory, eternal and plural marriage, and tithing.[18] Even the Mormon concept of the Trinity was first taught by Joseph Smith in later years.[19]

Gordon Wood has suggested that only nineteenth-century evangelical America could have produced Mormonism.[20] Yet, inconsistent with its social environment, only Mormonism appears to have incorporated two such paradoxical elements as the right to individual revelation and the necessity of institutional authority for the bestowal of this right. It is this idea of mediated authority within a church claiming primitive purity that has proved both a strength of Mormonism in attracting converts and a source of tension as the church faces the challenge of biblical scholarship.

For the Mormon church, the restoration of the pure gospel of Jesus Christ has remained its reason for being. Although other churches have also sought to incorporate elements of the original Christian church, LDS "primitivism," as this restoration is referred to by scholars, is unique in some ways.[21] For example, Mormons accept the Bible but only "as far as it is translated correctly."[22] Mormons also have a new scripture, the Book of Mormon, and they continue to receive additional revelations. This last element of Mormonism, latter-day revelation, published as the Doctrine and Covenants, implies that Joseph Smith's prophetic announcements assume the authority of scripture.

In addition to the Book of Mormon, the Doctrine and Covenants, and the Pearl of Great Price, Joseph Smith also took a revisionist look at the Bible. The organization revealed in Jesus' day, the Prophet declared, also existed in Adam's time and is now being restored during this last dispensation.[23] Joseph Smith revised portions of the Bible accordingly, deeming the editing necessary to correct errors in translation. Commonly referred to as the "Inspired Version" of the Bible, the book reveals the eternal nature of gospel principles. Faith, repentance, baptism in the name of Christ for the remission of sins, and the gift of the Holy Ghost were all part of Old Testament teachings, the Inspired Version shows. This version of the Bible not only serves to unify the central messages of the Old Testament and the New Testament but also underscores the harmony among the Bible, the Book of Mormon, and the tenets of Mormonism.

Peculiarly Mormon in this canon is the emphasis on the Old Testament patriarchs, all of whom knew of the same gospel principles during previous dispensations.[24] In this sense Mormonism can be seen as a restorer of elements of ancient Israel as much as a restorer of primitive Christianity.[25] A difficulty emerges, however, when one seeks some continuity between the Old Testament and the New Testament on the role and status of the patriarch. The Gospels refer to the ancient patriarchs when tracing lineage, but they do not give to any equivalent figure the primal role that Old Testament patriarchs had in their time. Joseph Smith's revelations resolved this apparent lack of continuity. They constituted a reinterpretation of Christian terminology and at the same time took care of an extension of the calling within an institutional setting. On June 27, 1839, the Prophet instructed the Brethren on doctrine. He referred to the list of offices Paul named in his epistle to the Ephesians 4:11: "He [Christ] gave some apostles; and some, prophets; and some, evangelists; and some, pastors and teachers." The Prophet explained, "An Evangelist is a Patriarch, even the oldest man of the blood of Joseph or of the seed of Abraham. Wherever the Church of Christ is established in the earth, there should be a Patriarch for the benefit of the posterity of the Saints, as it was with Jacob in giving his patriarchal blessing unto his sons."[26] This statement did two things: first, it confirmed the office of Patriarch as a recapitulation of the Old Testament and the New Testament; second, it established the principle that the church should always have this office.

Primitivism itself was an early nineteenth-century response to the religious pluralism of the day. Joseph Smith, like others, claimed to have reestablished the early Christian church in all its purity. The Mormon Prophet's charismatic "restoration of all things" included other dimensions, though. Crucial among these were the renewal of direct communication from God to a latter-day prophet; a dispensational view of sacred history, with Old Testament patriarchs, as well as Christ's apostles, serving as models for restored gospel principles; and the restoration of divine priesthood authority.[27]

These three aspects of a "restoration" that are peculiarly Mormon—revelation, a dispensational view of sacred history, and priesthood authority—are the phenomena responsible for the emergence of the patriarchate in the LDS Church. In response to the revealed word of God, Joseph Smith turned to the experience of former prophets. There he found the patriarchs, Abraham, Isaac, and Jacob, giving blessings to their people. In light of the united support of his own family, Joseph received divine authority for his own earthly father to occupy that same patriarchal role. Priesthood authority enabled him to ordain his father as Church Patriarch, an office with familial authority.

Soon after the formal organization of the church in 1830, traditional authority forms began taking shape. *Both* familial charisma and office charisma forms of authority were established side by side. The office of Patriarch was the longer lasting of the familial forms, but there is evidence Joseph intended, at certain times, that the office of prophet/president also pass by way of heredity. Certainly the family was an important part of the "Restoration."[28] Along with these ideas of familial charismatic authority, however, were structures within the church for office charisma authority. The first office was that of first elder, held by Joseph Smith himself. Then came a presidency (president with two counselors) and then priesthood groups, including high councils, a quorum of twelve apostles, seventies, and others, all receiving their authority through the laying on of hands by one whose higher office gave the power to ordain one to a position of lesser authority. Protectors of this type of traditional authority, when defending their relative positions of power after the death of Joseph Smith, made frequent reference to the inability of a stream to rise higher than its source.[29]

If Weber's types of authority are used as paradigms, it is clear that the Mormon church today depends on a combination of traditional (office charisma) authority and legal/rational authority. An important example is the selection process for the ultimate authority in the church. Traditional authority in the form of office charisma is utilized when apostles choose replacements to the Council of the Twelve upon the death of an incumbent. New members of the council are chosen by inspiration and ordained by the laying on of hands by the other apostles who have priesthood authority from God.[30] By contrast, the apostles choose a new president of the church from within the quorum based on what has become a legal/rational rule of seniority, to which the apostles themselves are subordinate. The new president is not chosen from the greater church membership by revelation, as new apostles are.

Weber does not suggest a simple chronological sequence from charismatic to legal/rational types of authority, and he notes that all three types of authority might coexist in varying degrees within an institution over time, although one type usually predominates. He does, however, see charisma as a revolutionary creative force in society, which, by its nature, will spawn tensions and the possibility of schisms in an established organization. Weber sees inevitable conflict between the maintainers of institutions and the charismatic innovators. He believes that charisma, along with other individual values, is losing the battle in an increasingly bureaucratized world because of what he calls "a parcelling-out of the soul."[31] Certainly the innovative charisma that gave birth to the hereditary office of Church Patriarch suffered from the bureaucratization of the Mormon church. Whether this constituted a spiritual loss is more difficult to assess.

Not all forms of charisma are antithetical to an ongoing institution. Edward Shils points this out in his writings. Voluntary compliance, stemming from shared beliefs, therefore, may be a stronger influence on society than objective authoritarian control through external rules or laws.[32] However, the reminder of the formational charisma that the office of Presiding Patriarch represented to the established and surviving institution created the very tension with which Weber dealt in his writings.

Consistent with the Weberian definition is the proposition, noted by Reinhard Bendix, that "the desire to preserve the original charisma, can only be satisfied by its transformation."[33] This is the inherent paradox involved in charismatic leadership. The transformation or routinization of the initial charismatic authority may result in authority's being passed on through hereditary succession, as in familial charisma, or it may result in the depersonalization represented by office charisma, where authority is transferred by the laying on of hands by those followers who have been functionaries for the original charismatic leader, thereby creating a chain of authority ensuring subsequent generations of leadership, as in apostolic succession.

After the death of Joseph Smith and Hyrum Smith, the authority of office charisma won decisively over familial charisma, consistent with Weber's assertion that one form of traditional authority will take precedence over the other.[34] A form of familial charismatic structure, however, continued to exist within the church until 1979—in the office of Church Patriarch. Had incumbents of the patriarchal office contented themselves with the *form* of office rather than what they conceived as historical rights of *substance*, the office might have survived in an impotent form, much the way some hereditary monarchies have survived in today's world of rational/legal political systems. There were, however, interesting and assertive patriarchs from time to time between 1833 and 1979. Familial charisma and office charisma cannot compete for authority without one conceding authority at some point. In the long run, they are mutually exclusive.

Chapter 4 unfolds in detail the problems Mormonism encountered during its transitional period, when its charismatic leader died. The need for these painful transformations is not unique to Mormonism. Methodism encountered problems when John Wesley died but in a different way. Wesley left a democratic legacy that opted for collective leadership when the innovative charismatic died. With Mormonism, Brigham Young continued with individual authority. Methodism and Mormonism show two of the different routes through which charismatic authority can be transferred.[35]

As Bendix points out in his discussion of Weberian theory, "charismatic leadership of the 'pure type' is approximated only at the time of its origin."[36] Even before the question of succession arises, a "charismatic aristocracy" will emerge in a movement that will be composed of disciples and privileged officeholders whose aim is to preserve this element of charismatic authority.[37] In Mormonism, the Quorum of the Twelve began to emerge as the predominant charismatic aristocracy during the years just before the death of the founder. After Joseph Smith's death, the apostles were able to effect the transition of authority to their own quorum with the express commitment to preserve the teachings and authority of Joseph Smith. For Mormons, the apostolic chain of authority (office charisma) remains the foundation for "the centralized and hierarchical structure of church organization laid down by Mormonism's founders in the nineteenth century," which has allowed for the development of the vast and complex bureaucracy operating today.[38]

By way of comparison, for Methodism there was no tribal tradition, no familial charisma, as had been established in Mormonism, and in 1791, when Wesley died, office charisma in the classic sense was not immediately approved by leading Methodists, despite Wesley's own unofficial ordinations. Over a period of years, short-term appointments by election evolved into a collective leadership that dispensed with a belief in charismatic leadership in favor of institutionally elected leaders.

In the Mormon church, the succession crisis following Joseph Smith's death presented several options. Mormonism's leadership included a "royal" founding family, and its doctrine allowed for at least two possible hereditary offices: (1) the presidency, vested in the oldest male offspring of Joseph Smith, Jr., and (2) the patriarchate, vested in the oldest male offspring of Joseph Smith, Sr., the first patriarch. This familial and hereditary aspect of leadership was immediately seen as a potential threat to the "institutional charisma" of chosen officeholders, who were believed to be divinely appointed.[39]

The resolution, eventually, was apostolic succession—transfer of power from the deceased prophet and president to the Quorum of the Twelve Apostles, who then selected the new prophet and president. Unlike the office of president or prophet, the office of Presiding Patriarch in the Utah church remained connected to the founding Smith family, specifically to the line of oldest sons descended from Joseph Smith, Sr., the first patriarch. The patriarchate would continue to illuminate the inevitable institutional strains involved in trying to accommodate both office charisma and familial charisma within the Mormon hierarchy. In the office of president those tensions were quickly muted and thereby permanently avoided as the early church worked out its succession traditions.

The essential incompatibility of an ancient primal hereditary office—the office of Patriarch—within the structure of a modern religious institution has been part of the continuing problem for Mormonism. The development of the church into a worldwide religious organization has served to highlight the tension provided by the office of Patriarch, as initially defined. The office is a concrete example of Weber's "familial charisma," dependent on kinship ties for its authority and primacy. Institutional predictability and efficiency, however, require greater control over the choice of suitable leaders, necessitating dispensing with lineal ties to inherent primal rights. The incongruity of institutional office and primal lineal rights became increasingly more difficult to reconcile as the church grew. The uneasy mix could be managed during the lifetime of Joseph Smith, who operated as a charismatic leader. It presented problems later, however, which would be perceived as personality clashes or competing claims to church leadership rather than as the result of intrinsic problems between office authority and lineal authority and the effect of that tension on the office of Patriarch. Partly because of this anomaly, the functions and importance of the office were slowly eroded through the years, until the office was finally retired in 1979. As far as the rest of the church leadership and structure were concerned, organizational procedures were developed that facilitated change, providing their own momentum and validity, while at the same time allowing belief structures to remain intact. The effort to retain the element of charisma—upon which the church itself is based—resulted in the adoption of office charisma as a viable solution and the abandonment of familial charisma as manifest in the calling of the Patriarch to the Church.

The history of the various incumbents and their relationship with other members of the hierarchy provides an interesting study of the changing emphases on different aspects of the office. This is not to say there has been an awareness, historically, of any inherent incompatibility. Perhaps it was the "primal aspect" that was "the central character of the office of Presiding Patriarch that defined it as well as doomed it."[40] The built-in unpredictability and independence of any hereditary calling, placing it beyond the control of the institution, would make the demise of the office inevitable.

The extent to which discord emerged depended on a number of factors. These included the willingness of any incumbent to discard tradition and reframe the nature of an office, to agree to an adjustment in ranking within the hierarchy in obedience to the needs of the institution, and to reinterpret or discount the value of past inconsistent revelations. In addition, any harmonization required some degree of tolerance on the part of the institution for an office that did not "fit" general organizational procedures.

The change in the status of the Presiding Patriarch in 1979 caused little concern throughout the general body of church members. Apart from the Twelve Apostles, who hold office for life, other general authorities—such as individual Seventies—had been made emeritus. The wording of the announcement about the Patriarch was ambiguous though. It was not made clear at the time whether the incumbent was being retired or whether the reason given—"in most parts of the world stakes now have their own patriarchs who provide the necessary blessings"—meant that the office itself was being terminated.

Only upon close examination can the office be seen as a casualty of the struggle for control and predictability in the transfer of authority. There are stated requirements that potential presiding patriarchs be morally sound and faithful and be called by the Prophet. Nonetheless, the hereditary nature of the office and its official designation as "prophet, seer, and revelator" allowed, at least in principle, for a degree of independence that proved troublesome. Short of immorality or apostasy there has been no real justification for rejecting the heir apparent to the office.

The severance of automatic kinship rights in the church has been accomplished in what may seem a relatively smooth and painless manner, yet history reveals the tensions and underlying struggles that brought the institution to this point. Our purpose is to trace the history of the office of Presiding Patriarch in the Mormon church from its initial position of primacy in a charismatic movement, through the difficulties encountered during evolutionary change and institutional growth within the church—including the interpretations of the office by individual patriarchs and their relationships with the other members of the hierarchy—to the phasing out and final demise of the office in 1979.

Notes

1. Max Weber, *Economy and Society: An Outline of Interpretive Sociology*, 3 vols., ed. Guenther Roth and Claus Wittich; trans. Ephraim Fischoff et al. (Berkeley: University of California Press, 1978), 3:1115–16.

2. Ibid., 1139.

3. Reinhard Bendix, *Max Weber: An Intellectual Portrait* (Berkeley: University of California Press, 1977), 311.

4. Peter M. Blau, "Critical Remarks on Weber's Theory of Authority," in *Max Weber*, ed. Dennis Wrong (Englewood Cliffs, N.J.: Prentice Hall, 1970), 151–52.

5. The myth of "first times" and the "cosmic" nature of Mormonism's "restoration" are explored in Richard T. Hughes and C. Leonard Allen, *Illusions of Innocence: Protestant Primitivism in America, 1630–1875* (Chicago: University of Chicago Press, 1988). Mormonism, the authors explain, encompassed "a constellation of sacred times" (133).

6. See, for example, Joseph Smith, *History of the Church of Jesus Christ of Latter-day Saints*, 2d rev. ed., ed. B. H. Roberts, 7 vols. (Salt Lake City: Deseret Book, 1978), 1:2–8; Lucy Mack Smith, *Biographical Sketches of Joseph Smith the Prophet and His Progenitors for Many Generations* (Liverpool, England: Published for Orson Pratt by S. W. Richards, 1853; New York: Arno Press and New York Times, 1969); Fawn Brodie, *No Man Knows My History* (New York: Alfred A. Knopf, 1945); Donna Hill, *Joseph Smith, the First Mormon* (Midvale, Utah: Signature Books, 1977); and Richard L. Bushman, *Joseph Smith and the Beginnings of Mormonism* (Urbana: University of Illinois Press, 1984). Early anti-Mormon literature attacked Joseph Smith's character, accusing him of fraud. Later studies, beginning perhaps with Brodie's analysis, looked for naturalistic explanations for the vision.

7. The event was not recorded until 1832. For a discussion of the developmental significance of his first vision, see Bushman, *Joseph Smith and the Beginnings of Mormonism*, 56–58; and Dean Jessee, "The Early Accounts of Joseph Smith's First Vision," *Brigham Young University Studies* 9 (Spring 1969): 275–94 (hereafter *BYU Studies*). D. Michael Quinn, *Early Mormonism and the Magic World View* (Salt Lake City: Signature Books, 1987), 112–49, provides a detailed discussion of another aspect of the vision.

8. James B. Allen, "Emergence of a Fundamental: The Expanding Role of Joseph Smith's First Vision in Mormon Religious Thought," *Journal of Mormon History* 7 (1980): 43–61. See also Marvin S. Hill, "A Note on Joseph Smith's First Vision and Its Import in the Shaping of Early Mormonism," *Dialogue: A Journal of Mormon Thought* 12 (Spring 1979): 90–99.

9. *Doctrine and Covenants of the Church of Jesus Christ of Latter-day Saints* (Salt Lake City: Deseret Book, 1955), section 13, May 15, 1829.

10. Thomas O'Dea, *The Mormons* (Chicago: University of Chicago Press, 1957), 160.

11. D. Michael Quinn, "The Evolution of the Presiding Quorums of the Church," *Journal of Mormon History* 1 (1974): 22, n.8. The account of the No-

vember 1831 revelation appeared in the first edition of the *Evening and Morning Star*, October 1832; the title of First Presidency was used in *Doctrine and Covenants* 68:22–23. Marvin S. Hill, "The Shaping of the Mormon Mind in New England and New York," *BYU Studies* 9 (Spring 1969): 363, points out that despite the evolution of the organization, "the principle of priesthood authority" was affirmed from the beginning. Greg Prince, "The Development of LDS Priesthood Authority and Organization, 1823–1844" (Paper presented at the Mormon History Association annual meeting, St. George, Utah, May 1992), provides the most comprehensive exposition.

12. See Peter Crawley, "The Passage of Mormon Primitivism," *Dialogue: A Journal of Mormon Thought* 13 (Winter 1980): 26–37.

13. Paul M. Edwards, "The Secular Smiths," *Journal of Mormon History* 4 (1977): 5, 11.

14. Gordon S. Wood, "Evangelical America and Early Mormonism," *New York History* 61 (October 1980): 368, 370. Hughes and Allen, *Illusions of Innocence*, xv–xvi, argue that "to explain the restoration impulse—restoration-oriented traditions—almost exclusively in terms of chaos or social disintegration implicitly suggests that the impulse is aberrant and will subside when order is restored." American history, the authors point out, shows that the myth of a pure "first times" persisted.

15. Wood, "Evangelical America and Early Mormonism," 373.

16. Timothy L. Smith, "The Book of Mormon in a Biblical Culture," *Journal of Mormon History* 7 (1980): 6. That the ideas of these groups not only survived within Mormonism but also were a source of continuing tension is addressed by Loretta L. Hefner, "From Apostle to Apostate: The Personal Struggle of Amasa Mason Lyman," *Dialogue: A Journal of Mormon Thought* 16 (Spring 1983): 90–104. Lyman was one of the apostles who espoused the "heresy" of Universalism.

17. Bushman, *Joseph Smith and the Beginnings of Mormonism*, 184, 174, argues that the Enlightenment had a greater influence on Campbell than on Joseph Smith and that "Rigdon's superior learning was of secondary importance" to Joseph's divine call.

18. James B. Allen and Leonard J. Arrington, "Mormon Origins in New York: An Introductory Analysis," *BYU Studies* 9 (Spring 1969): 270. The Mormon belief in continuous revelation can accommodate innovation and change in both policy and doctrine.

19. Thomas G. Alexander, "The Reconstruction of Mormon Doctrine: From Joseph Smith to Progressive Theology," *Sunstone* 10 (May 1985): 9.

20. Wood, "Evangelical America and Early Mormonism," 386.

21. Hughes and Allen, *Illusions of Innocence*, 133–52, discuss the uniqueness of the Mormon version of the myth. See also Grant R. Underwood, "The Millennarian World of Early Mormonism" (Ph.D. diss., University of California, Los Angeles, 1988). Richard D. Ouellette, "Authority and Ecclesiology in Primitive Christianity and Mormonism" (Paper presented at the Sunstone Theological Symposium, Salt Lake City, August 24, 1990), looks at two aspects of the early Christian church that Mormonism claims to have restored—

priesthood and church organization—and recounts the critical comments of biblical scholars who deny any early formalization.

22. The Articles of Faith of the Church of Jesus Christ of Latter-day Saints, appendix to Joseph Smith, *The Pearl of Great Price: A Selection from the Revelations, Translations, and Narrations of Joseph Smith* (Salt Lake City: Church of Jesus Christ of Latter-day Saints, 1955), no. 8.

23. Gordon Irving, "The Mormons and the Bible in the 1830s," *BYU Studies* 13 (Summer 1973): 474.

24. Ibid., 476. The idea that the Old Testament peoples taught the same gospel and church organization as is preached today is still current in the LDS Church. It includes the understanding that the ancient patriarchs all held the Melchizedek Priesthood and that they lived the law of polygamy. As early as 1831 Joseph Smith had talked privately of receiving a revelation about plural marriage, citing the Old Testament patriarchs. See Richard S. Van Wagoner, *Mormon Polygamy: A History* (Salt Lake City: Signature Books, 1986). The Mormon church was not alone in subscribing to unconventional marriage patterns, however. Orson Hyde, Diary, October 11, 1832, Archives of the Church of Jesus Christ of Latter-day Saints, Salt Lake City (hereafter LDS Church Archives), mentions preaching to another sect that taught spiritual wifery—the Cochranites in Maine. See also Lawrence Foster's *Religion and Sexuality: Three American Communal Experiments of the Nineteenth Century* (New York: Oxford University Press, 1981), and *Women, Family, and Utopia: Communal Experiments of the Shakers, the Oneida Community, and the Mormons* (Syracuse, N.Y.: Syracuse University Press, 1991).

25. According to Jan Shipps, *Mormonism: The Story of a New Religious Tradition* (Urbana: University of Illinois Press, 1985), 68, Christianity itself began as a restoration movement. "The Old Testament was its scripture, and its early claims were cast in an undeniably Judaic mode." The later developments in Christianity transformed and separated it from Judaism, despite its "reappropriation of Judaism's mythological dimension."

26. Joseph Smith, *History of the Church*, 3:381. The reference to the Patriarch is singular, which suggests that this requirement is not met by the many local patriarchs now serving. This distinction was noted in Franklin D. Richards and James A. Little, *A Compendium of the Doctrines of the Gospel* (1882; reprint, Salt Lake City: Deseret News, 1925), 73.

27. Hughes and Allen, *Illusions of Innocence*, 133–52.

28. For example, Lucy Mack Smith's *Biographical Sketches* uses the pronouns "we," "us," and "our" when referring to the actual activity involved in the restoration.

29. This particular phrase comes from John Taylor, "Patriarchal," *Times and Seasons* 6 (June 1, 1845): 922. The problem of primacy was still being debated in August 1847. According to Wilford Woodruff, Journal, August 15, 1847, LDS Church Archives, Brigham Young stated, "I want this Church to understand from this day henceforth & forever that an apostle is the highest office of authority that there is in the Church & kingdom of God on

earth . . . Joseph Smith gave unto me and to my brethren, the Twelve, all the priesthood keys, power and authority which he had and those are powers which belong to the apostleship. In Joseph's day we had to ordain patriarchs. Could we ordain men to authority greater than we held ourselves? No."

30. Although the First Presidency is very much involved in these decisions, we include them within the generic "apostle" designation, since the president is always the senior apostle.

31. Max Weber, "Some Consequences of Bureaucratization," in *Sociological Theory: A Book of Readings,* ed. Lewis A. Coser and Bernard Rosenberg (New York: Macmillan, 1957), 473.

32. Edward Shils, *Center and Periphery: Essays in Macrosociology* (Chicago: University of Chicago Press, 1975), 257–58, 261–62. See also Émile Durkheim, *The Elementary Forms of the Religious Life,* trans. J. W. Swain (London: Allen and Unwin, 1915). Shils points to a form of charisma that is alive and well and playing a conservative role in modern society, as well as the disruptive one described by Weber. Shils maintains that while charisma in the narrower, original sense is the state or quality of being produced by receipt of the gifts of grace, as in Corinthians 12:8–11, "an attenuated, mediated, institutionalized charismatic propensity is present in the routine functioning of society" (257). This type of charisma exists within subsystems of an organization and is generated by individuals who subscribe to a central core of transcendent values. Like Émile Durkheim before him, Shils notes a persistent human need for some predictable, moral ordering of the world. It is this need, he suggests, that provides what might be called a kind of "sacred glue" for society, maintaining order and continuity. It is this "glue," not simply the obedience to external rules or to a particular authority, that is the most powerful societal influence. Mormonism, perhaps, is a particularly good example of this in its "democracy of participation and its oligarchy of decision-making and command" (O'Dea, *The Mormons,* 149).

33. Bendix, *Max Weber,* 308.

34. Sixteen years after the death of Joseph Smith, Jr., his son Joseph Smith III, assumed the reins of a reorganization movement, members of which rejected the office succession personified by Brigham Young, and returned to a familial charismatic form of leadership, which has survived to the present time in the Reorganized Church of Jesus Christ of Latter Day Saints.

35. For a discussion of the historical development of Methodism, see Irene M. Bates, "Transformation of Charisma in the Mormon Church: A History of the Office of Patriarch, 1833–1979" (Ph.D. diss., University of California, Los Angeles, 1991).

36. Bendix, *Max Weber,* 300.

37. Ibid., 302.

38. Gordon Shepherd and Gary Shepherd, "Mormonism in Secular Society: Changing Patterns in Official Ecclesiastical Rhetoric," *Review of Religious Research* 26 (September 1984): 32.

39. In recording the ordination of Joseph Smith, Sr., as the Patriarch, Ol-

iver Cowdery disputed the primacy of the calling. Minutes in Joseph Smith, Sr., Patriarchal Blessing Book, vol. 1, 1835, LDS Church Archives; typescript in authors' possession.

40. D. Michael Quinn, "Comment on Patriarch Papers" (Response to papers presented by E. Gary Smith and Irene M. Bates at the Mormon History Association annual meeting, Salt Lake City, May 2, 1986). For a detailed discussion of the questions of "primacy," see E. Gary Smith, "The Office of Presiding Patriarch: The Primacy Problem," *Journal of Mormon History* 14 (1988): 35–47.

2

=⟫●⟪=

"Like the Patriarchs of Old"

Joseph Smith, Sr.—First Patriarch, 1833–40

> So shall it be with my father: he shall be called a prince over his posterity, holding the keys of the patriarchal priesthood over the kingdom of God on earth, even the Church of the Latter Day Saints, and he shall sit in the general assembly of patriarchs, even in council with the Ancient of Days when he shall sit and all the patriarchs with him and shall enjoy his right and authority under the direction of the Ancient of Days.
>
> —Joseph Smith, Jr., December 18, 1833

Even before the Mormon church came into being, with its attendant trials for all the Prophet's followers, Joseph Smith, Sr., was no stranger to hardship. Born in 1771 at Topsfield, Massachusetts, of hard-working parents, Asael and Mary Duty Smith, Joseph was at various times a teacher, a farmer, a cooper, and a money-digger. He married Lucy Mack on January 24, 1796, and fathered eleven children, two of whom died in infancy. Another, eldest son Alvin, died at the age of twenty-five. Joseph Smith, Jr., was their fifth child and third son.[1] Throughout her life, Lucy regarded her husband as "an affectionate companion and loving father."[2] The fortunes of the family, however, suffered many reverses because of poor crops, unwise investments, and bad debts. Joseph Sr. was forced to sell his farm at half its value and to use Lucy's wedding present of a thousand dollars (given to her by her older brother Stephen) to satisfy his creditors.[3]

When the Smith family moved to Palmyra, New York, Father Smith refused to become involved in formal religion, which caused his wife some concern. Joseph Sr. had several troubling visions illuminating the confusion of his religious life. In one he seemed to be wandering in a barren field, where there was no other living thing; in another he could see a box, which, if he could but open it, would give him understanding. Although he did not understand the dreams, he knew that he was waiting for "the ancient order, as established by our Lord and Savior Jesus Christ and His Apostles."[4]

Lucy, along with three of their children—Hyrum, Sophronia, and Samuel—joined the Presbyterian church, the only church with a meetinghouse in Palmyra. The whole family had been seeking religious direction during the upheaval of the revivals in western New York. Jan Shipps argues that the "positive reactions to the surprising information imparted to them by one of their own number [Joseph Jr.] makes the Smith family's response to the prophet so critical to the LDS story that accounts of Mormon beginnings are incomplete when so much emphasis is placed on Joseph Smith, Jr., that his family recedes into the background."[5] The original title of Lucy's own story underscores Shipps's interpretation. The copyright records the lengthy title of Lucy's book as *The History of Lucy Smith wife of Joseph Smith, the first Patriarch of Jesus Christ of Latter Day Saints, who was the father of Joseph Smith, Prophet, Seer, and Revelator; containing an account of the many persecutions, trials, and afflictions which I and my family have endured in bringing forth the Book of Mormon, and establishing the church of Jesus Christ of Latter Day Saints. . . .*[6]

The Prophet recorded that his father "was the first person who received my testimony after I had seen the angel, and exhorted me to be faithful, and diligent to the message I had received."[7] That Joseph Sr. believed his son is understandable within the context of his day, when there were many accounts of otherworldly experiences. Also, the son's inspired message provided a resolution of the father's own religious dilemma.[8] The earlier visionary experiences of Joseph Sr. had been representations of his religious questionings; the divine intervention in the life of his son must have seemed an answer to his prayers.[9] During an 1829 visit to his son at Harmony, Pennsylvania, where Joseph and his wife, Emma, were living with Emma's parents, Father Smith asked what the Lord would have him do in helping bring forth the restoration. In the revelation that followed there was no mention of the patriarchate. The Prophet simply called Father Smith to help in the "marvellous work . . . about to come forth among the children of men."[10] Both Joseph Sr. and Lucy, as well as the rest of the family, supported the enterprise that culminated in the translation and publication of the Book of Mormon. When the translation of that book was completed, Joseph Smith, Sr., and two of his sons, Hyrum and Samuel, were among the eight witnesses to testify that they had seen and handled the gold plates and had seen the engravings on them.[11]

The baptism of Father Smith, when the church was formally organized in 1830, demonstrated the close spiritual bond between Prophet/son and

Lucy Mack Smith, 1776–1856. Wife of Joseph Smith, Sr., and influential mother of the Prophet Joseph Smith, Jr. Courtesy of Eldred G. Smith.

what would become Patriarch/father. According to his mother, the younger Joseph cried, "Oh, My God! have I lived to see my own father baptized
into the true church of Jesus Christ!"[12] Joseph Knight said the Prophet
then "bast out with greaf and joy and seamed as tho the world could not
hold him. He went out into the Lot and appeared to want to git out of
site of every Body and would sob and Crie and seamed to Be so full that
he could not live. . . . [H]e was the most wrot upon that I ever saw any
man. But his joy seemed to Be full."[13]

About five months later, Joseph Sr. went on a mission to his family in
the East. With the exception of Jesse, the family was kindly disposed to
the message of the restoration. (Brothers Asael and John would later become patriarchs, and John would be the Presiding Patriarch after the
Saints arrived in the Salt Lake Valley.) Although his father, also named
Asael, died shortly after his visit, his mother, at age ninety-three, traveled to Kirtland in 1836 seeking baptism at the hands of her grandson,
the Prophet.[14]

In January 1831, just nine months after the church was organized, the
Smith family moved with the Saints to Ohio. Growth of the church was
slow in New York, and local religious leaders were persecuting the Prophet.
In Ohio, however, the converted Campbellite preacher Sidney Rigdon was
bringing his flock into the fold of Mormonism. Joseph Sr. and Lucy began operating a farm in Kirtland, which had been provided by Frederick
G. Williams. Lucy indicates in her history that they were to use all of the
surplus from working the farm for the "comfort of strangers or brethren, who were traveling through this place." Joseph and Lucy apparently
extended themselves too much for the benefit of those outside the family who were gathering to Kirtland. The Prophet received a revelation on
the subject in March of 1833: "And let mine aged servant, Joseph Smith,
Sen., continue with his family upon the place where he now lives; . . . Let
your families be small especially mine aged servant Joseph Smith, Sen, as
pertaining to those who do not belong to your families; That those things
that are provided for you, to bring to pass my work, be not taken from
you and given to those that are not worthy—And thereby you be hin-
dered in accomplishing those things which I have commanded you."[15]

By the time Joseph Smith, Sr., was ordained as the Patriarch at Kirtland, Ohio, on December 18, 1833, the Church of Christ (as it was called
until 1834) was three and a half years old. The concentration of members had moved from New York State to separate gathering places in Kirtland, Ohio, and Independence, Missouri. Although Missouri had been
designated as the ultimate gathering place, Joseph Jr. still lived in and governed the church from Ohio.

To understand the context of the birth of the patriarchate, we must talk of printing presses, mobs, and perseverance. In November 1831 a church conference took place at John Johnson's farmhouse near Hiram, Ohio, at which time the preface to the Book of Commandments was received by revelation. It was determined that printing these revelations was a task of prime importance. Oliver Cowdery was chosen to go to Jackson County, Missouri, to oversee the printing of ten thousand copies of the new book of scripture.[16] Cowdery and others established a press in the home of W. W. Phelps in Independence, Missouri, and by February of 1832 they began printing a prospectus for the *Evening and Morning Star*.[17] In May of 1832 a first edition of three thousand copies of the Book of Commandments (along with a book of hymns selected by Emma Smith) was ordered to be printed.[18]

However, in July of 1833, before the work could be accomplished, an anti-Mormon mob of Missouri residents entered the Phelps home and destroyed the press, type, and all of the other equipment. Several prominent Mormons sustained physical injuries.[19] Because of these and other hostilities, local church leaders were forced to sign a paper promising that they would move out of Jackson County and that no press would be set up "by any of the society in this County."[20] This was a considerable blow to the Mormon people, who desperately needed to have a means of communicating with the far-flung membership and the world at large. The Saints also needed a newspaper as a means of memorializing the revelations they held so dear and wished to follow.

Daunted by these developments, they were not ready to print from a press of their own for five months. At great sacrifice, arrangements were eventually made for a new press, which was to be located in the large brick inn recently built by John Johnson, located kitty-corner from the Whitney store in Kirtland, Ohio. "About the 1st of December [1833] Elder Cowdery and Bishop Whitney arrived at Kirtland [from the East] with a new press and type, and on the 4th commenced distributing the type."[21] With concern for the severe persecutions still being suffered by their Missouri brothers and sisters and joy over what the new press could do for uniting the church, they assembled in the printing office on December 18, 1833, and bowed their heads before the Lord, while Joseph dedicated the printing press "and all that pertained thereunto, to God."[22] They then proceeded to take the first proof sheet of the reprinted *Star* off the press.

To the participants, this was a historic moment. It represented victory over the enemies of the church in a significant arena, and the celebratory spirit manifested itself in blessings bestowed by the Prophet on his family and friends assembled there. Whether Joseph knew in advance he was going to create an office in the church before he began to speak to his father in blessing is unknown. It is also unknown whether Joseph placed his hands on the head of each recipient as he blessed them or whether this was a visionary pronouncement that was simply addressed to the appropriate person, in turn. Nevertheless, Cowdery recorded the words of the twenty-seven-year-old Prophet as he spoke on that important occasion: "Blessed of the Lord is my father, for he shall stand in the midst of his posterity and shall be comforted by their blessings when he is old and bowed down with years, and shall be called a prince over them, and shall be numbered among those who hold the right of patriarchal priesthood, even the keys of that ministry: for he shall assemble together his posterity like unto Adam; and the assembly which he called shall be an example for my father. . . ." The Prophet continued by recounting the time when Adam called his posterity together at Adam-ondi-ahman for the purpose of giving his descendants their last blessings. Among those gathered were Seth, Enos, Cainan, Mahalaleel, Jared, Enoch, and Methuselah, all of whom were high priests:

> And the Lord appeared unto them, and they rose up and blessed Adam, and called him Michael, the Prince, the Archangel. And the Lord administered comfort unto Adam, and said unto him, I have set thee to be at the head: a multitude of nations shall come of thee, and thou art a Prince over them forever. So shall it be with my father: he shall be called a prince over his posterity, holding the keys of the patriarchal priesthood over the kingdom of God on earth, even the Church of the Latter Day Saints; and he shall sit in the general assembly of patriarchs, even in council with the Ancient of Days when he shall sit and all the patriarchs with him—and shall enjoy his right and authority under the direction of the Ancient of Days. . . . Behold, the blessings of Joseph by the hand of his progenitor, shall come upon the head of my father and his seed after him, to the uttermost, . . . and his seed shall rise up and call him blessed. . . . His counsel shall be sought for by thousands, and he shall have a place in the house of the Lord . . . and his name shall be had in remembrance to the end.[23]

Father Smith thus became the first patriarch in the "dispensation of the fulness of times," when "every key, power, and authority ever dispensed from heaven to men on earth" would be restored. His ordination represented a stage in the "restoration of all things."[24] These two phrases are commonly used in the Church of Jesus Christ of Latter-day Saints to define the unique role of the church in bringing about the restoration. Mormons believe that there have been other dispensations when the gospel was preached and then ultimately lost in all its fullness and purity.[25] The nineteenth-century final restoration included priesthood authority, baptism by immersion for the living and the dead, the gift of the Holy Ghost, the ordinance of the sacrament, sacred temple ordinances, polygyny, tithing (introduced when the Law of Consecration failed), health laws, and the reality of continuous revelation, which allowed for addressing contemporary concerns.[26] It also included a patriarch to bless the people.

A new office within the Mormon hierarchy had been born. Father Smith was given the "keys of the patriarchal priesthood over the kingdom of God on earth, even the Church of the Latter Day Saints." It obviously was an office and position of importance. Hyrum Smith's blessing, received at the same time as his father's on December 18, indicated that he would be a shaft in the hand of his God "from generation to generation" and that "he shall stand in the tracts of his father and be numbered among those who hold the right of patriarchal priesthood, even the evangelical priesthood and power shall be upon him. . . ."[27] It was understood that the office would pass to the oldest son, Hyrum, and on to his descendants upon the death of Father Smith.

The position of patriarch, as well as that of president, was a form of lineal charismatic authority from the very beginning. In Weberian terms this was "traditional-familial" leadership, which was the real authority operating up until the death of Joseph Smith, Jr. It was only after the Prophet and the Patriarch were killed that what had been an embryonic, largely nominal "office" structure became the traditional authority with power and that the remnants of the "familial"—the office of Patriarch—became an impotent arm of the hierarchy.

Given the origins of Mormonism, it seems natural that young Joseph would see his father in a lineal role of primacy. The Prophet was restoring Old Testament primitivism, as that canon was interpreted through the New Testament, when he called his father to assume the patriarchate. Just as Joseph, ruler of Egypt, felt it necessary to bring his father, Jacob, to Egypt so that the patriarch could give blessings to the children of Israel over whom Joseph presided, so Joseph, the nineteenth-century prophet, felt it necessary to place his father in a patriarchal position within the hierarchy over which the younger Joseph presided.[28]

In the initial ordination blessing there was no explanation of the responsibilities that attended holding the keys of the patriarchal priesthood. This troublesome ambiguity would continue until the eventual elimination of the office. It was soon implicitly accepted that the calling included the right to bestow blessings on *all* members of the church,[29] as well as to preside over any other patriarchs who would be called on a local basis.[30]

The original ordination also did not indicate where, in a relative sense, the position fit in the existing hierarchy, except that it certainly was meant to have a dimension of primal importance in the familial authority structure then in existence. Being compared with Adam and serving as the figurative father of the church, the Patriarch was placed in an honorary primal position from the first.

In December 1833 the church hierarchy, as we know it today, had not yet taken form. At the beginning in 1830 there was only the simple designation of "first elder" and "second elder," applied respectively to the Prophet Joseph and his former scribe, Oliver Cowdery. By January of 1832 Joseph had been sustained as "President of the High Priesthood," and two months later two "Counselors" to Joseph were appointed: Jesse Gause and Sidney Rigdon. This "Presidency of the High Priesthood" was the extent of the governing hierarchy when Father Smith was designated holder of the keys of the patriarchal priesthood of the church in December 1833. Oliver Cowdery referred to Father Smith as being ordained "a president" and patriarch in 1833, which inferred presiding authority. Until the first high council was established in 1834, however, there was no well-defined hierarchy operating below the First Presidency.[31]

The *History of the Church* also recounts Joseph Jr.'s description of his father's ordination as both the Patriarch and the "President of the High Priesthood under the hands of Oliver Cowdery, Sidney Rigdon, Frederick G. Williams and myself, on the 18th of December, 1833."[32] It has been subsequently suggested that Father Smith was president of the high priests in Kirtland rather than of the "High Priesthood."[33] There is, however, no record of hierarchical authority over the high priests at that time, other than the First Presidency over the High Priesthood (i.e., no local High Priest quorums as such). The Saints thus probably understood Father Smith to have been given presidency rights over the High Priesthood— probably in an honorary sense only—when he was given the keys of the patriarchal priesthood. It is clear that Joseph Jr., having been ordained to the presidency in 1832, continued to hold the line-authority position above that of his father.[34]

When stakes were first formed in 1834, one in Kirtland and one in Missouri, Father Smith was called as a charter member of the first high council ("standing council") on February 17, 1834. He thus served in the line-authority structure at the same time he was serving as the Patriarch.[35] The First Presidency, with Joseph Smith, Jr., at the head, formed the presidency of the high council in Kirtland, and Oliver Cowdery was for a time president of the high council in Missouri.

In April the Prophet Joseph Smith left for Missouri with Zion's Camp, a Mormon army that anticipated the military redemption of their beleaguered fellow Saints. On December 6, 1834, following Zion's Camp, Father Smith was made an assistant president in the First Presidency. This gave him line-authority responsibilities, which he had been unable to exercise in his position as "honorary holder" of the keys of the priesthood in his calling as the Patriarch. At this time there were not yet any local patriarchs over whom he might preside.[36]

It is likely that Father Smith began giving blessings soon after he was ordained, but the first to be noted officially were those given to Joseph Smith, Jr., and his brother Samuel on February 19, 1834.[37] According to Benjamin F. Johnson, "In the summer of 1834 Father Joseph Smith, Sr., commenced to visit the families of the Saints and give patriarchal blessings, and greatly was the spirit of the Lord manifested among the Saints."[38] On December 9, 1834, the Patriarch blessed his own family and at least four other members of the church. Among other things he said to his son Joseph:

> The Lord has called thee by name out of the heavens. Thou hast heard his voice from on high, from time to time, even in thy youth. . . . Thou hast sought to know his ways and from thy childhood thou hast meditated much upon the great things of his law. Thou hast suffered much in thy youth and the poverty and afflictions of thy father's family have been a grief to thy soul. Thou hast desired to see them delivered from bondage for thou hast loved them with a perfect love. Thou hast stood by thy Father, and like Shem, would have covered his nakedness, rather than see him exposed to shame. When the daughters of the gentiles laughed, thy heart has been moved with a just anger to avenge thy kindred. Thou hast been an obedient son. . . . A marvellous work and a wonder has the Lord wrought by thy hand, even that which shall prepare a way for the remnants of his people to come in among the gentiles, with their fulness, as the tribes of Israel are restored. I bless thee with the blessings of thy fathers, Abraham, Isaac and Jacob; and even the blessings of thy father Joseph, the son of Jacob. Behold he looked after his posterity in the last days, when they should be scattered and driven by the gentiles and wept before the Lord. He sought diligently to know from whence the Son should come who should bring forth the word of the Lord by which they might be enlightened, and brought back to the true fold, and his eyes beheld thee, my Son. His heart rejoiced and his soul was satisfied, and he said . . . from among my seed, scattered with the gentiles, shall a choice Seer arise, whose bowels shall be as a fountain of truth.[39]

To Hyrum, his eldest son, the Patriarch said,

> Behold thou art Hyrum. The Lord has called thee by that name, and by that name has he blessed thee. Thou hast borne the burden and heat of the day, thou hast toiled hard and labored much, for the good of

thy father's family. Thou hast been a stay many times to them, and by thy diligence they have often been sustained. Thou hast loved thy father's family with a pure love, and hast greatly desired their salvation. Thou hast always stood by thy father, and reached forth the helping hand to lift him up, when he was in affliction, and though he has been out of the way through wine, thou hast never forsaken him, nor laughed him to scorn, for all these kindnesses the Lord my God will bless thee. I now ask my Heavenly Father, in the name of Jesus Christ, to bless thee with the same blessings with which Jacob blessed his son Joseph, for thou art his true descendant, and thy posterity shall be numbered with the house of Ephraim, and with them thou shalt stand up to crown the tribes of Israel, when they come shouting to Zion. Thou shalt live to see thy Redeemer come in the clouds of heaven. . . . The Lord will multiply his choice blessings upon thee, and upon thy seed after thee, and thou, with them shall have an inheritance in Zion, and they shall possess it from generation to generation, and thy name shall never be blotted out. . . .[40]

Patriarchal blessings to others followed.

Although there was concern about keeping records from the beginning, during its first decade the church was primarily concerned with the preservation and publication of the Prophet's revelations.[41] In 1835, however, a blessing book costing twelve dollars was purchased for the Patriarch in which a record could be kept of all blessings given by him. The book was lost or stolen at Far West, Missouri, but came to light several years later.[42] There was concern about not only records but also the Patriarch's livelihood. On September 14, 1835, the church departed from its tradition of an "unpaid clergy," at least in terms of the Patriarch: "It was decided that as the laborer is worthy of his hire whomever Joseph Smith, Senr. is called upon to pronounce patriarchal blessings upon the church he be paid for his time at the rate of ten dollars per week, and his expenses found. It was further decided that President Frederick G. Williams [a member of the First Presidency] be appointed and hereafter serve as scribe to attend blessing meetings, and that he receive for his service at the same ratio, having his expenses borne also."[43]

A variation on the custom is revealed by the high council trial of Elder Isaac McWithy, which charged him with "want of benevolence to the poor and charity to the Church." During the proceedings "Prest. J. Smith Senr. says that he blessed the accused with a patriarchal blessing but thinks that he received nothing from him [McWithy] for the poor as it was usual for him on such occasions."[44]

The blessing meetings spoken of were deeply spiritual events, followed

by celebratory feasts. Joseph Jr. tells of a large company assembled at Oliver Olney's house on December 29, 1835, "when Father Smith made some
appropriate remarks. A hymn was sung and father opened the meeting
by prayer. About fifteen persons then received patriarchal blessings under his hands. . . . A table was crowned with the bounties of nature; and
after invoking the benediction of heaven upon the rich repast, we fared
sumptuously."[45] B. Carmon Hardy has said that "there is something won-
derfully telling about the practice of the prophet's father, Joseph Smith,
Sr., who, when presiding at a meeting, would ask all to pray aloud at once,
'and there would be as many different prayers as there were persons.'"[46]

In the meantime, the ecclesiastical hierarchy was continuing to evolve.
In February 1835, over a year after Father Smith was called to be Patriarch, the Quorum of the Twelve Apostles was first created as a traveling
high council to preside over areas where the church was not yet established. At that time "the Twelve clearly ranked below the high council."[47]
The apostles had no presiding authority over the Patriarch to the Church,
and, indeed, their jurisdiction ended where that of the organized stakes
in the church began: "The twelve apostles have no right to go into Zion
or any of its stakes where there is a regular high council established, to
regulate any matter pertaining thereto: But it is their duty to go abroad
and regulate and set in order all matters relative to the different branches of the Latter Day Saints. No standing high council has authority to go
into the churches abroad and regulate the matters thereof, for this belongs to the Twelve."[48]

As one scholar explains, "Throughout Joseph Smith's lifetime the stakes
were the centers of the ecclesiastical mainstream. The hinterland of the
church [the only jurisdiction of the apostles] was comprised of compar-
atively small, isolated branches of members."[49] This must be remembered
to understand properly the later crisis between the Twelve and the office
of Patriarch upon the death of the Prophet Joseph Smith.

As the church was growing, it was recognized that the task of answering all requests for blessings would be beyond the capacity of Father
Smith. This concern was addressed on March 28, 1835, when a revelation
was announced taking the concept of patriarchal blessings beyond the
confines of a tribal responsibility and further into the realms of institutional procedure and jurisdiction. Doctrine and Covenants 107:39 states,
"It is the duty of the Twelve, in all branches of the church, to ordain evangelical ministers [patriarchs] as they shall be designated unto them by
revelation." While the revelation confirmed Joseph Jr. as the president in
the First Presidency, it gave the newly created Quorum of the Twelve
Apostles the duty to ordain patriarchs in all large branches of the church.
The revelation, curiously, does not mention the office of Patriarch over

the whole church; however, verses 53 through 55 of section 107, listing and describing the blessings of Old Testament patriarchs, are quoted verbatim from the December 18, 1833, ordination blessing of Joseph Smith, Sr.[50]

The distinction between the authority of the apostles to ordain patriarchs in the branches of the church and the authority of the First Presidency to ordain the Presiding Church Patriarch would become moot when the apostles later assumed the responsibilities of the First Presidency after the death of the Prophet. Prior to 1844, however, this distinction was very much in place. Although authorized to ordain local patriarchs in March 1835, the Twelve did not perform such ordinations until November 1837, and, although there are no records, the Prophet Joseph Smith, Jr., apparently ordained at least one priesthood father as a patriarch as early as 1834. Brigham Young's account of the ordination of his father, John Young, as a patriarch in 1834 following Zion's Camp is the prime example, one which has been problematic in its claim that Father Young, instead of Father Smith, was the first patriarch in the church. Brigham Young recalled in 1874 that when his father was ordained "so far as I am aware, Joseph had never received any intimation as to there being a Patriarch in the Church." Young continued:

> On our return home from Missouri, my brother Joseph Young, while conversing with me, asked if it would be right for our father to give us a blessing. . . . When we reached Kirtland we talked with Joseph on the subject, and he said, "Certainly," and . . . we met and ordained my father a Patriarch, and he was the first man ordained to the office of Patriarch in the Church, and he blessed his children; and soon after this Joseph ordained his father a patriarch. . . . Then Joseph had another revelation, that a record should be kept, and when this was revealed to him, he then had his father call his house together again, and blessed them over and a record was kept of it.[51]

Brigham Young's memory in 1874 appears to be inaccurate concerning the date of ordination of Father Smith.[52] The probable explanation for the confusion is that, although Father Smith was ordained in 1833, many might not have been fully aware of his activities in the office until he became generally active in giving blessings to those outside his own family in the summer of 1834.[53] Even Brigham Young was not consistent in his account of who the first patriarch was. Wilford Woodruff records Young saying on August 15, 1847, that "Father Smith was the senior patriarch in the Church and *first* patriarch in our day and afterwards Hyrum was the senior patriarch for his father sealed it upon his head . . ." (emphasis added).[54] At the funeral of Joseph Young, Brigham's brother, Wilford Woodruff stated that John Young was "the first ordained patriarch in this generation but he was ordained as patriarch of his own family, he did not officiate as the Patriarch to the Church, as Father Joseph Smith did up to the date of his death."[55]

There would be no reason for Oliver Cowdery to falsify the ordination date, even though the extant version of Father Smith's ordination was written by Cowdery in 1835.[56] The setting of the ordination at the gathering of the printing press dedication in Kirtland appears to be too detailed and historically contextual to have been a deliberate falsification, and there is no apparent motivation for such an error. Indeed, Cowdery's interests would be consistent with a later ordination date to preserve his own office status.

Despite all of this, D. Michael Quinn in *The Mormon Hierarchy: Origins of Power* posits that Joseph Smith, Sr., was not even present at the printing press meeting on December 18, 1833, and that he was not ordained Patriarch until December 9, 1834.[57] While the difference between the two dates is not critical to this study, and while Quinn's hypothesis is possible, it has not been established with any historical certainty. Indeed, a case for the traditional date of Joseph Sr.'s ordination is at least as credible. In choosing between Cowdery's date (December 18, 1833) given in 1835 and Brigham Young's date (after Zion's Camp in 1834) given in 1874, Quinn ignores the possibility that Young might have had a faulty or convenient memory and gives full credence to the idea that Cowdery was serving in "part of the larger pattern of revising the historical record to suggest orderly evolution of church priesthood and hierarchy."[58] One example of the tenuousness of Quinn's hypothesis is the conclusion that because Joseph Smith's diary does not list Joseph Sr. as being present at the meeting on December 18, 1833, then he was not there. The diary, however, makes no pretense of listing all those who were present. It states, "This day the Elders assembled togeth[er] in the printing office . . . and then proceded to bow down before the Lord and dedicate the printing press and all that per=tains thereunto to God by mine own hand and confirmed by bro Sidney Rigdon and Hyrum Smith and then proceded to take the first proof sheet of the star edited by Bro Oliv[ver] Cowd[er]y. . . ."[59]

The diary then proceeds to record blessings on Oliver Cowdery and members of the Prophet's family, including Joseph Smith, Sr. While it is possible that these blessings are simply an account of Joseph Jr.'s thoughts and are not related to those present at the December 18 meeting discussed in the same diary entry, there is no way to draw that conclusion from the record. Further, the reference to "the Elders" assembling together suggests that more were present than just the Prophet, Sydney Rigdon, Hyrum Smith, and Oliver Cowdery.

Moreover, Quinn states that Father Smith did not give any blessings prior to December 9, 1834, which is not correct. As discussed earlier in this chapter, Joseph Sr. blessed his sons Joseph Jr. and Samuel on February 19, 1834, and began visiting families to give blessings in the summer of 1834.[60]

Whether the date is 1833 or 1834, in 1835 the Quorum of the Twelve was not yet in tension with the office of Presiding Patriarch (as would later be the case). It seems Oliver Cowdery did have some concerns, however. When he copied the 1833 ordination blessing of Joseph Smith, Sr., in 1835, Cowdery editorialized as follows:

> Joseph Smith, Jr., [was] the *first elder and first patriarch* of the church; for although his father laid hands upon and blessed the fatherless, thereby securing the blessings of the Lord unto them and their posterity, *he was not the first elder,* because God called upon his son Joseph and ordained him to this power and delivered to him the keys of the Kingdom, that is, of authority and spiritual blessings upon the church. . . . Let it suffice that others had authority to bless, but after these blessings were given [December 18, 1833] Joseph Smith, Sen. was ordained a president and patriarch. . . .[61]

Cowdery apparently felt it necessary to point out that being the Patriarch did not make Joseph Sr. the "first elder," a designation given to Joseph Jr. as the ultimate hierarch. In a revelation Cowdery claims to have received, also in September 1835, he quotes God as saying, "For behold, [Joseph Smith, Jr.,] is the first patriarch in the last days."[62] There is no record of Cowdery's making similar protestations that Joseph Jr. was the first apostle, bishop, or high counselor, even though a similar argument could have been made at that time based on Joseph Jr.'s possession of the keys and authority of all other offices in the church. Cowdery likely pressed this point because he perceived the Patriarch to be a primal office in the organization, one that might dilute his own status. Cowdery himself had, once again, been declared "second elder" on December 5, 1834, and his protestations suggest a protective attitude.

Oliver Cowdery's attempts to distinguish Joseph Jr. as the first elder *and* first patriarch and to emphasize the two separate titles also might have been an attempt to promote church institutional/office authority over the unstructured and de facto familial authority of the Smith family, a difficult task in those charismatic times.

Another possible reason for Cowdery's concern, one that was to present itself repeatedly throughout the history of the patriarchy, was the difficulty or unwillingness of other leaders to accept an honorary "first" office, with limited power, as consistent and coexistent with an ultimately powerful, line-authority "first" office. As unworkable as such an arrangement eventually became, there were always proponents and opponents. Some members of the Smith family have, on and off and with varying degrees of intensity, been proponents. Cowdery seems to have been the earliest of the opponents to record his feelings on the subject.

In 1836 the office of Patriarch was again associated with the Old Testament prophets. On January 21, the Prophet Joseph and the First Presidency, after attending to the ordinance of washing their bodies in pure water in the attic of the printing office, removed to the west schoolroom of the Kirtland Temple to complete the ordinance by anointing their heads with holy oil. The Prophet Joseph noted, "I took the oil in my left hand, Father Smith being seated before me, and the remainder of the Presidency encircled him round about." They then consecrated the oil and "laid our hands upon our aged Father Smith, and invoked the blessings of heaven." Joseph Jr. "sealed many blessings upon him," including "to be our Patriarch, to anoint our heads, and attend to all duties that pertain to that office. The Presidency then took the seat in their turn, according to their age, beginning at the oldest, and received their anointing and blessing under the hands of Father Smith." In his turn, Joseph Sr. then blessed and anointed his son Joseph Jr. and sealed upon him the blessings of Moses "to lead Israel in the latter days, even as Moses led him in days of old; also the blessings of Abraham, Isaac, and Jacob."[63] Thereafter a vision of the celestial kingdom was opened up to the younger Joseph, in which he saw his brother Alvin and other family members.

This appears to have been an occasion when Father Smith received further powers and instruction in connection with his patriarchal calling. The record unfortunately does not record the details of the "many blessings" that he received; however, he apparently received sufficient authority to, in turn, bless his son with the blessings of Moses and Abraham. This mutual giving and receiving between the Prophet and the Patriarch of significant blessings suggests, at least with respect to the perception at that time, that son and father shared power and authority of a primal nature.

Through all of the organizational developments, Father Smith also had the responsibility of supervising the temporal needs of his family. In 1836, because of the hardships his parents encountered, the Prophet asked them to move into the home he and Emma were occupying.[64] At that time, in addition to giving patriarchal blessings to his family and church members, Father Smith continued in other forms of church activity. He presided over high council meetings in Kirtland,[65] and he continued in his calling to collect donations for the building of the Kirtland Temple. Both Father Smith and Hyrum were very much involved in the building of that edifice, which was dedicated on Sunday, March 27, 1836, amidst great spiritual experiences for the Saints.[66] It was said that an angel sat between Joseph Smith, Sr., and Frederick G. Williams during the dedication services.[67]

After the dedication, the temple was used for a variety of meetings. In addition to the regular Sunday services, on the first Thursday of each month Father Smith would preside at fast meetings:[68] "and there [in the temple], under his teachings have the meek and the humble been instructed, while the widow and the orphan have received his patriarchal blessings. . . . [He] saw the elders of Israel go forth under his blessing . . . and hailed them welcome when they again returned bringing their sheaves with them."[69]

Father Smith and his brother John went on a mission to New Portage in May 1836 to preach and give patriarchal blessings. Soon after their arrival they learned that their ninety-three-year-old mother, Mary Duty Smith, had arrived in Kirtland from the East. According to Eliza R. Snow, Mary told Lucy Mack Smith that she wanted to be baptized by her grandson the Prophet, and she wanted her son Joseph Sr. to bless her.[70] They returned only two days before Mary died. On June 22 the brothers left for the East to inform relatives of their mother's death and to, again, give patriarchal blessings. The Prophet went to see them off as far as Painsville, where they "procured a bottle of wine, broke bread, ate and drank, and parted after the ancient order, with the blessings of God."[71]

Their encounters with their relatives were pleasant, except for the one with their brother Jesse, who not only continued to oppose the church but actually arranged for the arrest of Joseph Sr. for a twelve dollar debt. Their brother Silas paid the debt, and Joseph Sr. and John moved on.[72] They covered twenty-four hundred miles and visited dozens of eastern branches before they returned in early October.

Patriarch Smith was not unaffected by the economic troubles of the time. In November 1836 the Mormon leadership attempted to create the Kirtland Safety Society Bank to solve the financial chaos that had devastated northern Ohio. When temporary political reverses in January 1837 prevented the issuing of a charter for the bank, the Mormons reorganized the enterprise into the Kirtland Safety Society Anti-Banking Company to issue notes and take in money. There was a short boom, but within three weeks the company failed. Joseph Smith, Jr., accused Warren Parrish, who had succeeded the Prophet as cashier, of absconding with a large sum of money, and many of the Saints suffered great financial losses.[73] Inevitably, this led to apostasy by many of the Saints.

Warren Parrish, consistently maintaining his innocence, was especially bitter. While Joseph was on a mission in Canada in August, Father Smith was presiding at meetings in the Kirtland Temple in the Prophet's absence. Warren Parrish and other apostates arrived with weapons and threatened to take the temple by force. Attempting to protect his father, William Smith "sprang forward and caught Parrish, and carried him in his arms nearly out of the house."[74] At sword point William released Parrish, and eventually order was restored.

The next day Father Smith was arrested on the complaint of the apostates and charged with riot. Eliza R. Snow wrote, "I found the court scene as amusing as the Temple scene was appalling. The idea of such a man as Father Smith—so patriarchal in appearance—so circumspect in deportment and dignified in his manners, being guilty of riot, was at once ludicrous and farcical to all sane-minded persons."[75] After the hearing, the court dismissed the case.

Because of such internal dissension in Kirtland, the Prophet declared that "God revealed to me that something new must be done for the salvation of His Church." The answer was expansion of the church to England, "the first foreign mission of the Church of Christ in the last days."[76] Apostles Heber C. Kimball and Orson Hyde, along with the recent convert Willard Richards, were sent to Britain, and they succeeded in bringing fifteen hundred converts into the church by April 1838. Although many of the converts were impoverished, the British transfusion brought such people as William Clayton and others who became stalwarts in the faith. Strength was certainly needed during the years of persecution and hardship awaiting them when they emigrated to "Zion."

By September 1837 the Prophet Joseph was back from Canada and presiding over a general conference at Kirtland. He presented Sidney Rigdon and Frederick G. Williams for a sustaining vote as counselors in the First Presidency. The congregation did not sustain Williams, however. Joseph then introduced Oliver Cowdery, Joseph Smith, Sr., Hyrum Smith, and his uncle John Smith as assistant counselors, telling the congregation that they and the three in the First Presidency, "are to be considered the heads of the Church."[77] Once again Father Smith was participating in the line-authority aspects of primal leadership, at the same time holding his position as the Patriarch. The more overlap, the less clear the lines of distinction were between the two positions. That this ambiguity would be allowed is understandable. Father Smith was the father of the Prophet and head of the "royal family." He was also providing comfort and reassurance to the persecuted Saints with his patriarchal blessings.

As 1837 came to a close, there was a significant step in the calling of patriarchs in the church. The first local patriarch, Isaac Morley, was ordained on November 7, 1837; however, it was not the apostles who ordained the first patriarch in a branch of the church, despite the 1835 revelatory authorization to do so. Morley was ordained by Joseph Smith, Jr., Sidney Rigdon, and Hyrum Smith. Morley was a relatively well-to-do member of the church, who had been associated with Sidney Rigdon's group of Campbellite believers when Parley P. Pratt first came to Kirtland with the message of the restored gospel. "Father Morley," who served long and with distinction in his patriarchal calling, was understood to be subordinate to "Father Smith" within the ranks of patriarchs in the church.[78]

It should be noted that local patriarchs have never claimed or been given administrative authority. Their role is to give blessings within the geographical boundaries of their particular stake, have the blessings recorded, and transmit the recorded blessing to the recipient as well as to the church for archiving in the official records. They have variously reported to the Presiding Patriarch, the First Presidency, the Quorum of the Twelve, and, most recently, the stake president of their particular stake.

In the spring of 1838 Joseph Smith, Sr., was once again arrested, this time for marrying a couple without a license. He was placed in the police custody of Luke Johnson, who, although disaffected from the church at the time, nevertheless thought warmly of Father Smith. Johnson volunteered his services to be Father Smith's legal counsel (an interesting example of conflict of interest) and promptly arranged for Father Smith's escape. Before the court proceeded to business, Johnson said he would like a few minutes of private conversation with his client. Permission was granted for him to take the prisoner into a room adjoining the court. He then helped Father Smith out the window with instructions to go to Oliver Snow's house. Johnson then walked back into court. After a moment he acted as though he had just discovered that his client had not followed him and rushed back into the adjoining room to see what was detaining him. "After hunting about there a short time, he came back to the court room, apparently very much disconcerted, and reported the unaccountable fact that the prisoner was not to be found."[79]

Father Smith stayed two or three weeks at the home of Oliver Snow, the father of Lorenzo Snow and Eliza R. Snow. Lucy sent him money and clothes to travel, and he then made his way to New Portage, despite handbills posted prominently for his arrest. Father Smith remained there until his family could go with him to Missouri.

During these years severe persecution was continuing in Missouri, as well as in Kirtland. In 1838 the bitterness of the spirit of "apostate mobocracy" caused most of the Saints to leave Kirtland, Ohio, for Far West, Missouri. Joseph Smith quoted Jesus, who said, "When they persecute you in one city, flee to another."[80] Father Smith and his family suffered sickness and hardships because they were forced to move during inclement weather during the summer of 1838. Upon arriving in Far West, Missouri, the family settled in a small, one-room log house. Shortly after, Joseph arranged for his parents to move into a tavern house, which was more comfortable.

The persecution increased in Missouri, and the Mormons were eventually driven entirely from the state. Joseph Sr. and his wife, Lucy, watched as their sons Joseph and Hyrum were taken prisoners by a Missouri mob in November 1838. They then once again traveled under adverse circumstances to a new home.[81]

Father Smith and Lucy arrived in Quincy, Illinois, on March 6, 1839, while Joseph and Hyrum were still imprisoned in the jail at Liberty, Missouri. Two months later Father Smith moved his family up the Mississippi River to the town of Commerce. In June, after Joseph and Hyrum's escape from jail, the settlement at Commerce was renamed Nauvoo and became the new gathering place for the Saints. Joseph Smith, Sr., lived with his wife in this new home in relative peace, but in failing health, until his death.

In 1839, shortly before the departure of the Twelve on their missionary trip to England, the Prophet taught the apostles that "an Evangelist is a Patriarch, even the oldest man of the blood of Joseph or of the seed of Abraham. Wherever the Church of Christ is established in the earth, there should be a Patriarch for the benefit of the posterity of the Saints, as it was with Jacob in giving his patriarchal blessing unto his sons, etc."[82]

When the apostles arrived in England, they finally followed up on their 1835 charge to ordain patriarchs. On April 16, 1840, at the Temperance Hall in Preston, Lancashire, Apostle Heber C. Kimball "laid before the conference the importance and propriety of ordaining a Patriarch to bestow Patriarchal blessings on the fatherless," and he referred to the Twelve, whose business was to select one and ordain him according to the directions of the spirit. The next day the Twelve met, and it was "moved by elder H. C. Kimball and seconded by elder W. Richards, that elder Peter Melling be ordained as an evangelical minister in Preston."[83]

Melling was undoubtedly taught by the apostles to follow the pattern set by Father Smith in having blessing meetings. Indeed, Melling presided at gatherings where a feast was prepared at a private house and several persons were invited to attend. After refreshments, the meeting was opened by singing and prayer; then Melling laid hands on the head of a brother or sister and, a sentence at a time, pronounced the blessing while his scribe, a Brother Whitehead, wrote it down.[84]

While still on their mission in England, and after Joseph Sr., had died, the apostles ordained a second patriarch for that country. Brigham Young was speaking at a conference and "proceeded to make some remarks on the office of patriarch, and concluded by moving that Elder John Albiston be ordained to that office." It was seconded by Elder Kimball and carried unanimously. Apparently they felt it necessary first to give the candidate his own patriarchal blessing, because "the Patriarch P[eter] Melling was then called upon to pronounce a patriarchal blessing upon the head of John Albertson [sic] previous to his being ordained to the office of patriarch." Albiston was then ordained as a patriarch before the congregation. Melling and Albiston were the only patriarchs ordained while the apostles were in England, and Melling was the only patriarch ordained by the apostles during the incumbency of Joseph Smith, Sr.[85]

Father Smith continued to give patriarchal blessings until the time of his death. His blessings throughout his life were poetic and otherworldly, as well as prophetic. One blessing given on March 26, 1836, for example, promised the recipient, "Thou shalt see thy Redeemer and behold the prints of the nails in his hands and feet, and thou shalt weep when thou seest him, and seek to wash his feet with thy tears, and to wipe them with the hairs of thy head like Mary: he shall lay his hands upon thee and bless thee with all the feelings of a father, and then thy soul shall be satisfied."[86] Lorenzo Snow received an interesting blessing. In December 1836 he was told by the Patriarch, "Thou shalt have the power to translate thyself from one planet to another—power to go to the moon if thou shalt desire it." He was also promised that "the diseased shall send to thee their handkerchiefs and aprons and by thy touch their owners shall be healed."[87]

Elijah Abel, a black convert born in Maryland on July 25, 1808, was given a particularly significant patriarchal blessing in Kirtland in 1836 by Joseph Smith, Sr. Abel's blessing describes a scene that could well be understood as a prophetic vision of the Civil War:

> Thou has been ordained an Elder and anointed to secure thee against the power of the destroyer. Thou shalt see His power in laying waste the nations, and the wicked slaying the wicked, while blood shall run down the streets like water, and thy heart shall weep over their calamities. Angels shall visit thee and thou shalt receive comfort. They shall call thee blessed, and deliver thee from thine enemies. They shall break thy bands and keep them from affliction. . . . Thou shalt be made equal to thy brethren, and thy soul be white in eternity and thy robes glittering; thou shalt receive these blessings because of the covenants of thy fathers.[88]

Some women were also promised they would be "made equal to thy brethren" or that they would be not "one single whit behind thy brethren in knowledge and understanding."[89] Several were also told they would have power to heal the sick.[90]

When Father Smith attended blessing meetings, he invariably asked Lucy to accompany him. Lucy tells of one occasion when she had been hurt in a fall and did not feel like going with him. "I told him that I was afraid that I should take a cold and it would affect me seriously on account of my fall, but as he refused to go without me . . . I went."[91] That Joseph wanted Lucy to be with him at blessing meetings and that they actually shared in the giving of blessings attest to the close spiritual bond between the parents of the Prophet. There was more to it than that, though. In the blessing given to Father Smith on December 18, 1833, when he was given the "keys of the patriarchal kingdom," the Prophet included Mother Lucy Mack Smith: "And blessed also is my mother, for she is a mother in Israel, and shall be a partaker with my father in all his patriarchal blessings." Caroline Barnes Crosby tells of receiving a blessing from the Patriarch in 1836, and she adds, "Mother Smith was in the room. She also added her blessing or confirmed what we have already received."[92]

In many of the Patriarch's blessings he uses the phrase "I seal you up unto eternal life." At the time the "sealing power" was a power associated with the High Priesthood. The Prophet Joseph Smith, Jr., told a gathering on October 25, 1831, that "the order of the Highpriesthood is that they have power given them to seal up the Saints unto eternal life. And said it was the privilege of every Elder present to be ordained to the Highpriesthood."[93] Elders who were members of the High Priesthood used this sealing power in the early 1830s. Reynolds Cahoon, for example, sealed an entire congregation to eternal life in November 1831.[94] Orson Hyde, during an unsuccessful house-to-house missionary journey in 1832, sealed "many to the day of rath, bound the tares and bundles, blessed some. . . ."[95]

A decade later the Prophet recorded a revelation that is now Doctrine and Covenants 132:7: "and I have appointed unto my servant Joseph to hold this power in the last days, and there is never but one on earth at a time on whom this power and the keys of this priesthood are conferred." It seems likely that Joseph was talking about other kinds of sealings at that time, especially plural or eternal marriage. But throughout his tenure as the Patriarch, Father Smith had sealed individuals to eternal life (as well as sealing blessings on recipients). Much later the phrase would be adjusted to "I seal you up to come forth on the morning of the first resurrection."[96] Although with Hyrum Smith the sealing powers would become an important part of his calling as the Patriarch, they were not specifically mentioned in the original ordination of Joseph Smith, Sr. He was admonished to bless his own posterity, give counsel, and hold "the keys of the patriarchal priesthood" within the church organization. The sealing authority of the patriarchate became of record in 1841 with the revelation set forth in Doctrine and Covenants 124:93 and 124.

The power to "curse," as well as "bless," was evidently believed to be part of the patriarchal calling.[97] Once, when on a missionary journey and a farmer refused them shelter in a storm, Father Smith "removed his hat and with uplifted hands he prayed: 'In the name of the Lord whom we serve, let that man be cursed in his basket and in his store, and let this man's name be cut off from under heaven.'"[98]

Although Father Smith did not keep a journal, his brother John's written accounts tell of many experiences the two had as they traveled together many hundreds of miles giving blessings.[99] Father Smith had suffered much during the ten years that the church had existed. While in Illinois, "whenever he had a short respite from pain, he felt a pleasure in attending to his patriarchal duties."[100]

When Father Smith realized his condition was such that he would not long survive, "he called his children and grandchildren around him and like the ancient Patriarchs gave them his final benediction. Although his strength was far gone, and he was obliged to rest at intervals, yet his mind was clear, perfectly collected, and calm as the gentle zephyrs."[101] On September 14, 1840, a year after arriving in Nauvoo, he died, "the first family martyr of the Missouri persecutions."[102]

Before dying, the Patriarch blessed his wife and all of his family, and, in keeping with his understanding of the familial nature of his calling, he conferred the office of Church Patriarch upon his eldest son, Hyrum.

Beginning with Joseph Sr.'s tenure, and largely defined by it, the hereditary calling of the Patriarch in the LDS Church was modeled on the Old Testament patriarchs. Father Joseph performed in a familial, tribal role of primacy. As incumbents and other general authorities repeatedly stated later, *patri* means "father" and *arch* means "chief." Joseph Smith, Jr., confirmed this when he ordained Father Joseph as the Patriarch on December 18, 1833: "[Joseph Sr.] shall be called a prince over his posterity holding the keys of the patriarchal priesthood over the kingdom of God on earth, even the Church of the Latter-day Saints, and shall sit in the general assembly of Patriarchs, even in council with the Ancient of Days when he shall sit and all the Patriarchs with him and shall enjoy his right and authority under the direction of the Ancient of Days."[103]

Within the statement are the seeds of tension. The Prophet might well have tied the calling to both lineal primacy and an institutional role. There is a built-in ambiguity in the definition of the office itself and in terms of the framework of the organization within which the office would function.

The office of Patriarch might have been ill-defined, but it was clearly one of primal importance, bound within a familial relationship with the Prophet—a line-authority figure. As for the institution, it was still in the process of evolving, so it was difficult to say where the office of Patriarch belonged within the hierarchy during the years when the organization was being formalized.

Joseph Smith, Sr., was the central figure for whom the office was created, and his was the family that had a hereditary right to the office of Patriarch. While the Prophet was alive, the patriarchate did not present any problems, and there was no clue that serious conflicts might lie ahead. Why, where, and how the difficulties arose is discussed in the chapters that follow.

Notes

1. Joseph Sr. and Lucy Mack Smith's children were Alvin, born February 11, 1799; Hyrum, February 9, 1800; Sophronia, May 18, 1803; Joseph Jr., December 23, 1805; Samuel, March 13, 1808; Ephraim, March 13, 1810; William, March 13, 1811: Catherine, July 8, 1812; Don Carlos, March 25, 1816; and Lucy, July 18, 1821.

2. Lucy Mack Smith, *Biographical Sketches of Joseph Smith the Prophet and His Progenitors for Many Generations* (Liverpool, England: Published for Orson Pratt by S. W. Richards, 1853; New York: Arno Press and New York Times, 1969), 163, 269.

3. Ibid., 67–68.

4. Ibid., 57.

5. Jan Shipps, *Mormonism: The Story of a New Religious Tradition* (Urbana: University of Illinois Press, 1985), 9. Shipps maintains that Lucy's Mormonism "is familial, even tribal, rather than organizational and institutional. It is the Mormonism of the early 1830s . . . the church the prophet founded in the beginning not the one he led at the end of his life" (104).

6. Illinois copyright records, vol. 18, cited in Shipps, *Mormonism,* 104. The book was published by Orson Pratt in England in 1853 and was condemned by Brigham Young as inaccurate. In 1902 there was a revised edition: Lucy Mack Smith, *History of the Prophet Joseph Smith,* revised by George A. Smith and Elias Smith (Salt Lake City: Improvement Era, 1902), which included only minor alterations. There was also a later version: Lucy Mack Smith, *History of Joseph Smith by His Mother, Lucy Mack Smith,* with notes and comments by Preston Nibley (Salt Lake City: Bookcraft, 1958).

7. Joseph Smith, *History of the Church of Jesus Christ of Latter-day Saints,* 2d rev. ed., ed. B. H. Roberts, 7 vols. (Salt Lake City: Deseret Book, 1978), 4:190.

8. For accounts of parallel mystical experiences, see Neal E. Lambert and Richard H. Cracroft, "Literary Form and Historical Understanding: Joseph Smith's First Vision," *Journal of Mormon History* 7 (1980): 31–42. It is believed that Joseph Sr. might have been involved with Nathaniel Wood's New Israelites and the group's ill-fated prediction that "the destroyer would pass through the land and slay a portion of unbelievers, and that a great earthquake would obliterate the remaining unfaithful." Stephen A. Marini, *Radical Sects of Revolutionary New England* (Cambridge, Mass.: Harvard University Press, 1982), 55, citing Barnes Frisbie in *The History of Middletown, Vermont* (Rutland, Vt.: Tuttle, 1867).

9. Lucy Mack Smith, *Biographical Sketches,* 57. Lucy tells how her husband

refused to go to the local Methodist church after his father, Asael Smith, had insisted he read Thomas Paine's *Age of Reason.*

10. *Doctrine and Covenants of the Church of Jesus Christ of Latter-day Saints* (Salt Lake City: Deseret Book, 1955), 4:1–7.

11. See preliminary pages of the Book of Mormon, fifth unnumbered page.

12. Lucy Mack Smith, *Biographical Sketches,* 151.

13. Quoted in Dean Jessee, "Joseph Knight's Recollection of Early Mormon History," *Brigham Young University Studies* 17 (Autumn 1976): 29, 37 (hereafter *BYU Studies*).

14. Edward W. Tullidge, *The Women of Mormondom* (New York: Tullidge and Crandall, 1877), 98, quoting Eliza R. Snow.

15. Lucy Mack Smith, *History of the Prophet Joseph Smith,* 184; Doctrine and Covenants 90:20, 25–27. The "aged" Father Smith was sixty-one years old at the time.

16. Joseph Smith, *History of the Church,* 1:222, 229, 235.

17. Ibid., 1:259.

18. Ibid., 1:270. The Book of Commandments became the Doctrine and Covenants in later editions.

19. Ibid., 1:390–93.

20. Ibid., 1:394.

21. Ibid., 1:448.

22. Ibid., 1:465.

23. Manuscript History of the Church, December 18, 1833, Oliver Cowdery, clerk and recorder, Archives of the Church of Jesus Christ of Latter-day Saints, Salt Lake City (hereafter LDS Church Archives). The event is erroneously dated December 18, 1834, in B. H. Roberts, *A Comprehensive History of the Church of Jesus Christ of Latter-day Saints: Century I,* 6 vols. (Salt Lake City: Deseret News Press, 1930), 1:387. The blessings were published in Joseph Fielding Smith, comp., *Teachings of the Prophet Joseph Smith* (1938; reprint, Salt Lake City: Deseret Book, 1969), 38–40. The most contemporaneous account extant is in the Joseph Smith Diary, 1832–34, 30–42, LDS Church Archives, as reproduced in Dean C. Jessee, comp. and ed., *The Personal Writings of Joseph Smith* (Salt Lake City: Deseret Book, 1984), 23–25. A slightly altered version of the diary account was printed in the *Times and Seasons* 6 (July 1, 1845): 947–48. However, this earliest account in the Joseph Smith Diary, penned by Frederick G. Williams, does not include the language where Father Smith is made the Patriarch. Because Doctrine and Covenants 107, which was written in 1835, uses the same Adam-ondi-Ahman language as that in the 1835 Oliver Cowdery version of the 1833 blessing, Robert J. Matthews, "Adam-Ondi-Ahman," *BYU Studies* 13 (Autumn 1972): 29, n.6, has suggested the possibility that the version of the 1833 blessing copied by Oliver Cowdery in 1835 was an edited version containing information that was not actually given at the time of the 1833 blessing.

24. Quoted in Bruce R. McConkie, *Mormon Doctrine* (Salt Lake City: Bookcraft, 1958), 186. Joseph Smith, *History of the Church,* 1:xxiii, explains that "the Dispensation of the Fulness of Times is the dispensation which in-

cludes all others and gathers to itself all things which bear any relation whatsoever to the work of God . . . the one in which will be gathered together in one all things in Christ, both which are in heaven, and which are on earth; even in Him." See also Ephesians 1:10.

25. Richard T. Hughes and C. Leonard Allen, *Illusions of Innocence: Protestant Primitivism in America, 1630–1875* (Chicago: University of Chicago Press, 1988), 138, explain that compared with the many restoration movements of the early nineteenth century, which sought to restore primitive Christianity, the Mormon restoration was "cosmic in its scope, that penetrated space to the ends of the earth and the outer bounds of the universe itself."

26. Baptism for the dead was not introduced until 1840 in Nauvoo. John Smith [1781–1854], Journal, October 15, 1840, LDS Church Archives (copy in George A. Smith Family Collection, Manuscripts Division, Special Collections, Marriott Library, University of Utah, Salt Lake City), notes his first experience when members underwent "22 baptisms as agents for their departed friends and then for themselves." Apostle George Albert Smith, in a letter to John R. Boynton, September 6, 1911, George A. Smith Family Collection, Manuscripts Division, Special Collections, Marriott Library, University of Utah, Salt Lake City, remarked that baptism for the dead was practiced among the Montanists of Africa, that the Druids of Wales "probably practiced this also," and that First Corinthians 15:29 alludes to it. See also M. Guy Bishop, " 'What Has Become of Our Fathers?': Baptism for the Dead at Nauvoo," *Dialogue: A Journal of Mormon Thought* 23 (Summer 1990): 85–97.

27. Manuscript History of the Church, December 18, 1833.

28. D. Michael Quinn, "Comment on Patriarch Papers" (Response to papers presented by E. Gary Smith and Irene M. Bates at the Mormon History Association annual meeting, Salt Lake City, May 2, 1986).

29. Joseph Fielding Smith maintained in the twentieth century that Father Smith was appointed on December 18, 1833, "to hold the keys of blessing on the heads of all members of the Church, the Lord revealing that it was his right to hold this authority." Joseph Fielding Smith, *Essentials in Church History* (1922; reprint, Salt Lake City: Deseret Book, 1966), 168–69. Apostle Franklin D. Richards clarified the latter phrase in 1882: "From this we learn that Joseph Smith, Sen., inherited the Patriarchal Priesthood, by right from the fathers over the house of Israel in this dispensation. For this right to have descended to him, by lineage, he must of necessity be an Ephraimite, for Ephraim, by the right of appointment and ordination by his (grand)father Jacob, is the head of Israel." Franklin D. Richards and James A. Little, *A Compendium of the Doctrines of the Gospel* (1882; reprint, Salt Lake City: Deseret News, 1925), 74–75.

30. The presiding right over other patriarchs only became a question when local patriarchs were called four years after the original calling of Father Smith. However, Oliver Cowdery, the scribe at the original ordination in 1833, said that Father Smith had been "ordained Patriarch and President of the High Priesthood" under the hands of his son. Quoted in Joseph Smith, *History of the Church*, 4:190. John Taylor, "Patriarchal," *Times and Seasons* 6 (June

1, 1845): 920–22, maintained that the Church Patriarch would preside over local patriarchs.

31. Joseph Sr. had been ordained a high priest prior to December 1833 and was "ordained to the High Priesthood" on June 3, 1831, along with the first group to be so ordained. Although the office of high priest later became synonymous with "presidency," this was not the case prior to 1834. See minutes in Donald Q. Cannon and Lyndon W. Cook, eds., *Far West Record: Minutes of the Church of Jesus Christ of Latter-day Saints, 1830–1844* (Salt Lake City: Deseret Book, 1983), 3, 6, 9, 11, etc.

32. Joseph Smith, *History of the Church,* 4:190.

33. See brackets added, "[in Kirtland]," and footnote to Joseph Smith, *History of the Church,* 4:190. After Joseph Jr. and Hyrum were killed in 1844, the official history of the church was "revised" into its present form. The brackets and footnote were probably added later.

34. Ibid., 190–91.

35. Ibid., 190.

36. The first local patriarch was Isaac Morley. He was ordained at Far West, Missouri, on November 7, 1837. Ibid., 2:524.

37. Ibid., 2:32, refers to these two blessings, when Joseph Smith, Sr., laid his hands on the heads of Joseph Jr. and Samuel. The occasion was a meeting of the newly formed high council in Kirtland. The Prophet himself had placed hands on the heads of the members of the high council and "commanded a blessing to rest upon them." On June 21, 1874, Brigham Young claimed that after the return from Zion's Camp in June 1834 his father became the first patriarch ordained by the Prophet. *Journal of Discourses by Brigham Young, President of the Church of Jesus Christ of Latter-day Saints, His Two Counsellors, the Twelve Apostles and Others,* 26 vols. (Liverpool, England: Latter-day Saints Books Depot, 1855–86), 18:240–41. The blessings cited above provide evidence that Joseph Sr. was already functioning as Patriarch at that time.

38. Benjamin F. Johnson, *My Life's Review* (Independence, Mo.: Zion's Printing and Publishing, 1947), 17.

39. Blessing of Joseph Smith, Jr., by his father, Patriarch Joseph Smith, Sr., December 9, 1834, Eldred G. Smith Personal Records, Salt Lake City.

40. Blessing of Hyrum Smith by his father, Patriarch Joseph Smith, Sr., December 9, 1834, Eldred G. Smith Personal Records.

41. Dean C. Jessee, "Priceless Words and Fallible Memories: Joseph Smith as Seen in the Effort to Preserve His Discourses," *BYU Studies* 31 (Spring 1991): 23.

42. The high council debated whether the book should be purchased. Finally it was decided that such a record was important enough to warrant the cost.

43. Kirtland High Council Minute Book, September 14, 1835, LDS Church Archives.

44. Ibid.

45. Joseph Smith, *History of the Church,* 2:346–47. Father Smith's bless-

ing meetings were often held in the basement of the printing office, and, according to Catherine Barnes Crosby, so many attended that latecomers had to be turned away. Cited in Margaret F. Maxwell, "They Also Served: Women and the Building of the Kingdom at Kirtland" (Paper presented at the Mormon History Association annual meeting, Salt Lake City, May 2, 1986).

46. B. Carmon Hardy, *Solemn Covenant: The Mormon Polygamous Passage* (Urbana: University of Illinois Press, 1992), 3, which cites a sermon by Brigham Young in *Journal of Discourses*, 6:42.

47. Thomas G. Alexander, *Things in Heaven and Earth: The Life and Times of Wilford Woodruff, a Mormon Prophet* (Salt Lake City: Signature Books, 1991), 87.

48. Minutes of a Grand Council at Kirtland, Ohio, May 2, 1835, manuscript, included in Patriarchal Blessing Book 2, LDS Church Archives, as quoted in D. Michael Quinn, "The Evolution of the Presiding Quorums of the LDS Church," *Journal of Mormon History* 1 (1974): 28.

49. Quinn, "The Evolution of the Presiding Quorums of the LDS Church," 28.

50. Doctrine and Covenants 107:39–53 raises the question of whether local patriarchs were also to have their priesthood handed down from father to son, as it had been done with the Presiding Patriarch.

51. *Journal of Discourses*, 18:240–41. It is not known what happened to the record of John Young's ordination as the Patriarch. A similar account, worded a little differently, was given by Brigham Young at Logan, on June 30, 1873. See *Deseret Evening News*, July 19, 1873.

52. Joseph Fielding Smith wrote in a footnote in "Presiding Patriarchs," *Improvement Era* 38 (April 4, 1935): 216, that the entry in the *Doctrine and Covenants Commentary*, 869, was incorrect where it said that John Young, father of Brigham Young, was the first man ordained to the office of Patriarch "after the return of Zion's Camp in 1834." Joseph Smith, Sr., he notes, "was ordained December 18, 1833, nearly one year before the ordination of John Young."

53. Johnson, *My Life's Review*, 17, stated, "In the summer of 1834, Father Joseph Smith, Sr., commenced to visit the families of the Saints and give patriarchal blessings, and greatly was the Spirit of the Lord manifested among the Saints in the gift of tongues, with interpretation, prophecy, and the gift of healing."

54. Wilford Woodruff, Journal, Special Collections, Marriott Library, University of Utah, Salt Lake City. Also in LDS Church Archives and in Scott G. Kenney, ed., *Wilford Woodruff's Journals, 1833–1898*, 9 vols. (Salt Lake City: Signature Books, 1983–85), 3:258.

55. *Millennial Star* 34 (August 22, 1881): 531.

56. The reason for rewriting the 1833 ordination blessing in 1835 appears to have been connected with the purchase of a patriarchal blessing book at that time, within which book Father Smith was to record his blessings. Oliver Cowdery copied the original account into the first pages of that book.

57. D. Michael Quinn, *The Mormon Hierarchy: Origins of Power* (Salt Lake

City: Signature Books, 1994), 46–51.

58. Ibid., 48.

59. Joseph Smith Diary, in Jessee, comp. and ed., *Personal Writings of Joseph Smith*, 23.

60. Joseph Smith, *History of the Church*, 2:32; Johnson, *My Life's Review*, 17.

61. Oliver Cowdery, Minutes in Joseph Smith, Sr., Patriarchal Blessing Book, vol. 1, 8, 1835 (emphasis added); photocopy of original in possession of authors.

62. Ibid., 15–16.

63. Joseph Smith, *History of the Church*, 2:379–80. Abraham 1:2–3 in the Pearl of Great Price indicates some of the great blessings promised to Abraham.

64. Earnest M. Skinner, "Joseph Smith, Sr., First Patriarch to the Church" (M.S. thesis, Brigham Young University, 1958), 156; Lucy Mack Smith, *History of Joseph Smith by His Mother, Lucy Mack Smith*, 237.

65. Kirtland Elders Quorum Minutes, April 29, 1836, Archives of the Reorganized Church of Latter Day Saints, Independence, Mo. (hereafter RLDS Archives).

66. The certificate issued by the Kirtland High Council on May 21, 1836, read, "This is to certify that John Smith and Joseph Smith Sen. are authorised to Collect donations for the finishing the Hous of the Lord, also to lone moneys to pay depts that have all ready been contracted to build said hous. [signed] Reynolds Cahoon, Hyrum Smith, Jared Carter." John Smith [1781–1854], Journal.

67. Joseph Smith, *History of the Church*, 2:427.

68. James B. Allen and Glen M. Leonard, *The Story of the Latter-day Saints* (Salt Lake City: Deseret Book, 1976), 101.

69. Robert B. Thompson, "An Address Delivered at the Funeral of Joseph Smith, Sen.," *Times and Seasons* 1 (September 15, 1840): 170–73.

70. Edward W. Tullidge, *The Women of Mormondom*, 98, cited in Skinner, "Joseph Smith, Sr., First Patriarch to the Church," 132.

71. Joseph Smith, *History of the Church*, 2:446–47.

72. Lucy Mack Smith, *History of Joseph Smith by His Mother, Lucy Mack Smith*, 244–45; Joseph Smith, *History of the Church*, 2:441–42.

73. Allen and Leonard, *The Story of the Latter-day Saints*, 110–15.

74. Lucy Mack Smith, *Biographical Sketches*, 211.

75. Eliza R. Snow, *Biography of Lorenzo Snow* (Salt Lake City: Deseret News Press, 1884), 20–24, as quoted in Skinner, "Joseph Smith, Sr., First Patriarch to the Church," 163–65.

76. Joseph Smith, *History of the Church*, 2:489. This seems reminiscent of the direction taken by English Methodism in the late eighteenth century. The Methodists' decision to open up foreign missions has been interpreted as a reaction to internal dissent, as was the case for Mormonism.

77. Ibid., 2:509.

78. Brigham Young, Journal History, 7 November 1837, as quoted in Ri-

chard Henrie Morley, "The Life and Contributions of Isaac Morley" (M.A. thesis, Brigham Young University, 1965). This thesis tells Morley's life story. There is also the account in John Clifton Moffitt, "Isaac Morley on the American Frontier," n.d., Historical Department of the Church of Jesus Christ of Latter-day Saints, Salt Lake City.

79. Eliza R. Snow, *Biography of Lorenzo Snow*, 20–24, as quoted in Skinner, "Joseph Smith, Sr., First Patriarch to the Church," 164.

80. Joseph Smith, *History of the Church*, 3:1.

81. Joseph Sr. and Lucy sold nineteen acres of land in Caldwell County, Missouri, to William Robinson on July 16, 1839. Photocopy of indenture in possession of authors; original with the Eldred G. Smith family.

82. Joseph Smith, *History of the Church*, 3:381. This statement was consistent with the understanding Father Smith imparted on December 9, 1834, when he blessed his oldest son, Hyrum. Phillip Barlow, in his preface to his *Mormons and the Bible* (New York: Oxford University Press, 1991), points out that Mormonism tends to offer its own reinterpretation of traditional scriptures.

83. John Taylor, "From England," *Times and Seasons* 1 (June 1840): 121. See also British Mission Manuscript History, March 8, 1839, to January 15, 1843, LDS Church Archives.

84. J. Blakeslee, "For the Times and Seasons," *Times and Seasons* 2 (July 15, 1841): 484.

85. Joseph Smith, *History of the Church*, 4:334. Subsequently, the policy was to await stakehood before ordaining patriarchs. Only when the first stake (similar to a diocese) was formed in England in 1960 was another patriarch appointed in Britain.

86. Patriarchal blessing of Stephen Post, March 26, 1836, by Joseph Smith, Sr., at Kirtland, LDS Church Archives; copy in authors' possession. For further discussion of patriarchal blessings, see Irene M. Bates, "Patriarchal Blessings and the Routinization of Charisma," *Dialogue: A Journal of Mormon Thought* 26 (Fall 1993): 1–29.

87. Blessing of Lorenzo Snow by Joseph Sr., December 15, 1836, at Kirtland, LDS Church Archives. D. Michael Quinn, *Early Mormonism and the Magic World View* (Salt Lake City: Signature Books, 1987), 221, notes "the magic dimensions of [the Apostle] Paul's sending a blessed handkerchief to heal people. (Acts 19:12; chap. 1)"

88. Blessing of Elijah Abel by Joseph Sr., sometime during 1836, at Kirtland, Joseph Smith's Patriarchal Blessing Record, 88, LDS Church Archives, cited in Lester E. Bush, Jr., "Mormonism's Negro Doctrine: An Historical Overview," *Dialogue: A Journal of Mormon Thought* 8 (Spring 1973): 52n.30. Elijah Abel was one of the few black members of the church to receive both the priesthood and a patriarchal blessing prior to the 1978 revelation that changed church policy and allowed black male members of the church to be ordained to the priesthood.

89. Blessing of Amanda Rogers by Joseph Sr., August 11, 1837, Archives and Manuscripts Division, Harold B. Lee Library, Brigham Young University, Provo, Utah (hereafter BYU Archives); blessing of Bathsheba Bigler by Joseph

Sr., February 7, 1839, Record Book of Bathsheba Bigler Smith, 1822–1906, BYU Archives.

90. See, for example, the blessing of Flora Jacobs by Joseph Sr., June 13, 1837, Archives of the Reorganized Church of Jesus Christ of Latter Day Saints, Independence, Mo.

91. Preliminary manuscript of Lucy Mack Smith's *History*, n.d., unpaginated, LDS Church Archives.

92. Caroline Barnes Crosby, Journal and Memoirs, February 21, 1836, Utah State Historical Society, Salt Lake City. This appears to be the only recorded instance where a woman participated giving patriarchal blessings.

93. Minutes of a general conference held at the dwelling of Brother Sirenes Burnet in Orange, Cuyahoga County, Ohio, October 25, 1831, as quoted in Cannon and Cook, eds., *Far West Record*, 19–21, as reported by Oliver Cowdery.

94. Reynolds Cahoon, Journal, November 1831, LDS Church Archives.

95. Orson Hyde, Diary, March 15, 1832, LDS Church Archives.

96. In one early blessing, December 9, 1834, Joseph Smith, Sr., promised Mary Smith, his daughter-in-law, wife of Samuel Smith, "Thou art sealed up unto eternal life." Quoted in Ruby K. Smith, *Mary Bailey* (Salt Lake City: Deseret Book, 1954), 43. Many other blessings contained similar promises, including one given to Simeon Dunn, June 22, 1840, just three months before the Patriarch died. Knecht Family Records, in possession of William L. Knecht, Moraga, Calif.

97. Although there is no available record that Joseph Sr. was given this power, it was said of Hyrum, as Patriarch, "That whoever he blesses shall be blessed, and whoever he curses shall be cursed." Doctrine and Covenants 124:92–93.

98. Perregrine Sessions, Diary (typescript), Huntington Library, San Marino, Calif.

99. John Smith [1781–1854], Journal.

100. Thompson, "An Address Delivered at the Funeral of Joseph Smith, Sen."

101. Ibid.

102. Ruby K. Smith, *Mary Bailey*, 85, quoted in Skinner, "Joseph Smith, Sr., First Patriarch," 189.

103. Joseph Fielding Smith, comp., *Teachings of the Prophet Joseph Smith*, 39.

3

"By Blessing and Also by Right"

Hyrum Smith—Second Patriarch, 1841–44

> The order of this [patriarchal] priesthood was confirmed to be handed down from father to son, and rightly belongs to the literal descendants of the chosen seed, to whom the promises were made. This order was instituted in the days of Adam, and came down by lineage.
>
> —Doctrine and Covenants 107:40–41

Before the sixty-nine-year-old patriarch Joseph Smith, Sr., passed away in September 1840, his final blessing to his eldest son, Hyrum, fulfilled the Prophet's own 1833 promise to his brother that Hyrum would "stand in the tracks of his father and be numbered among those who hold the right of Patriarchal Priesthood."[1] The aged patriarch said to Hyrum, "I seal upon your head your patriarchal blessing which I placed upon your head before, for that shall be verified. . . . I now seal upon your head the patriarchal power, and you shall bless the people."[2] This ordination of the eldest son by his father faithfully replicated the traditions of the Old Testament patriarchs. Four months later Hyrum was given official confirmation in a revelation, which was read at the April 1841 General Conference in Nauvoo.

The spring of 1841 was a time of optimism and stability for a people who had endured repeated hardships. The persecutions in New York, Ohio, and Missouri were behind them. The Prophet had survived Liberty Jail and now stood before them, seemingly invincible. The state of Illinois had just granted their new city a charter that empowered, among other things, their own militia and university. During the years of persecution, simply surviving had been an all-consuming task. But 1841 was different.

On the first day of the April conference, the Nauvoo Legion marched in grand procession to the temple site, where, with appropriate ceremony, the cornerstones were laid. On the second day of the conference, a revelation on church government, received by Joseph Smith three months earlier, was read to the assembled Saints directly from the first entry made in Joseph's Book of the Law of the Lord. The Lord set forth the order of sustaining church officers as follows: "Verily, I say unto you, I now give unto you the officers belonging to my Priesthood, that ye may hold the keys thereof, even the Priesthood which is after the order of Melchizedek." The revelation then proceeded to list the officers of the church: "First, I give unto you, Hyrum Smith to be a patriarch unto you, to hold the sealing blessings of my church even the Holy Spirit of Promise, whereby ye are sealed up unto the day of redemption, that ye may not fall notwithstanding the hour of temptation that may come upon you."

Listed next in order were Joseph, "to be a presiding elder," and the other men and priesthood offices they held, as they were to be presented for the vote of the members at conference. Hyrum was promised that henceforth he would "hold the keys of the patriarchal blessings upon the heads of all my people."[3] This revelation was canonized as section 124 of the Doctrine and Covenants. Hyrum, by virtue of his new calling, was designated as "a prophet, and a seer, and a revelator unto my church as well as my servant Joseph," to act "in concert also with" the Prophet-President.[4]

The wording of this institutional confirmation would only contribute to the ambiguity that would continue to surround the office. In this major revelation on church government, Hyrum, who was succeeding his father at that time as the Church Patriarch, was designated "first" in the sustaining order of the church. Was this an acknowledgment of primal characteristics to the patriarchy? Of some "first" place in church order? Certainly the ordination of Joseph Smith, Sr., would suggest that might be the case. In 1833 the first patriarch in this dispensation had been told that he would be like unto Adam: "So shall it be with my father; he shall be called a prince over his posterity, holding the keys of the patriarchal priesthood over the kingdom of God on earth, even the Church of the Latter Day Saints."[5]

Joseph Sr., as Patriarch to the Church, was to have a primal, titular role in the restoration, in much the same way that the Old Testament and Book of Mormon patriarchs did (Jacob/Israel is such an example in the Old Testament, Lehi in the Book of Mormon).

The conclusion seems inescapable. Something more—and perhaps something more fundamental—was intended for and embodied in the patriarchy as it was held by Joseph Smith, Sr., and Hyrum Smith than was evident in its succeeding generations. Certainly in the case of the first patriarch the primal characteristics appear to have been mostly honorary, with the exception of whatever presiding authority he had over local patriarchs. Isaac Morley was the first local patriarch, appointed in 1837, and was the only one Father Smith could have logistically supervised during his seven-year tenure. Now, Hyrum was being told that he would

> take the office of Priesthood and Patriarch, which was appointed unto him by his father, by blessing and also by right. That from henceforth he shall hold the keys of the patriarchal blessings upon the heads of all my people. That whoever he blesses shall be blessed, and whoever he curses shall be cursed; that whatsoever he shall bind on earth shall be bound in heaven, and whatsoever he shall loose on earth shall be loosed in heaven. And from this time forth I appoint unto him that he may be a prophet, and a seer, and a revelator unto my church as well as my servant Joseph, that he may act in concert also with my servant Joseph, and that he shall receive counsel from my servant Joseph, who shall show unto him the keys whereby he may ask and receive, and be crowned with the same blessing, and glory, and honor, and priesthood, and gifts of the priesthood, that once were put upon him that was my servant Oliver Cowdery.[6]

This was clearly an enlargement of the concept of the office of Church Patriarch. Whatever primal notions might have been present with Joseph Sr.'s calling, they did not equal, functionally, those given to Hyrum.

It has been argued that Hyrum really received two separate callings—as the Patriarch (Doctrine and Covenants 124:91–94) and as second elder (the calling of the disaffected Oliver Cowdery) or associate president (Doctrine and Covenants 124:94–96)—and that these two offices were not to be confused with each other. This explanation argues that Hyrum's office of Patriarch had no primal or line-authority characteristics and that all jurisdictional authority was attached solely to Hyrum's concurrent second elder calling. Such attempts to define the separate functions of the two positions during the time they were held by Hyrum, however, were not undertaken until after Joseph and Hyrum were killed, at which time presidential succession interests colored the objectivity of the analysis.[7]

The proposition that the office of Patriarch, at the time Hyrum held the office, assimilated the second elder powers has considerable historical support. First, the language and the context of the revelation itself appear to merge all of Hyrum's authority and responsibility into one calling. The only mention of office in the text is that of Patriarch. The verses that now separate parts of the text in the Doctrine and Covenants were not present in the early edition, and the entire text was paragraph twenty-nine of section 103.

The second evidence that the two offices were assimilated into one is in the same revelation. It is Hyrum as Patriarch who is first in the order of church offices. The only reference to Hyrum in all of section 124 is in the context of his calling as Patriarch. The office of second elder, or associate president, is not mentioned or referred to at all. (It hardly seems likely that a "second" elder, or "associate" president, would be placed ahead of the first elder, or president.) By contrast, when Joseph Sr. held the office of Patriarch along with that of assistant to the president, the two callings were always referred to separately.

Third, Hyrum had served as a counselor in the First Presidency prior to his call as Patriarch. His calling as Patriarch was seen as a promotion. Elder LeGrand Richards of the Quorum of the Twelve noted, "The importance of this calling is evident from the fact that the Lord, by revelation, took Hyrum Smith, the brother of the Prophet, Joseph Smith, out of the First Presidency of the Church and called him to be Patriarch of the Church."[8]

Fourth, on several subsequent occasions Joseph confirmed the importance of Hyrum's patriarchy. The earliest of these was during a meeting of the Quorum of the Twelve Apostles recorded by Willard Richards on May 27, 1843, when Joseph said that "the patriarchal office is the highest office in the Church."[9] This statement came one day after Hyrum, after considerable resistance, had accepted the concept of plural marriage.[10] Joseph's comment could have been an honorific thank you for Hyrum's valuable support or a reaffirmation of the 1841 revelation's description of the patriarchal office, public comment about which had been suspended during Hyrum's opposition to plural marriage. The latter seems more likely.

A similar but much more problematic comment came two months later when, on July 16, 1843, Joseph stated in a sermon in the Grove at Nauvoo that he "would not prophesy any more, and proposed Hyrum to hold the office of prophet to the Church, *as it was his birthright*. I am going to have a reformation," he said, "and the Saints must regard Hyrum, for he has the authority, that I might be a Priest of the Most High God."[11] The only office Hyrum held that was associated with a birthright was that of Patriarch. To quote Michael Quinn, "When Joseph Smith publicly declared on 16 July, 1843, that Hyrum Smith should 'hold the office of prophet to the Church, as it was his birthright,' he obviously referred to Hyrum's lineal role as successor to his father in the office of Presiding Patriarch."[12]

When Joseph suggested that Hyrum should be *the* prophet, however, it went beyond what had been, and what would be, the actual relationship between the two. All previous references were consistent with Hyrum's acting "in concert" with Joseph but always being subject to him in line-authority—sort of an aide-de-camp. To the extent that Hyrum had been first, or ahead of Joseph Jr., it had always been in honor, not in governing institutional authority. Now, it appeared, Joseph was suggesting that Hyrum would actually take over the role of *first* elder.

On the next Sunday, July 23, Joseph clarified his earlier statements when he gave his Sunday sermon in the Grove:

> It has gone abroad that I proclaimed myself no longer a prophet. I said it last Sabbath ironically: I supposed you would all understand. It was not that I would renounce the idea of being a prophet, but that I had no disposition to proclaim myself such. . . . Last Monday morning certain brethren came to me and said they could hardly consent to receive Hyrum as a prophet, and for me to resign. But I told them, "I only said it to try your faith; and it is strange, brethren, that you have been in the Church so long, and not yet understand the Melchizedek Priesthood."[13]

The explanation lies in Joseph's political dilemmas of the moment, which deserve some attention to place his statement in context. Joseph had previously committed his vote in the 1843 congressional election to Cyrus Walker, a Whig candidate, and it was assumed that the Mormon bloc would follow. As election time approached, however, Joseph became convinced that the candidate of the Democratic party, Joseph P. Hoge, would better suit the interests of the Saints. On August 5, two days before the election and three weeks after Joseph's comments about Hyrum's taking over as prophet, Hyrum announced to a large assembly that it was the will of God that the Saints should vote for the Democratic candidate. The next day, before the election, Joseph preached at the Sunday gathering and said, "Brother Hyrum tells me this morning that he has had a testimony to the effect that it would be better for the people to vote for Hoge; and I never knew Hyrum to say that he had a revelation and it failed. Let God speak and all men hold their peace."[14]

Joseph thus was able to vote for Walker, thereby keeping his promise, while the bloc of Mormons voted for Hoge, swinging the election to the Democrats. This incident uniquely illuminates Hyrum's position. While the office embodied sufficient primal dimensions to be used convincingly for the exigencies of the moment, the incident made it very clear that Hyrum's jurisdictional responsibilities remained subject to those of Joseph.

A fifth evidence of Hyrum's primal responsibilities lies in the day-to-day de facto authority he exercised with Joseph during the Nauvoo period. They were brothers and close lifelong allies. Joseph wanted Hyrum to act and function with substantial authority, and defining parameters of church offices was no doubt secondary in Joseph's mind. During the last few years of their lives, official church communications were often signed "Joseph Smith, Jr., [and] Hyrum Smith, Presidents of the Church."

To understand the relationship that Hyrum had with his younger brother Joseph, the Prophet, we return to the beginnings of Mormonism.

Hyrum Smith, who was born February 9, 1800, at Tunbridge, Vermont,
the second son of Lucy Mack and Joseph Smith, Sr., was more than five
years older than Joseph. He was sent to Moore's Academy in Hanover for
a time, while the rest of the children went to local common schools. In
1816 the family, which included eight children, moved to Palmyra, New
York. There Hyrum became a member of the local Presbyterian church,
along with his brother Samuel, sister Sophronia, and his mother. Yet when
Joseph told of his vision, Hyrum, along with the rest of the Smith family, immediately accepted Joseph's story.

Hyrum was one of the eight witnesses permitted to view the gold plates
from which the Book of Mormon was translated. He was one of the six
members who constituted the organization of the church on April 6, 1830.
He presided over the Colesville, New York, Saints, who made up the first
branch of the church created outside the initial organization at Fayette,
New York. Throughout the years of persecution and constant uprooting,
Hyrum remained a faithful supporter of the Prophet and shared impris-
onment in Liberty Jail with his brother. In the Book of the Law of the
Lord, Joseph had once written this tribute to his brother: "Brother Hyrum
what a faithful heart you have got . . . Oh how many are the sorrows we
have shared together! and again we find ourselves shackled by the unre-
lenting hand of oppression. Hyrum, thy name shall be written in the Book
of the Law of the Lord, for those who come after to look upon, that they
may pattern after thy works."[15]

Hyrum's first wife, Jerusha Barden, whom he married on November
2, 1826, died on October 13, 1837, leaving a family of six children.[16] On
December 24, 1837, he married Mary Fielding, and they had a son and a
daughter. In November 1837 he became a counselor in the First Presidency
of the church, following the disaffection of both Oliver Cowdery and Frederick G. Williams. Hyrum was both an important member of the church
hierarchy and, as Doctrine and Covenants 23:3 reminds us, heir to a lineal office. The April 1830 revelation had advised Hyrum, "Wherefore thy
duty is unto the church forever, and this because of thy family." When
his father died, Hyrum was forty years of age. An article in the *New York
Herald* described him as "five feet, eleven and a half inches high, weigh-
ing one hundred and ninety-three pounds" and as "one of the most pi-
ous and devout christians in the world."[17]

Hyrum's life shows a pattern of loyalty and support for his younger
brother's calling, proven time after time. Perhaps that explains why the
lineal calling of Church Patriarch appears to take precedence over
Hyrum's institutional appointment, at least for Joseph and Hyrum, and

Jerusha Barden Smith, 1805-37. Wife of the second presiding patriarch, Hyrum Smith. Courtesy of Eldred G. Smith.

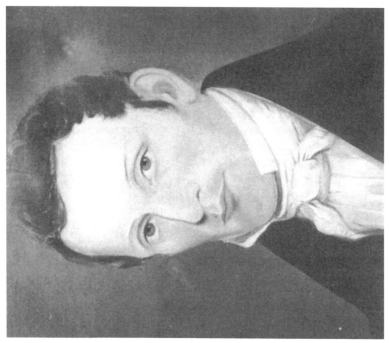

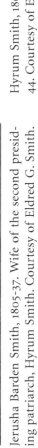

Hyrum Smith, 1800-1844. Second presiding patriarch, 1841-44. Courtesy of Eldred G. Smith.

that it remained, to some extent, outside the patterns of organizational procedures. An example of the idiosyncratic nature of the "office" was the way in which a successor was to be chosen. In December 1840 Joseph Smith, Jr., sent a letter to the Twelve Apostles then engaged in missionary work in Britain. The Prophet informed his apostles of the death of his father, saying "Hyrum succeeds him [Joseph Smith, Sr.] as Patriarch of the Church, according to his last directions and benedictions."[18] The choice of successor and the right to ordain him therefore belonged to the dying patriarch, not the ongoing institution. Another example is the way in which Hyrum, as the Patriarch, was perceived as having real authority. An excerpt from the *New York Herald* on February 19, 1842, reproduced in the May 1842 edition of the *Millennial Star* in England, describes "the first presidency of the Mormon hierarchy which consists of four dignitaries—to wit, a principal prophet, a patriarch, and two councillors."[19]

None of these interpretations of the nature of the office of Patriarch created any sense of dissonance during Hyrum's lifetime, except in the case of Oliver Cowdery, who in 1835, to maintain Cowdery's own calling as second elder, had deemed it necessary to note that the Patriarch, Joseph Sr., did not hold a primal position. The only instance of Hyrum's being overruled by Joseph was in the case of plural marriage. As late as May 1843 Hyrum was not privy to any official, if secret, disclosures about plural marriage. When he became aware of rumors about the practice, he preached against it, saying, "If an angel from heaven should come and preach such doctrine [you] would be sure to see his cloven foot and cloud of blackness over his head."[20]

The Prophet was disturbed by Hyrum's remarks and the following Sunday he issued a rebuttal, referring to the doctrine—however obliquely—in public for the first time. Hyrum was troubled and vowed to trap Brigham Young by confronting him with his own involvement. Instead, Brigham Young convinced Hyrum that it was indeed a revelation from God. Hyrum "went to Joseph and told him what he had learned, and renewed his covenant with Joseph, and they went heart and hand together while they lived."[21] It was Hyrum who insisted that the revelation on eternal and plural marriage be put in writing.[22] On April 7, 1844, he spoke at the Nauvoo General Conference with a caution to the Saints that perhaps related to the secret practice:

> Never undertake to destroy men because they do some evil thing; it is natural for a man to be lead [*sic*] and not driven. Put down iniquity by good works. Many men speak without any contemplation but when they have a little contemplation it would not be spoken. We ought to

be careful what we say and take the example of Jesus, cast over the mantle of charity and try to cover their faults. We are made to enlighten and not darken one another; save men but not destroy men. Do unto others as ye would have them do unto you. . . . Humble yourself before God and ask him for his spirit; and pray to him to judge it for you. It is better not to have so much faith than to have so much as to believe all the lies.[23]

Yet Brigham Young tells us that when Hyrum took it upon himself to officiate in plural marriages, he was chastised by Joseph, who said that if Hyrum did that again without authorization, "he would go to hell and all those he sealed with him."[24]

Among Hyrum's responsibilities was the planning of additions to the city of Nauvoo.[25] According to Paul Edwards, Hyrum institutionalized the sacred experience of the Prophet. Edwards contends that the Mormon church is "a bureaucracy designed to sustain ritual arising from the mystical experience of Joseph Smith. It is a product of the organizational mind of Hyrum Smith and a host of inspired secular leaders."[26]

Despite his other duties, Hyrum still actively pursued his calling as Church Patriarch, giving blessings to all who requested them. In the November 19, 1841, *Times and Seasons* there was an announcement that Hyrum would be available to give blessings on Monday, Wednesday, and Friday or on any other day if urgent circumstances required him "to perform the duties of his high and holy calling." Hyrum's blessings differed from those of his father in that they appear more intellectual and formal in their phrasing, although not lacking in spirituality.

A particularly beautiful blessing was given to Susanna White on September 8, 1841:

> Susanna, I lay my Hands upon your head, in the name of Jesus of Nazareth, to bless you with a Blessing which is called Patriarchal, for your benefit, and for the benefit of your Posterity and Kinsfolk, that you might have a Name in Israel, as Daughter of Abraham in the lineage of Joseph, in the tribe of Ephraim, & as a Mother in Israel, in the due time of the Lord, to receive the Honors of that Blessing in the fullness of times, which is the glory of the Celestial, with a Diadem enriched with the Honors of glittering Glories, in Comparison with the Moon under your feet. . . . The Lord has looked upon your integrity, & moved upon by his Spirit, & called you from your native country, in answer to the prayers of your Fathers, & for a wise purpose unto himself . . . tribulation awaiteth you, Trials, Sorrowings, in them you shall be sustained, & shall be supported by the Grace of God in the hour of your deepest affliction.[27]

In blessing a ten-year-old girl, Hyrum said, "Your mind shall be enlightened, your judgement informed through the light of the smiling countenance of a lovely Savior who looketh after the pure and the youthful and obedient scholar under his tuition."[28]

The comfort and beauty of blessings bestowed by Hyrum and the spiritual benefit the recipients felt must be understood within the context of difficult times. Conditions in Nauvoo became an increasing challenge for Joseph and Hyrum during the two years before their assassination. By the 1840s, Marvin Hill explains, "the Mormon dream of a kingdom had become such a concrete social and political entity in Illinois that notable Americans, including [governor] Thomas Ford, Josiah Quincy, and even the itinerant preacher Peter Cartwright, remarked on the unusually ambitious temporal designs of the Mormons and their prophet."[29] By 1843 there was gentile hostility and internal dissension in the wake of disclosures about plural marriage, the newly revealed doctrine of a plurality of gods, and the idea of man's being co-eternal with God, all of which led some of the Saints to see Joseph as a fallen prophet.[30] Dissenting former leaders of the church published their first and only edition of the *Nauvoo Expositor*, condemning the policies of the church that were attempting to "Christianize the world by political schemes and intrigue."[31] Joseph, as mayor of Nauvoo, declared the *Expositor* a public nuisance, and the city council ordered the press destroyed. Joseph and Hyrum were arrested and incarcerated in the Carthage, Illinois, jail. While awaiting trial, they were killed by a mob that stormed the jail on June 27, 1844.[32]

There is little doubt that Hyrum Smith would have succeeded his brother as prophet and president had he survived Joseph. Brigham Young, at an October 1844 general conference, said, "Did Joseph ordain any man to take his place? He did. Who was it? It was Hyrum, but Hyrum fell martyr before Joseph did."[33] Joseph Smith himself gave Young reason to say this. Just before the two brothers were arrested, Joseph said, "I want Hyrum to live to lead the church, but he is determined not to leave me."[34] Questions are raised by this possibility. Who would then have been Patriarch to the Church? Would Hyrum have combined two roles, as he did when serving as both the Patriarch and associate president? This could have reconciled the two positions of leadership within a lineal framework, at least for that one generation. The question of primacy would have reemerged in subsequent generations, however, unless the offices of patriarch, president, and prophet had been permanently combined.

Although speculation may be futile today, there was certainly a great deal of it during the years following the murders of Joseph Smith and Hyrum Smith. Joseph's eldest son, Joseph Smith III, was not yet twelve years old. Hyrum's shortened life not only prevented his succession to the presidency but also left his oldest son, John, a boy of eleven, the heir-apparent to the patriarchal office. The result was an unexpected and sudden organizational adjustment.

Jan Shipps has suggested that whereas the early Christian church's developmental struggle for leadership was between charisma (i.e., Paul) and office (i.e., the original apostles at Jerusalem), among the Mormons the struggle was between lineage (i.e., the Smith family) and office (i.e., Brigham Young and the Quorum of the Twelve).[35]

The office of Patriarch during Hyrum Smith's lifetime wielded more influence than it did during the life of Father Smith, reaching its zenith in power and status during Hyrum's tenure. Despite the fact that Hyrum held the office for less than four years, his status as the Presiding Patriarch established precedents that would prove troublesome in the years to come.

Notes

1. Joseph Fielding Smith, comp., *Teachings of the Prophet Joseph Smith* (1938; reprint, Salt Lake City: Deseret Book, 1969), 40.

2. Lucy Mack Smith, *History of the Prophet Joseph Smith,* revised by George A. Smith and Elias Smith (Salt Lake City: Improvement Era, 1902), 266. Joseph Fielding, Diary, December 9, 1840, Archives of the Church of Jesus Christ of Latter-day Saints, Salt Lake City (hereafter LDS Church Archives), states, "Joseph Sen, who died a short time ago, just before he died, called his children together and blessed them, and ordained his son, Hyrum, Patriarch, as his Successor."

3. *Doctrine and Covenants of the Church of Jesus Christ of Latter-day Saints* (Salt Lake City: Deseret Book, 1955), 124:92. On July 16, 1843, the Prophet proposed that his brother Hyrum "hold the office of prophet to the church, as it was his birthright." Joseph Smith, *History of the Church of Jesus Christ of Latter-day Saints,* 2d rev. ed., ed. B. H. Roberts, 7 vols. (Salt Lake City: Deseret Book, 1978), 5:510.

4. Doctrine and Covenants 124:94–95.

5. Manuscript History of the Church, December 18, 1833, clerk and recorder, Archives of the Church of Jesus Christ of Latter-day Saints, Salt Lake City, cited in Joseph Fielding Smith, comp., *Teachings of the Prophet Joseph Smith,* 39.

6. *A Book of Commandments for the Government of the Church of Christ* (Zion [Independence, Mo.]: W. W. Phelps, 1833; reprint, Independence, Mo.: Herald Publishing, 1971), 103:29 (now Doctrine and Covenants 124:91–95).

7. John Taylor, "Patriarchal," *Times and Seasons* 6 (June 1, 1845): 920–22; Glen Mouritsen, "The Office of Associate President of the Church of Jesus Christ of Latter-day Saints" (M.A. thesis, Brigham Young University, 1972).

8. LeGrand Richards, "A Chosen Vessel unto Me," *Instructor* 99 (December 1964): 466.

9. Minutes of the Quorum of the Twelve, May 27, 1843, Brigham Young Collection, LDS Church Archives.

10. Ibid. William Clayton, Diary, May 26, 1843, LDS Church Archives, recorded that "Hyrum received the doctrine of priesthood."

11. Joseph Smith, *History of the Church,* 5:510 (emphasis added).

12. D. Michael Quinn, "The Mormon Succession Crisis of 1844," *Brigham Young University Studies* 16 (Winter 1976): 187–233.

13. Joseph Smith, *History of the Church,* 5:516–18. There were those who not only understood but also took things in good-humored stride. Willard Richards met Hyrum in the street midweek and said, "I am writing to the brethren, has our new prophet anything to say to them? 'Give my respects to them,' replied Hyrum.'" Ibid., 5:513.

14. Ibid., 5:526. Charlotte Haven, a nonresident living in Nauvoo in 1843, also refers to this on September 8, 1843. "A Girl's Letters from Nauvoo," *Overland Monthly* 16 (December 16, 1890): 635.

15. Quoted in B. H. Roberts, *A Comprehensive History of the Church of Jesus Christ of Latter-day Saints: Century I,* 6 vols. (Salt Lake City: Deseret News Press, 1930), 2:161.

16. Lucy Mack Smith, *History of the Prophet Joseph Smith,* 246, said, "About one year after my husband returned from this mission, a calamity happened to our family that wrung our hearts with more than common grief. Jerusha, Hyrum's wife, was taken sick, and after an illness of perhaps two weeks, died while her husband was absent on a mission to Missouri. She was a woman whom everybody loved that was acquainted with her, for she was every way worthy. The family were so warmly attached to her, that, had she been our own sister, they could not have been more afflicted by her death."

17. Veritas, "The Mormon Prophets," *Millennial Star* 3 (May 1842): 8, quoting from the *New York Herald,* February 19, 1842.

18. Joseph Smith, *History of the Church,* 4:229. Joseph Fielding, Diary, December 9, 1840, refers to the ordination.

19. Veritas, "The Mormon Prophets," 8.

20. Andrew F. Ehat, "Joseph Smith's Introduction of Temple Ordinances and the 1844 Mormon Succession Question" (M.A. thesis, Brigham Young University, 1981), 56. The exposé concerning John C. Bennett's sexual misconduct had alerted Hyrum to the practice and had led him, along with William Law and William Marks, to initiate "a crusade to purify Nauvoo of all such immoralities." Ibid., 46–47.

21. Ibid., 59. Hyrum had two wives sealed to him in August 1843, Catherine P. Smith and Mercy Thompson. See Danel W. Bachman, "Mormon Plural Marriages before the Death of Joseph Smith" (M.A. thesis, Purdue University, 1975), Appendix H.

22. Ehat, "Joseph Smith's Introduction," 71. As late as May 24, 1845, church leaders were issuing public denials of the practice of polygamy in *The Prophet,* a Mormon newspaper in New York, Newspaper Collection, New York Public Library.

23. "Conference Minutes," *Times and Seasons* 5 (August 1, 1844): 596–98.

24. Brigham Young to William Smith, August 10, 1845, Brigham Young Collection, LDS Church Archives. Brigham Young used this to show William that the power of the office of Patriarch was limited.

25. Original sketches of Hyrum's proposed layouts for the city of Nauvoo are in the possession of Eldred G. Smith.

26. Paul M. Edwards, "The Secular Smiths," *Journal of Mormon History* 4 (1977): 3–17. It is unclear from Edwards's essay how Hyrum played any major role in the creation of the bureaucracy, and contributions to that end may well be better laid at the feet of such leaders as Sydney Rigdon.

27. Blessing of Susanna White by Hyrum Smith, Nauvoo, September 8, 1841, Archives of the Reorganized Church of Jesus Christ of Latter Day Saints, Independence, Mo. (hereafter RLDS Church Archives).

28. Blessing of Phebe S. Merrill by Hyrum Smith, January 2, 1841, RLDS Church Archives.

29. Marvin S. Hill, *Quest for Refuge: The Mormon Flight from American Pluralism* (Salt Lake City: Signature Books, 1989), xv.

30. Robert E. Paul, "Joseph Smith and the Plurality of Worlds Idea," *Dialogue: A Journal of Mormon Thought* 19 (Summer 1986): 13–36, shows the context within which some of Joseph Smith's ideas evolved.

31. A facsimile of the *Nauvoo Expositor*, vol. 1, June 7, 1844, can be seen at the Huntington Library, San Marino, Calif.

32. An account of the assassinations, the events leading directly to them, and subsequent developments can be found in the official *History of the Church*, 7:22–139, as well as in other general treatments of Mormon history, several of which are cited above.

33. "October Conference Minutes," *Times and Seasons* 5 (October 15, 1844): 683.

34. Edward Tullidge, *Life of Joseph, the Prophet,* Reorganized Church edition, 491, cited in Roberts, *A Comprehensive History of the Church,* 2:424, n.20. Differing versions of this statement would surface later during debates about succession.

35. Jan Shipps, *Mormonism: The Story of a New Religious Tradition* (Urbana: University of Illinois Press, 1985), 105.

4

Office in Crisis

William Smith—Third Patriarch, May 1845–October 1845

> It will be his privilege when he [William] arrives, to be ordained to the office of patriarch to the church, and to occupy the place that his brother Hyrum did, when living; and he will stand in the same relationship to the Twelve, as his brother Hyrum did to the First Presidency, after he was ordained patriarch. . . .
>
> —*Times and Seasons*, December 1, 1844

William Smith was on a mission in New York at the time of the martyrdom. On July 8, 1844, Brigham Young had not yet learned of the Prophet's murder when he reported from Salem, Massachusetts, to Apostle Willard Richards, "The Twelve have been faithful in all things. William Smith is a great man in his calling in this country."[1] When the apostles were informed of the death of Joseph and Hyrum, they were summoned back to Nauvoo immediately, but even though he was one of the Quorum of the Twelve Apostles, William was advised not to return for the time being in the interests of his own safety.[2] As a member of the Smith family, they felt he might be in danger from the mobs that had killed his brothers. In addition, his ailing wife, Caroline, was thought to be too ill to travel.[3]

Back in Nauvoo, as early as July 6, 1844, William Clayton expressed his concern about the situation. "The greatest danger that now threatens us is dissensions and strifes amongst the Church," he wrote in his diary. "There are already 4 or 5 men pointed out as successors to the Trustee and President & there is danger of feelings being manifest. All the brethren who stand at the head seem to feel the delicacy of the business."[4] Clayton was still thinking in familial terms, however, as far as leadership of the church was concerned. On July 12 he wrote, "The trustee must of necessity be the first president of the Church & Joseph said that if he and Hyrum were taken away Samuel H. Smith [brother of the Prophet] would be his successor."[5] Samuel, however, died on July 30, 1844, one month following the martyrdom, leaving only one son remaining in the Smith family—Apostle William Smith. William unexpectedly found himself the standard-bearer for the Smith family.

At a historic conference in Nauvoo on August 8, 1844, a debate between Brigham Young and Sidney Rigdon took place. Neither contender for leadership claimed the full authority of the martyred Joseph, but each claimed to be guardians of the church. Brigham Young, as head of the Quorum of the Twelve Apostles, claimed legitimacy through the body of apostles chosen by the fallen prophet. Rigdon claimed rights through his position as counselor to Joseph. Young dealt with Rigdon by addressing two concerns of the members: the feeling that no one could take the place of the Prophet and the notion that any successor to leadership in the church should come from the Smith family. Wilford Woodruff noted in his journal that the Saints "felt like sheep without a shepherd, as being without a father, as their head had been taken away."[6] Young satisfied the first concern not by claiming the office of president in the Quorum of the First Presidency but by proposing that the Twelve, as a quorum, lead the church without filling Joseph's charismatic position. Young satisfied their second concern by pointing out the right the Smith family had to succeed to the office of Patriarch. In doing so, he had to consider possible inheritors of the office, given that Hyrum's oldest son was only twelve years old: "Do you want a patriarch for the whole church? To this we are perfectly willing. If Brother Samuel H. Smith had been living, it would have been his right and privilege, but he is dead. . . . Do you want a patriarch? Here is Brother William [Smith] left; here is Uncle John Smith, uncle to the Prophet Joseph Smith left; it is their right. The right of patriarchal blessings belongs to the Smith family."[7]

In the afternoon session, Brigham Young again addressed the issue of the office of Patriarch:

> We shall have a patriarch, and the right is in the family of Joseph Smith, his brothers, his sons, or some one of his relations. Here is Uncle John, he has been ordained a patriarch. Brother Samuel would have taken the office if he had been alive; it would have been his right; the right is in Uncle John, or one of his brothers. . . . I know that it would have belonged to Samuel. But as it is, if you leave it to the Twelve, they will wait until they know who is the man. Will you leave it to the Twelve, and they dictate the matter. (A unanimous vote). I know it will be let alone for the present.[8]

William Clayton recorded that "the Church universally voted to sustain the Twelve as such in their calling as next in presidency & to sustain Er [elder] Rigdon and A. Lyman as councillors to the Twelve as they had been to the First Presidency. The Church also voted to leave the regulation of all the church matters in the hands of the Twelve."[9] "Church matters" included the decision about which surviving adult male of the Smith family was to be called to be Church Patriarch. Hyrum's oldest son, like Joseph's, was only twelve years old at the time. William was the nearest adult male blood-relative, but Young was obviously probing the possibility of selecting a more satisfactory Smith. Aware of William's independent nature, the other eleven of the Quorum of Twelve probably perceived him as less than totally committed.

Historians have found William Smith difficult to deal with and therefore easy to dismiss. Survivors within the leadership of the institution have described him as violent, wicked, unstable, and licentious. Despite the truth in some of those unflattering characterizations, William was a creature of his time and place and possessed a complex set of characteristics. He was three-dimensional, not the ogre created by those who wrote the official histories. Indeed, there is evidence that William's sins were no more grievous than those of other church leaders of his time.[10]

William Smith was more than five years the Prophet's junior, born March 13, 1811, at Royalton, Vermont. When William was seventy years old, B. H. Roberts, one of the General Authorities, described him as "an unusually tall man and, though emaciated, disclosed a symmetrical physical manhood. . . . He stood erect, full of form, with an aggressive appearance and boldness that would well nigh surpass understanding . . . the features were strong and fine. . . . The eyes were soft, but deep blue, easily converted by the depth of them to almost dark eyes, when animated or stirred by emotion."[11] William was baptized into the church in June 1830 in Seneca Lake, made a high priest in 1833, went to Missouri with Zion's Camp in 1834, and was ordained an apostle on February 15, 1835, at Kirtland. He accompanied the Twelve on their first mission through the eastern states and returned with them to Kirtland in the fall of 1835. William married Caroline Amanda Grant, the sister of Jedediah M. Grant, in 1833. Although Jedediah probably regarded this as a special connection with the Smith family, his relationship with William after Caroline's death would become permanently bitter. William and Caroline had two children, Mary Jane and Caroline L.

When Joseph Jr. blessed William on December 18, 1833 (during the meeting when Joseph Sr. was ordained as the Patriarch), the words he used were recalled often during William's more difficult moments: "Brother William is as the fierce lion, which divideth not the spoil because of his

William Smith, 1811–93. Third presiding patriarch, May to October 1845. Courtesy of the RLDS Church Archives.

strength; and in the pride of his heart he will neglect the more weighty matters until his soul is bowed down in sorrow; and then he shall return and call on the name of his God, and shall find forgiveness, and shall wax valiant therefore he shall be saved unto the uttermost . . . therefore, the blessings of the God of Jacob shall be in the midst of his house, notwithstanding his rebellious heart."[12]

The patriarchal blessing given by his father on December 9, 1834, cautioned William, "Thou has greatly desired to see thy father's family redeemed from trouble, and from the power and dominion of those who oppressed them . . . but thou has not altogether desired this thing in meekness because thou hast not always known God."[13]

Yet there were other sides to William. His mother, Lucy Mack Smith, tells of his courage. Several times he faced his persecutors, sometimes in defense of his father, and risked being tarred and feathered or worse. In about 1837 William returned to his parents' home to find four men plundering the house. According to his mother, William "seized a large handspike, sprang upstairs and in one instant, cleared the scoundrels out of the chamber. They scampered down stairs; he flew after them and, bounding into the very midst of the crowd, he brandished his handspike in every direction exclaiming 'Away from here you cut throats, instantly, or I will be the death of every one of you.'. . . They seemed to believe what he said and fled in every direction, leaving us again to ourselves."[14]

William also reported having had visions.[15] His eloquence as a speaker is on record.[16] A report of a conference at Walnut Grove, January 30, 1841, refers to the branch's being "highly gratified with the labors of Brother [William] Smith since with us he having delivered several excellent discourses, and it was moved, seconded and carried unanimously, that a vote of thanks be given by this Conference to Brother William Smith for his zealous services at this Conference."[17] As representative for Hancock County in the Illinois legislature, William was regarded as a fluent and persuasive speaker.[18]

As editor of the Mormon newspaper *The Wasp*, however, William took on Mormonism's adversaries with even more colorful language than that which occasionally embellished his oratory, and he proved a source of embarrassment at times to the Saints. For example, in answer to an attack by Thomas Sharp printed in the *Warsaw Signal*, in which Sharp said *The Wasp* should have been named "Pole-Cat," William simply replied, "Well done, THOM-ASS."[19] When Joseph became concerned about his brother's abrasiveness, William was persuaded to resign as editor on December 10, 1842.[20]

While William's personality certainly played a part in Brigham Young's reluctance to call him as the Patriarch, the more basic problem was that the Quorum of the Twelve, as the new governing body of the church, would not tolerate William's assertions of Hyrum's primal patriarchal prerogatives for himself. This would have placed him above the Twelve, something the other eleven apostles would not accept.[21]

William's troubles with the Quorum of the Twelve began much earlier, though. His colleagues were irked either by what they perceived as special privileges being given to William because of his family connection with the Prophet or by what they saw as disrespect in William's brotherly familiarity and sometimes hostility toward the Prophet.[22] Twice in 1835 William had serious differences with his brother. The other members of the Quorum of the Twelve did not think well of him for this. The first involved a high council trial of a Sister Elliot held on October 29, 1835. William had instigated the trial, accusing Brother and Sister Elliot of beating their fifteen-year-old daughter. Charges against Brother Elliot had been dismissed. Later, Lucy Mack Smith, the Prophet's mother, testified against Sister Elliot, but Joseph denied her evidence on the grounds that the court had ruled previously on it. William became angry with Joseph, accusing him of doubting his own mother's testimony. Joseph ordered William to sit down but he refused, saying Joseph would have to knock him down first.[23] William became so angry with his brother that he turned in his "license." The remaining eleven apostles had to be humbled by a "Revelation to the Twelve" before they would open their minds to William's reinstatement: "As for my servant William, let the Eleven humble themselves in prayer and in faith, and wait on me in patience, and my servant William shall return, and I will yet make him a polished shaft in my quiver, in bringing down the wickedness and abominations of men."[24]

A month after that, on December 6, 1835, another altercation took place. William was conducting a debating school in his home, and Joseph questioned if good could come of the school and whether it should continue. William became enraged at Joseph's interference. He laid violent hands on the Prophet, the unspecified consequences of which, it is said, Joseph "occasionally felt until his death."[25]

Two days after the attack William wrote a letter of apology to Joseph offering his resignation from the Quorum ("then I would not be in a situation to bring so much disgrace upon the cause"), but he asked to remain a member of the church. He also sent a letter to Hyrum asking his forgiveness.[26] Ten days later, December 29, 1835, the Quorum of the Twelve called William to account for this disastrous breach in hierarchical unity. Orson Johnson preferred formal charges against him for speaking disrespectfully of, and attempting to inflict personal violence on, the Prophet. Orson Hyde also expressed resentment over William's "superior privileges."[27] William was ordered to stand trial on January 2, 1836. After confessing his fault, however, William was forgiven.[28] Four years later William was suspended from office until the next general conference, where he was to give an account of his conduct while in Missouri.[29]

The persons recounting these incidents do so with scarcely veiled disgust at William's conduct. Yet during the nineteenth century this easy resort to anger and fisticuffs was far from unusual in the church and in American society in general.[30] The atmosphere in Kirtland at the time might well have led to such demonstrations within the church, for a Journal History entry on January 1, 1836, states that there was "a division among the Twelve also among the Seventy and bickering and jealousies among the Elders and the official members of the Church."[31] All but two of the apostles rebelled during this time. Even the elderly Joseph Smith, Sr., was not free from the violent nature of the community. Warren Parrish about this time tried to drag Joseph Sr. from the stand during a church meeting because of some remark the Prophet's father had made, and William Smith alone of those present went to his father's aid.[32]

William's violence was not the only thing to which his fellow apostles objected. In later years William's refusal to serve missions as did others in the Quorum of the Twelve prompted William to write a defensive letter published in the *Times and Seasons* in 1840. The hardships in caring for his family William offered as excuses were not regarded by the other apostles as greater than those they suffered when they had responded to the calls.[33]

During the early 1840s William traveled between Nauvoo and the East several times. After returning to Nauvoo on April 22, 1844, he left again on May 21 to promote Joseph's candidacy as president of the United States. During that spring visit at Nauvoo Joseph introduced William to the Council of Fifty and also to the Quorum of the Anointed. Caroline was not with him, so he did not receive the second anointing at that time, but he was most probably introduced to polygamy.

The May 25, 1844, issue of *The Prophet* in New York, quotes the newspaper *Nauvoo Neighbor* regarding William:

> We are happy to say that our well-beloved brother William Smith, has returned once more to our goodly city, in first-rate health and spirits, the same old champion of the rights of man "the world for all and all for the world." He certainly has a great many Mormon notions in his mind. . . . He is the same unyielding advocate for the extension of "Mormonism Unveiled"—power, dominion, grace and glory, not only in this world but in worlds without end. And with the blessing of God and the saints may continue so in company with the servants of the "exalt-

ed" till the morning stars sing together again at the second creation of the earth.[34]

William did not have the full respect of Brigham Young, however, and it is not surprising that Uncle John and Uncle Asael, both brothers of Joseph Sr., were more acceptable to Young and the rest of the Quorum as possible successors to Hyrum's patriarchal office. Young frequently associated Samuel's name with the office of Patriarch, even after Samuel's death, probably to emphasize the fact that it was the patriarchal office, not the presidency, that belonged to the Smith family. To follow through with his commitment in this regard, he was prepared to give the office to William if need be.

After his brothers died, Apostle William Smith was concerned about his own place in the church. One can presume that he was aware of the outcome of the August 8 conference establishing the Quorum of the Twelve as the ultimate leaders of the church when he wrote to Brigham Young from Boardentown, New Jersey, on August 24, 1844:

> Will the bretherin remember me & my clames in the Smith family. I do not mean succession as a prophet in Joseph's place for no man on Earth can fill his place he is our prophet seer, revelator, priest & king in time & in Eternity & hence the 12 come next to him on earth or in heaven. Concequently they must act in Joseph's place on Earth as presiding officers and govern the Church in all things temporaly & spiritualy recieving revelation from Joseph as the antient apostles did from Christ . . . this duty then involves upon you Brother Young as head and revelator to receive revelations from Joseph for the government of the Church . . . as you are the president of the Quorum. . . . The next in order is the Patriarch of the Church this singular personage stands as father to the whole church, a patriarch can be a prophet and revelator not to the church as government but to the church as his children in Patriarchal Blessings upon their heads . . . a patriarch can be an apostle as well as a prophet as in the case of Hyrum . . . and all I have to say farther is that this office of Patriarch must continue in the Smith family while they live and are in the faith.[35]

At the October 1844 General Conference at Nauvoo, it was moved and seconded that Asael Smith, oldest priesthood-holding brother of Joseph Smith, Sr., be ordained a local patriarch. Young might have wanted a ready fallback position in the event it was possible to bypass William when he returned from the East. At the General Conference, however, Young "went on to show that the right to the office of Patriarch to the whole Church belonged to William Smith as a legal right by descent." Young added, with respect to Asael's role as a patriarch, that "Uncle Asael ought to receive the office of (a) [sic] Patriarch in the Church."[36] Brigham Young's commitment to follow what he acknowledged were William's family rights might not have excluded, in Young's mind, the possibility that another Smith might yet take William's place, and having Asael ordained a patriarch ahead of time would help smooth any such transition. On September 28, 1844, Brigham Young wrote the following to William: "As regards a Patriarch for the whole church . . . the right rests upon your head there is no doubt and all will remain as it is until we have further connections from you, but if you feel disposed you can bestow it upon Uncle John or Uncle Asael; and if not disposed to do so but feel to have it yourself we wish you to come to Nauvoo as soon as possible to receive your ordination of Patriarch by the proper authorities, so that you may officiate in giving the saints their patriarchal blessings."[37]

Brigham Young's concern about William was further fueled by reports from Wilford Woodruff, who wrote from the East in October 1844 complaining that William, along with others, had been "crowding their spiritual wife claims . . . until some of the strongest pillars were shaking. . . ."[38] It seems that William Smith and George Adams had been advocating plural marriage indiscriminately during their stay in the East, and it had caused some disaffection among the Saints. Yet, publicly, kind words were spoken about William. In a December 1, 1844, issue of the *Times and Seasons*, the editor reports receiving a communication (probably the one dated August 24) from William Smith and states:

> It will be his privilege when he arrives, to be ordained to the office of patriarch to the church, and to occupy the place that his brother Hyrum did, when living; and he will stand in the same relationship to the Twelve, as his brother Hyrum did to the First Presidency, after he was ordained patriarch . . . yet we can assure him that his old friends the Twelve have not forgotten him; he yet lives in their remembrance, and though with him they mourn the loss of departed friends, they will rejoice to shake him again by the hand, and to enjoy his company, and share his counsels in the city of Nauvoo.[39]

In December Wilford Woodruff again wrote to Brigham Young from the East complaining that William and George Adams were in opposition to the Twelve and were using money they collected for the temple for their personal purposes. He reported that warrants had been issued against them.[40] This problem was not William's alone, however. At one time Joseph had suggested that the Brethren be put under bonds to make sure they turned in the monies collected.[41]

Parley P. Pratt, by contrast, wrote in the January 1845 issue of *The*

Prophet, "I highly approve of the course pursued by Elder Wm. Smith and the presiding officers in general in this region . . . they have preserved the church in union by the aid of the Spirit of God."[42] That this did not reflect his true personal view of things, at least later on, is evidenced by the fact that nine months later Pratt would be the one to object formally to William's being sustained as the Patriarch because of his conduct in the East.

Just two weeks prior to Pratt's editorial in *The Prophet,* he had announced in the same organ that the church was to be reorganized into districts under the direction of the Twelve when "every elder etc. will be accountable for doctrine, labors and conduct."[43] These early efforts to control any kind of independent action would appear to be consistent with Max Weber's theory that after the death of the charismatic innovator, an organization would routinize charisma, accomplishing conformity by introducing general institutional rules. Ironically, the need for such reorganization was probably a response to what they perceived as irresponsibility in William, the very one who would wage a battle for lineal rights.[44]

It becomes quite clear that William's outspokenness, his recalcitrance, his zealousness, his stated conviction that the Smiths constituted the "royal family" of Mormonism, his insistence that the Church Patriarch be independent of hierarchical control, and his claim to visionary experiences all conspired to illuminate the difficulties inherent in hereditary callings. William's words and actions alerted Brigham Young and the Quorum to the dangers in the Patriarch's lineal claims to primacy and in the challenge the Smith family presented to leadership through its familial charisma. Hereditary callings suggested that unsuitable candidates could be waiting in the wings. Within days of William's return to Nauvoo on May 4, 1845, he was perceived as a threat.

Upon his return, William faced dangers from outside and within. The enemies of the church were still threatening the lives of the Smith leaders, and William was prime among them. In addition, with Brigham Young installed as de facto president of the church through his position as president of the Quorum, William did not have the fraternal protection in the hierarchy that he enjoyed when his brothers were alive. The church could no longer be seen as the exclusive province of the Smith family.

William arrived in Nauvoo the evening of May 4 with his mortally ill wife, Caroline. He was taking precautions against assassination and yet actively attempting to undertake the role he saw as his at the headquarters of the church. The day after his arrival he told some of the Brethren that he was "satisfied with the present organization of the church—& state of things in Nauvoo."[45] On May 11, 1845, just one week later, William preached a sermon. James Monroe, an educated man who recorded some of William's blessings after he became the Patriarch, reported in his diary, "He [William] seemed determined to live up to his privilege and stand in his place" and furthermore "did not seem to approve of the harsh measures now going on to get rid of our enemies but advised the Saints to leave judgment in the hand of God." Monroe recounted that Brigham Young was present and "spoke in a commendatory manner of William, but I thought rather coolly."[46]

Caroline Smith died eighteen days after arriving in Nauvoo.[47] As feared earlier, the trip home was more than her weakened condition could withstand. Her funeral was on the morning of May 24, but, fearing for his life, William did not attend.[48] At 3:00 P.M. the same day, the Twelve met at John Taylor's home to consider the case of Samuel Brannan, a friend of William's in the eastern states who had been disfellowshipped for polygamy. Brannan was restored to fellowship, and then "the brethren present expressed their feelings toward Elder William Smith, to which he responded by lifting both hands to heaven and expressing the same."[49] "The Twelve then laid their hands upon him and ordained him to be a Patriarch to the whole church" of Jesus Christ of Latter-day Saints and to preside over the patriarchs. Those assembled shared a bottle of wine, and there was a "warm interchange of good feeling between William Smith and the Quorum."[50]

The good feelings were short-lived. Despite earlier statements that he was content with the leadership he found in place in Nauvoo, William was not satisfied. William Clayton, on the day before the Patriarch's ordination, commented in his diary: "Wm. Smith is coming out in opposition to the Twelve in favor of Adams. The latter has organized a church at Augusta, Iowa Territory with young Joseph Smith for President, Wm Smith for Patriarch . . . and himself for spokesman to Joseph. William says he has sealed some women to men and he considers he is not accountable to Brigham nor the Twelve nor any one else. There is more danger from Wm. Smith than from any other source, and I fear his course will bring us much trouble."[51]

William's ordination the next day did not settle the relationship of the Presiding Patriarch to the rest of the church hierarchy. Within days two articles appeared on the subject in the May 15 issue of the *Times and Seasons* (the publication was running about three weeks late, so it probably reached the public in June, after William's ordination). One article by William Smith was entitled "Patriarchal"; the other, untitled, was signed simply "[Ed.]."[52] Within the context of the times, both articles were disturbing. William's article did not refer to Joseph individually but instead attributed the ac-

complishments of the church to "the family." He then referred to his own
sufferings and sacrifices, his continuing trust in God, and the fact that he,
as "the last of the family," had now settled in Nauvoo. He asked, "Shall I be
sustained by this community?" William also advised, "Support and uphold
the proper authorities of the church—when I say authorities, I mean the
whole, and not a part; the TWELVE and not one, two, six, eight, ten, or elev-
en, but the whole TWELVE follow me as I follow Christ."

The Twelve chose to read a message between the lines of William's article: he was now Patriarch over the whole church. He held the position
of his late brother Hyrum, a man who would have succeeded Joseph as
president had he lived. Hyrum had never been below or subject to the
Quorum of the Twelve in either his capacity as the Patriarch or his position as associate president. William stood before the membership as one
of the Twelve Apostles and at the same time held authority previously seen
as superior to that of the Quorum of the Twelve. If William could persuade the people that Brigham Young's authority was limited to one-
twelfth of the Quorum, then William could match that one-twelfth and
add his churchwide authority through the historical, primal dimensions
of the patriarchal calling. Would that not lead to William as Joseph's eventual successor?

Privately, William was being more explicit. Monroe's diary quotes William on May 27 as saying that Brigham Young was "not a whit beyond
himself or any other of the Twelve, that he is more president by courtesy,
that he has no higher keys and that the whole twelve are presiding over
the church not Brigham Young and that he does not stand in Joseph's
shoes. . . . I hardly know how it will come out. Most probably to his dis-
advantage as the authority of the Twelve is too firmly rooted to be bro-
ken up very easily."[53]

As if William's published comments were not disturbing enough, the
article by the "[Ed.]," appearing immediately below William's, declared
that William had inherited by right of lineage the same office that Joseph
Sr. and Hyrum had held; it eulogized the Smith family; and it emphasized William's role as the family representative, calling him "a father to
the church." It confirmed that William had been called to "the office of
Patriarch over the whole church."

John Taylor was the editor of the paper, and it is probable that the read-
ership thought the article reflected the position of the influential apostle
on behalf of the Quorum. In fact, the article was written by W. W. Phelps,
an articulate and knowledgeable church leader but nevertheless an *assistant* editor. Appearing in combination, these two articles raised serious
questions about leadership in those critical times. Members were confused, and the Quorum felt a need to respond immediately.

John Taylor, speaking for the Quorum as well as for Brigham Young, quickly published an article in the next edition of the *Times and Seasons*. Also entitled "Patriarchal," it read in part:

> Since the publication of the last *Times and Seasons* we have frequently been interrogated about the meaning of some remarks made by Eld. Wm. Smith . . . and also concerning some expressions in the editorial connected therewith; and as the nature of the office of Patriarch does not seem to be fully understood, we thought a little explanation on this point might not be amiss. So far as the editorial is concerned it was written rather hastily by our junior editor, W. W. Phelps, and did not come under our notice until after it was published. There are some expressions contained in it, which might have been worded better and have rendered it less subject to criticism; but he assures us that no such intention was intended to be conveyed as that which is conceived by some. And concerning Brother Wm. Smith, we are better acquainted with him, and with his views, than to believe that he intended to convey any such idea as the one which some persons would put upon, or gather from his sayings.[54]

Then Taylor began to disarm the perceived threat to the Quorum's leadership by limiting the definition of the office of Patriarch. He first discussed the name of the office. It was to be "Patriarch *to* the Church." To identify the name of the office was a somewhat difficult undertaking because of the numerous conflicting titles given to the office previously. William Smith's ordination by Brigham Young indicates he was to be "a Patriarch *to the whole* church" (emphasis added);[55] Brigham Young, in the August and October conferences of 1844, referred to the office as "patriarch *for the whole* church" and "*to the whole* church" (emphasis added).[56] Young used the same phrase in his September 1844 letter to William. On the occasion of Joseph Sr.'s death, the Prophet Joseph referred to his father as having been ordained "Patriarch and President of the High Priesthood."[57] Joseph Jr. ordained his father on December 18, 1833, to hold "the keys of the patriarchal priesthood over the kingdom of God on earth, even the Church of the Latter Day Saints."[58] In Joseph's official history Joseph Sr. is called the "Presiding Patriarch of the church."[59] Nevertheless, the Taylor article maintained that William was not "patriarch *over* the *whole* church."

Taylor did concede that William would act as a "senior Patriarch," have "priority and presidency," hold the keys of the patriarchal priesthood, and in a council of patriarchs preside by right of office. (These concessions would much later be withdrawn by the Twelve Apostles.) Taylor hastened to say, however, that William "is not the only Patriarch" and that "his labors would be more especially connected with the church in *Zion.*" Although this implied a geographical restriction, Taylor seemed to attribute these restrictions more to logistical limitations than to jurisdictional boundaries. There were no geographical restrictions on either Hyrum or Joseph Sr., and this is one limitation that the office remained free of until its demise in 1979. Taylor, in reference to William, in fact quoted the language of Hyrum's revelatory calling: to hold "the keys of the patriarchal blessings upon the heads of *all* my people" (emphasis added).[60]

Another point Taylor made in his article was that William, as Patriarch, had only the restricted authority to give blessings to those who did not have a worthy priesthood-holding father to do so: "A Patriarch to the church is appointed to bless those who are orphans, or have no father in the church to bless them. Not as stated inadvertently in the editorial above alluded to, 'bless all, and such as have not a father to do it' for this he could not do, where the church is so extensive; the burthen would be too onerous; hence other Patriarchs have been ordained, both in this country, and in England, to assist the Patriarch to the church." Taylor was obviously attempting to demonstrate the absence of unique priesthood authority in the office of Patriarch by pointing out the parallel authority of all worthy fathers.

John Taylor's article continues:

> We now proceed to answer some of the remarks which we have heard: But does not the Patriarch stand in the same relationship to the church as Adam did to his family, and as Abraham and Jacob did to theirs? No. This is another mistake which is made by our junior. . . . Adam was the *natural* father of his posterity, who were his family and over whom he presided as patriarch, prophet, priest, and king. Both Abraham and Jacob stood in the same relationship to their families. But not so with Father Joseph Smith, Hyrum Smith, or William Smith. They were not the natural fathers of the church and could not stand in the same capacity as Adam, Abraham or Jacob.[61]

Taylor's answer, in making the distinction between lineal family and organizational family, begs the question as to what the calling of Patriarch Joseph Smith, Sr., and the callings of the patriarchs Adam, Abraham, and Jacob *did* have in common. That the ancient and modern callings were meant to correspond to each other in some way was made clear in the ordination blessing of Father Smith: "So shall it be with my father: he shall be called a prince over his posterity, holding the keys of the patriarchal priesthood over the kingdom of God on earth, even the Church of the Latter Day Saints; and he shall sit in the general assembly of patriarchs even in council with the Ancient of Days when he shall sit and all the patriarchs with him—and shall enjoy his right and authority under the direction of the Ancient of Days. . . ."[62]

Members probably accepted themselves as "children" of the "Father-Patriarch" of the organization, just as if they had been literal descendants of the ancient patriarchs, and thus regarded Taylor's argument as a distinction without a difference. Indeed, Taylor admitted elsewhere in his article that, since there had been none to give blessings for generations, the current patriarchs were set apart for that purpose, to hold the keys of that priesthood, to unlock the door that had so long been closed to the human family, and to act as proxy for the natural fathers.

Taylor went on, "We have been asked, Does not 'patriarch over the whole church' place Brother William Smith at the head of the whole church as president?" The answer, of course, was "no." Taylor maintained that William was ordained as Patriarch "*to* the church," not "*over* the *whole* church."

As discussed earlier, Taylor's recollections of the semantics of William's ordination differ from those recorded in the *History of the Church*. The Quorum, however, certainly did not now wish to emphasize the "whole church" aspect of the position. Taylor continued:

> But does not the Book of Doctrine and Covenants say, "First, I give unto you Hyrum Smith to be a Patriarch unto you to hold the sealing blessings of my church, even the Holy Spirit of promise whereby ye are sealed up unto the day of redemption, that ye may not fall." Yes. But that is in regard to seniority not in regard to authority in priesthood, for it immediately follows, "I give unto you my servant Joseph to be a presiding elder over all my church. . . ." And from this it is evident that the president of the church, not the patriarch, is appointed by God to preside.

This quotes what is now Doctrine and Covenants 124:124. This is the only scriptural source for the sustaining order of the General Authorities of the church. The answer insightfully notes the separation during the lives of Joseph and Hyrum of the honorary "seniority" of the patriarchal office from the administrative authority of the Prophet Joseph.

Taylor then discussed another test for determining seniority within the hierarchy: the one with greater authority ordains (or grants) authority to the one with lesser authority. Although Taylor acknowledged that Father Smith was ordained by the Prophet and that Hyrum had been ordained by Father Smith, he pointed out that William was ordained by the Twelve, and he asked, "Can a stream rise higher than its fountain?" implying that William must, therefore, be subject to the Twelve.[63] Taylor referred to the charge in Doctrine and Covenants 107:39, which states, "It is the duty of the Twelve in all large branches of the church, to ordain evangelical ministers." William's calling, however, was not as a "branch" or "local" patriarch.

Taylor's extension of apostolic authority over the office of Church Patriarch was a fundamental change—one that would continue to create tension between patriarchal incumbents and the Quorum of the Twelve for generations. Taylor knew that neither Joseph Sr. nor Hyrum had been subject to the Twelve, only to the Prophet/president of the church. With the elimination of the Quorum of the First Presidency, however, the office William was receiving *had* to be subject to the Quorum as the new line-authority head of the church.[64]

Apostle Taylor then went on to point out that "the president of the church presides over all patriarchs, presidents, and councils of the church; and this presidency does not depend so much upon genealogy as upon calling, order, and seniority."[65] That one sentence documents and signals the transformation from innovative, familial, charismatic leadership to traditional leadership, a leadership deriving its authority from office ("office charisma") rather than from lineage ("lineal charisma"). Taylor ends with this assurance (which turned out to be more accurate than he could have guessed): "We think that everyone will see that Br. William Smith's patriarchal office will not exalt him higher in regard to priesthood than he was before, as one of the Twelve; but will rather change the nature of his office."[66]

Things became progressively worse between William Smith and the Quorum of the Twelve. William even feared for his own safety. "News has come to me that certain men are forming a conspiracy to put me out of the way in this city," he said in a letter to Brigham Young.[67] William's fear was undoubtedly real, even if there was, in fact, no danger. He had to know that his open opposition to the Twelve was known by the apostles and that they would like to see it stop. The Quorum was meeting without inviting William to be present, and the lines were clearly drawn.[68]

William asked for protection from Brother Elbridge Tufts, the chief of police in Nauvoo. When Tufts refused to honor William's directive, William "beat brother Tufts shamefully."[69] William then wrote to Brigham Young on June 25, 1845 (probably before the publication of the Taylor article in the *Times and Seasons*). Young discussed William's letter with George A. Smith at the home of Willard Richards, after which George A. gave William notice to meet at 6:00 P.M. to work things out. That evening, John Taylor noted that "we there prayed for William that God would overrule every evil principle; that his violent spirit might be curbed by the Spirit of God."[70] According to George A., William "made a very long and pathetic speech against Bro. Tufts and family."[71] John Taylor told William that he was wrong and that his life was not in jeopardy. Taylor reported that William said "he would go quietly & let the people here remain in peace, that he was one of the last remnants of the Smith family to whom the priesthood had come; and that if he went away he would take along with him his sisters, his mother, and the last remains of the family; and that where he and they went there the priesthood, authority, and the church would be; he made other remarks of an unpleasant nature."[72]

Taylor noted that Brigham Young replied by pointing out that

> he [Young] knew as much about the power and authority of the priest-hood as William Smith or any other man in the Church. He stated that he did not receive his priesthood from William Smith but from his brother and he understood the power of that priesthood, neither is this Church indebted to William Smith for the priesthood; that Joseph had made some expressions about a year ago upon the stand, that . . . there were certain principles connected with the priesthood, genealogy, and blood which would be unfolded in their proper time, that Hyrum, al-though he was older than Joseph, had no right to the presidency, nei-ther had Samuel, Don Carlos, William, or any of the brothers but Joseph. . . . We could live in peace here before William came, and since he came there has been the devil to pay.[73]

Brigham had apparently forgotten that a few months before, in October 1844, he himself had acknowledged that if Hyrum had lived he would have been Joseph's heir to the presidency of the church.[74]

After these later remarks of Brigham Young, William agreed to "com-pare his statement with Bro. Tufts' and be satisfied. We thought we could then settle the whole matter in a few minutes."[75] As on other occasions with William, what began as a burst of anger ended with a surprisingly amicable, if temporary, reconciliation. Taylor wrote that William appeared humbled by Brigham Young's remarks.

On June 27, 1845, two days after this confrontation, Brigham Young wrote a letter to Wilford Woodruff, expressing his concern about William Smith: "Since his return to Nauvoo . . . he seems to think he ought to be President of the Church, and since he was ordained a Patriarch to the whole church he has endeavored to get up an influence among the saints to persuade them that the office of Patriarch necessarily makes him president. . . . He seems determined to cause us trouble, but our prayers continually ascend to our heavenly father to overrule William and save him if possible."[76]

On June 28, the confrontation between William and the Quorum was accelerated by news that Lucy Mack Smith, mother of the martyred prophet, had received a vision in which William was to be a presiding authority in the church. She described the vision as having to do with her husband, "the first patriarch of this church," as well as all of her sons and daughters. Her sons were "the first founders, fathers, heads of this Church," and her daughters had a part as "daughters of Israel." Lucy was mother of the church. The vision then spoke of William:

> He shall raise up this Church. . . . Thy son, William he shall have pow-
> er over the churches, he is father in Israel over the patriarchs, and the
> whole of the Church; he is the last of the lineage that is raised up in
> these last days. He is Patriarch to regulate the affairs of the Church. He
> is President. . . . The Presidency of the Church belongs to William, he
> being the last of the heads of the Church, according to the lineage, he
> having inherited it from the family from before the foundation of the
> world. . . . Brother and children, I want you to take notice that the bur-
> den of the Church rests [on William].[77]

When Brigham Young heard of Mother Smith's vision, he arranged a meeting at her home.[78] William refused to attend the meeting, telling his cousin George A. Smith and his uncle John Smith that he "had the right, by birth, to lead the church and that all he wanted was his rights and he would have them at all events."[79] At the meeting with Mother Smith, William Clayton asked for a copy of the vision. Lucy refused, maintaining that it was "not all correct and she wanted it sealed up as it only pertained to her own family."[80] Brigham Young told Mother Smith that William Smith was attempting to assume priesthood authority that was not his and that John Taylor's recent article in the *Times and Seasons* was correct in its conclusions. Lucy replied that she did not profess to be a revelator except for her own family and that she only wanted "peace, union, and harmony. The Twelve all expressed the same feeling and manifested the greatest kindness to Mother Smith together with the Bishops."[81]

Although William did not attend the meeting at his mother's house, he did have a lengthy letter delivered to those of the Twelve who were assembled there. The letter was dated June 30 and was directed more to the June 1 *Times and Seasons* article by John Taylor than to Lucy's vision. (Although the *Times and Seasons* issue was dated June 1, it probably reached the public the latter part of June.) William's letter shows he had no more expected Taylor's article than Taylor had expected William's:

> It has been my purpose from the first to do all I could for peace. I said
> in a short note to you the other day that I would stand by you till death.
> But it might be asked upon what principle? I will answer, on the prin-
> ciple that I am dealt justly by in the church. The next morning after
> our meeting I notice an article that appears under the head of the Pa-

triarch. It is not so much the doctrine that I care about; it is the spirit of the article, a disposition that appears in the brethren to cut and shave me down to the last cent, every hour and minute in the day. I do not like it. . . . Why was the article not shown to me? . . . [He complained of abuse since returning from the East, and added:] I have often said . . . it was my wish that you should stand as the President of the church, but I claim to be patriarch over the whole church, this gives me my place and proper standing, and what I inherit . . . no man being my head . . . I want all men to understand that my father's family are of the royal blood and promised seed and *no man* or set of *men* can take their crown or *place* in time or in eternity.[82]

The letter went on to claim that when they met at Taylor's house on May 24, there was an understanding that William was Patriarch over the whole church. "This is what I claim and must have. . . ." William then asked them to publish in the *Times and Seasons* "the true state of the case" so he could visit all branches of the church, adding that "no man being my head. . . . I will reconcile all difficulties and Elder Young can stand as the president of the church, and by my most hearty wish and consent."

Young's reply, written the same day, was read to Mother Smith and obtained her approval: "We have had considerable talk with mother Smith and find her possessing the best of feelings toward the church." Young went on to concede the right of the Patriarch to operate throughout the world and no one to dictate or control "excepting the Twelve, which body of men must preside over the whole church in all the world." Young also reiterated that

there are some ordinances in the church that cannot be administered by any person out of this place at present, but must be done here. As to your having the right to administer all ordinances in the world, and no one standing at your head, we could not sanction. . . . We hope and trust there will be no feelings. Say nothing about matters and things. If you want peace, so do we; and let us walk together in peace, and help to build up the kingdom. If this does not meet with your feelings brother William, write me again, or come and see me, and we will make all things right, for we surely want peace and the salvation of the people. P.S. We have read this to mother Smith, Catherine, Lucy and Arthur [Milliken] and they express their satisfaction with it as well as those of the council who are present.[83]

Despite William's apparent rebellion, the Twelve seemed to demonstrate considerable patience and even goodwill. In July the church paid for a Smith family feast that nearly all of the Smiths, including William, attended.[84]

On August 9, 1845, however, William again wrote to Brigham Young complaining that Young and the other apostles were interfering with his exercise of the sealing rights connected with the office of Patriarch, to wit, "to seal on earth and it would be sealed in heaven" (see Doctrine and Covenants 124:93). "When the Brethren[85] call on me to be sealed to their wives, their dead friends &c also to get patriarchal blessings for their dead—what shall I say to them?"[86]

The next day Young wrote to William, saying that all sealings, including patriarchal blessings for the dead, should be held in abeyance until the temple was available, since, for the sealings to be valid, they would all have to be done over again anyway in that edifice. He also pointed out that the sealing power is always vested in only one man and that man is the president of the church. Whether Young meant *he* was the president, or whether he meant no one could seal until a new president was designated, is not clear. Young went on to declare that William did not inherit sealing authority by reason of his succession to Hyrum Smith's former authority, because Hyrum had sealing power only to the extent Joseph delegated it to him. This probably referred to officiating in plural marriage sealings.[87]

On August 17 William gave a talk on the subject of plural marriage to an assembly of Saints in Nauvoo. It was entitled "The First Chapter of the Gospel by St. William." Speaking within a church community where plural marriage was still a secret, though suspected, practice, William spoke as "one of these sort of independent soldiers of the Cross that will do all things in daylight." He said, "If a Sister gives me her hand upon the Spiritual Wife system to share with me the fate and destinies of time and eternity, I will not be ashamed of her before the public." He also talked of Jacob and his four wives: "if the Twelve Tribes were God's peculiar people were they all legitimate or lawful seed . . . and sprang from Four Women? The Scriptures command me to love all men, and women too." John Taylor, who was the only other apostle present, "felt pained and distressed when Wm. was speaking, as did a great many of the congregation, and many of the people left, being disgusted at the remarks he made."[88]

If William ever had a chance of undermining the leadership of the Twelve, this public discourse certainly ended any such possibility. Although perhaps not a clear turning point, it did place him beyond the point of no return. William Clayton opined that the speech "hurt him in the estimation of the saints more than any thing he has done before."[89]

As the month of August wore on, William continued to battle for "Smith family rights" by arguing that Joseph's twelve-year-old son should eventually be the proper successor as president. Many in the church at

that time felt the Quorum of the Twelve was acting as a temporary head
of the church until young Joseph III grew up and took his rightful place.
On August 20, 1845, William wrote to a Brother Little:

> Emma is well and also little Joseph, his father's successor, although
> some people would fain make us believe that the Twelve are to be per-
> petual heads of this church to the exclusion of the Smith family, but
> everyone who has read the book of Doctrine and Covenants must be
> aware that priesthood authority is hereditary and descends from father
> to son, and therefore Joseph's oldest son will take his place when he
> arrives at the age of maturity. The Twelve are, however, the president
> for the *time being* but when Joseph's successor comes they take their
> former place.[90]

William continued, "There seems to be a severe influence working
against me and the Smith family in this place." Many things *were* working against William. As James Monroe had observed back in May, the
apostles were simply too well rooted in their leadership roles before William returned from the East. But William's own lack of discretion was
working against him, too.

Toward the end of August the Quorum of the Twelve decided to let William return to the East to give patriarchal blessings. It changed its mind,
however, when Parley P. Pratt contended that William had alienated the
affections of the eastern Saints and would not be welcome. Willard Richards wrote to William of the decision of the Quorum of the Twelve.[91]

Since Mother Smith was accepting the authority of the Twelve, many
of the Smiths were now opposed to William's course of action. Uncle John
Smith, who was the brother of Joseph Smith, Sr., and had been ordained
a local patriarch on January 1, 1844, showed his loyalty to Brigham Young
and the Quorum of the Twelve when he instigated a sting operation
against his nephew William. In September Uncle John sent a man to William posing as one "privey to the mob" with instructions to report William's sentiments. It was reported that William told the man "he was going East & he would let him know more before next spring. By God I'll
let this people know who their ruler is."[92] Uncle John reported the results
to the Twelve.

Long before October William was not even attempting a working relationship with the rest of the Quorum. His defiance was outright. On
October 5 he wrote to a Brother Robbins and asserted that "no man need
tell me that Brigham Young does not claim to be the prophet, seer and
perpetual head of the Church for I know that he dos, and you know that
it lawfuly and legaly belongs to litle Joseph. . . . I shall not resign the Smith
family rights."[93]

The inevitable culmination of William's rebellion was about to occur. On October 6, one day after the letter to Robbins, at the General Conference of the church, the membership assembled rejected William Smith as an apostle and as Patriarch to the Church. Orson Pratt's journal records the customary sustaining of authorities: "It was next moved [by local patriarch, Isaac Morley[94]] that William Smith be continued and sustained as one of the Twelve Apostles; seconded. Whereupon Elder (Parley P.) Pratt arose and said 'I have an objection to Brother William continuing in that office.'"[95] The *History of the Church* gives Apostle Pratt's reasons for his objection: "I have proof positive that he [William] is an aspiring man; that he aspires to uproot and undermine the legal Presidency of the church, that he may occupy the place himself. . . . In the second place, while Brother William was in the east . . . his doctrine and conduct have not had a savory influence; but have produced death and destruction wherever he went."[96] On Sunday, October 19, 1845, William Smith was excommunicated from the church by unanimous vote.[97]

Some historians have seen William as such an embarrassment that they have either left him off the list of Patriarch incumbents without explanation or have claimed he never legally held the office because he was never sustained in his position at a general conference.[98] Since William was ordained after the April General Conference and was excommunicated in the October General Conference, this argument has superficial credibility. It does not, however, accurately reflect church practice. D. Michael Quinn has noted that other "important ordinations of General Authorities had not only occurred without a prior vote of the Church but had also continued in force for weeks, months, and years before being officially presented for a public vote of common consent."[99]

There is an epilogue to the story of William's rise and fall. His fury can be measured by the tone of a letter he wrote to Lewis Robbins of St. Louis on November 7, 1845. He describes members of the Quorum of the Twelve as "mean enough to steel if they could get the chance eaven Christ's supper off his plate or seduce the Virgen Mary or Rob an orphan child of 25 cts and so damnable are their acts & conduct that old Judas . . . would be a perfect genteelman to these men. . . ."[100] In November James Kay of St. Louis tells of William's endeavors to "make a raise in this city." William, Kay reports, contended that "the church is disorganized, having no head, that the twelve are not, nor ever were, ordained to be head of the church, that Joseph's priesthood was to be conferred on his posterity to all future generations, and that young Joseph is the only legal successor to the presidency of this church."[101]

While William was living in St. Louis for a time in the fall of 1845, he stayed at the home of an unmarried woman. When Jedediah Grant, William's brother-in-law, came through St. Louis on his way to Nauvoo, he concluded that William's relationship with his landlady was a compromising one. Grant was aware of William's differences with Brigham Young, and this was reason enough for Jedediah, a loyal follower of the new leadership, to place William firmly within the camp of the enemy. When William heard of Grant's reports to the people in Nauvoo, he wrote an angry letter to Emma, Joseph's widow, in which, among other things, he rebuked Emma for refusing to help him "reform" the church: "After the many times I have talked with you in this subject and asked what I should do to save my father's family and all my friends and the answer was for me to come out and proclaim against the spiritual wife doctrine, the userpation of the Twelve etc. etc. Now Emma, I have don it and all hell is in rage and every lie that can be set on foot is on hand and will you believe them. . . ."[102]

The pathos of this letter reveals the bitter disappointment William must have felt. He thought he had failed to uphold the Smith family honor, a concern shared by some of his successors in the office. Also, other younger brothers of the "eldest son" in the patriarchal line would be victims of the attention given to their older sibling. A lineal patriarchal office not only presented inherent difficulties for the organization but also placed unfair expectations and consequences on William and other Smith descendants.

As for the church organization, the internal threat represented by William's claim of Smith family rights of succession was shelved with the help of William's irascible temper and his unwillingness to relinquish the independence of the office of Patriarch. It was "shelved" insofar as immediate Smith family claims were neutralized, but the leaders as well as members continued to hold out some expectation that someday an adult son of Joseph might step forward to assume presidential leadership and that the patriarchate would go to the line of Hyrum's oldest sons.

William Smith's shadow became "a reference point for more than a century of ecclesiastical misgivings many general authorities had about the [patriarchal] office."[103] In fairness to William, however, his personality simply highlighted the inherent tension between two competing strains of authority within the church and dramatically illustrated the possibility of other incompatible successors waiting in the wings to inherit the lineal office of Patriarch.

Once William was outside the structure of the church, he could be seen by the followers of Brigham Young and the Twelve simply as a disruptive influence. Yet, with respect to the giving of patriarchal blessings, he had faithfully fulfilled his calling, giving almost three hundred blessings during his four months as the Patriarch, many of them quite beautiful.

Even as an excommunicant, William continued to oppose the Twelve. He sought a money or property inheritance for the Smith family from the Twelve, he lobbied against admitting the state of Deseret to the Union, and he continued to assert his right to be Patriarch over the whole Church. William's efforts, however, had little impact on the institution that had developed during the fourteen years of Joseph's ministry and that now provided some degree of community and security for the beleaguered Saints. William Smith ultimately joined the Reorganized Church, led by the Prophet Joseph's son Joseph Smith III.

The controversy between William Smith and Brigham Young resulted in modifications of the office of Patriarch to the Church. The heart of the controversy was over whether William was receiving the same position as that held by his brother Hyrum. The Quorum of the Twelve claimed it was. In fact, it was not the same, nor could it be. Either the office had to become subject to the Twelve for the first time, with far less stature, or it must expand its former authority and become the most important single position in the church, outside the authority of the Twelve.

William spoke of having, in essence, two heads of the church—one with line and priesthood authority to manage the organizational needs and another with staff or spiritual authority to minister to the responsibility of blessing the church and its members. This latter office would not make William subject, within his sphere, to the Quorum. The duality William spoke of, which Young and the Twelve thought would dilute the authority needed for leading the Saints during this difficult time, illustrates the Weberian axiom suggesting the inherent incompatibility between office and lineal charismatic leadership. Indeed, Weber says it would be impossible for both to exist without one predominating.

Subsequent holders of the patriarchal office would inherit an office encumbered by the baggage of the 1845 conflicts between William and the Quorum of the Twelve. The Twelve, especially Brigham Young, would thereafter manifest a defensive posture to any suggestion that the *family* of Joseph Smith, Jr., as opposed to the Prophet Joseph as an individual, had any part in the founding of the church or the restoration of authority within it. The Taylor article in the *Times and Seasons,* spawned by the conflict of that time, would continue to be, selectively, the authoritative text for defining the office. Never again would a Smith hold the office without a catch-22 dilemma: assert the premartyrdom dimensions of the office and invite hostilities from the Brethren; or be passive in the calling and invite criticism for not magnifying the office. The specter that William Smith had illumined never completely faded away but would reappear in various guises in the years to come.

Notes

1. Brigham Young to Willard Richards, Salem, Mass., July 8, 1844, Journal History, Archives of the Church of Jesus Christ of Latter-day Saints, Salt Lake City (hereafter LDS Church Archives).

2. Willard Richards to Brigham Young, Nauvoo, June 30, 1844, Manuscript History of the Church, LDS Church Archives.

3. Caroline died on May 22, 1845, just eighteen days after their arrival in Nauvoo.

4. William Clayton, Diary, July 7, 1844, LDS Church Archives. See also James Whitehead's testimony in the Temple Lot Suit, 33, Special Collections, Marriott Library, University of Utah, Salt Lake City.

5. Clayton, Diary, July 12, 1844. During his lifetime the Prophet Joseph Smith had named several successors, including, but not limited to, Hyrum, Joseph Smith III, and the Quorum of the Twelve. Other successors proposed by Joseph had either left the church by 1844 or else were deceased. D. Michael Quinn, "The Mormon Succession Crisis of 1844," *Brigham Young University Studies* 16 (Winter 1976): 193.

6. Scott G. Kenney, ed., *Wilford Woodruff's Journal, 1833–1898*, 9 vols. (Salt Lake City: Signature Books, 1983–85), 2:434.

7. Joseph Smith, *History of the Church of the Church of Jesus Christ of Latter-day Saints*, 2d rev. ed., ed. B. H. Roberts, 7 vols. (Salt Lake City: Deseret Book, 1978), 7:234. Uncle John Smith, brother of Joseph Sr., was a local patriarch at the time, ordained by the Prophet Joseph on January 10, 1844. In October 1844 he was called to be president of the Nauvoo Stake.

8. Joseph Smith, *History of the Church*, 7:241–42.

9. Clayton, Diary, August 8, 1844. See also John Taylor, Journal, December 26, 1844, LDS Church Archives; copy in authors' possession; original in private collection.

10. For example, Jedediah Grant, a member of the First Presidency, in a Sunday Tabernacle Discourse on March 23, 1856, in Journal History, March 23, 1856, referred to William as "the profligate brother" of Joseph Smith, Jr. Orson Hyde in a letter to Brigham Young, April 25, 1850, in Journal History, June 26, 1850, noted "the hypocrisy, licentiousness, treachery, deceit, slander and lies of William Smith." Most of such references to William came after his excommunication in 1845, but the Prophet himself, on December 18, 1833, had characterized William as having "a rebellious heart." Quoted in Joseph Fielding Smith, comp., *Teachings of the Prophet Joseph Smith* (1938; reprint, Salt Lake City: Deseret Book, 1969), 41. A majority of the apostles were disfellowshipped for rebellion, adultery, or licentiousness at least once and in most cases several times. See Joseph Smith, *History of the Church*, especially vol. 3, for details. The *Deseret News 1989–1990 Church Almanac* (Salt Lake City: Deseret News, 1988), 42–50, gives dates of excommunications of early church leaders. Even Joseph Smith, Jr., resorted to physical violence in tense situations. Benjamin F. Johnson, a great admirer of the Prophet, said of him, "In

the early days at Kirtland and elsewhere one or another of his associates were more than once, for their impudence, helped from the congregation by his foot and at one time at a meeting at Kirtland for insolence to him he soundly thrashed his brother William who [had] boasted himself as invincible." Benjamin F. Johnson to George S. Gibbs, 1903, 4, typescript, Huntington Library, San Marino, Calif. Apostle David Patten tells of being slapped and kicked out of the yard by the Prophet. David Patten, Journal, 1832–34, LDS Church Archives. (The last part of Patten's journal, undated, is written by Wilford Woodruff, probably after Patten's death, October 25, 1838). Brigham Young threatened an apostate with a cowhide whip. Told by George A. Smith in *Journal of Discourses by Brigham Young, President. of the Church of Jesus Christ of Latter-day Saints, His Two Counsellors, the Twelve Apostles and Others*, 26 vols. (Liverpool, England: Latter-day Saints Books Depot, 1855–86), 7:114.

11. Quoted in Truman G. Madsen, *Defender of the Faith: The B. H. Roberts Story* (Salt Lake City: Bookcraft, 1980), 121.

12. Joseph Smith, *History of the Church*, 1:467; reproduced in *Times and Seasons* 6 (July 15, 1845): 968.

13. Blessing Book II, 9–10, LDS Church Archives, cited in Calvin Rudd, "William Smith, Brother of the Prophet Joseph Smith" (M.A. thesis, Brigham Young University, 1973), 31.

14. Lucy Mack Smith, *Biographical Sketches of Joseph Smith the Prophet, and His Progenitors for many Generations* (Liverpool, England: Published for Orson Pratt by S. W. Richards, 1853; New York: Arno Press and New York Times, 1969), 163, 218, 241.

15. Joseph Smith, *History of the Church*, 2:387, 392. On January 28, 1836, in the upper loft of the Lord's House, William saw the heavens opened and the Lord's host protecting the Lord's anointed. On February 6 of the same year he had another vision.

16. Lucy Mack Smith, *Biographical Sketches*, 218, tells of William addressing a crowd and managing to convert a Mr. Bear, one of the most belligerent anti-Mormons.

17. William Smith, "Minutes of a Conference Held at Walnut Grove, Knox Co., Ill., January 30th, 1841," *Times and Seasons* 2 (March 1, 1841): 338.

18. There are cordial references to William's performance in the legislature in Parley Pratt's correspondence in the *Millennial Star* 3 (April 1843): 207. One of his speeches in the House is quoted in full in Joseph Smith, *History of the Church*, 5:201–4. When William withdrew his candidacy for re-election because of his wife's sickness, tribute was paid to him. "William Smith . . . proved to be a man of talent and of genius, a patriot and a statesman, and a man every way qualified to maintain the interests of the people he represented." "For the Neighbor," *Times and Seasons* 5 (May 15, 1844): 534.

19. Fawn M. Brodie, *No Man Knows My History* (New York: Alfred A. Knopf, 1945), 288. William's articles in the *Times and Seasons* included imaginative phrasing a little less crude but still belligerent. For example, see his answer to Governor Boggs's "Extermination Order," in 2 (February 15, 1841):

314–16. Colorful language was not exclusive to William, however. The speeches of Heber C. Kimball and Brigham Young showed a lack of delicacy typical of their environment.

20. Joseph Smith, *History of the Church*, 5:204. When John Taylor took over the editorship of *The Wasp*, the tone became more civil and cultivated. For a discussion of Sharp's relationship with the church, see Marshall Hamilton, "Thomas Sharp's Turning Point: Birth of an Anti-Mormon," *Sunstone* 13 (October 1989): 16–22.

21. See Irene M. Bates, "William Smith, 1811–1893: Problematic Patriarch," *Dialogue: A Journal of Mormon Thought* 16 (Summer 1983): 11–23

22. Abraham H. Cannon, Diary, April 9, 1890, LDS Church Archives, tells of Brigham Young, as president of the Twelve, conducting a trial against William on charges of adultery and other sins. Joseph had asked Brigham to conduct the proceedings. In the meantime Emma talked to Joseph, and said the charge preferred against William was with a view to injuring the Smith family. When Joseph attended the trial, he arose, filled with wrath, and said, "'Bro. Brigham I will not listen to this abuse of my family a minute longer. [I] will wade in blood up to my knees before I will do it.'" Brigham instantly said, "'Bro. Joseph I withdraw the charge.'"

23. Kirtland High Council Minute Book, October 29, 1835, LDS Church Archives. See also Joseph Smith, *History of the Church*, 2:294–95.

24. Joseph Smith, *History of the Church*, 2:300–301.

25. Andrew Jensen, *Latter-day Saints Biographical Encyclopedia*, 4 vols. (Salt Lake City: Andrew Jensen Historical Co., 1901–36), 1:87. See also the "Orson Hyde Biography" by his son Joseph Hyde, MS 193, Special Collections, Marriott Library, University of Utah, Salt Lake City: "It was, however, obvious knowledge . . . that one, William Smith, . . . all but beat his brother to death in a common fist fight and dog-fashion battle. . . . It was said William Smith (big local bully) had received from the bishop's storehouse materials and merchandise to the amount of six hundred dollars and he, as an apostle, not having stirred a foot or travelled a mile or preached a sentence in the interests of the church . . . (19)." Joseph's own account, referred to in Joseph Smith, *History of the Church*, 2:335, states that William used "violence upon my person . . . for which I am grieved beyond measure."

26. Joseph Smith, *History of the Church*, 2:338–43, 353.

27. Ibid.; "Orson Hyde Biography," 19.

28. Kirtland High Council Minute Book, January 2, 1836, LDS Church Archives. See also Joseph Smith, *History of the Church*, 2:354.

29. Minutes of General Conference, Quincy, May 4–5, 1839, LDS Church Archives; Joseph Smith, *History of the Church*, 3:345, 364. The ease with which church leaders were disfellowshipped and reinstated during the early years of the church suggests that these procedures were not regarded with the same seriousness as they are today. For example, on October 22, 1837, "the Church in Kirtland disfellowshiped twenty-two brethren and sisters until they make satisfaction for uniting with the world in a dance the Thursday previous." Joseph Smith, *History of the Church*, 2:519.

30. See Bates, "William Smith, 1811–1893."

31. Joseph Smith, *History of the Church*, 2:352; Journal History, January 1, 1836.

32. Lucy Mack Smith, *Biographical Sketches*, 211. Violent conduct on the part of Joseph was not uncommon. For example, when Ira Spaulding was riding in a carriage with the Prophet, a man who came to collect a note insulted Joseph. The Prophet simply handed the reins to Spaulding, "just stept outside the carriage and knocked him down as flat as a beef, not speaking a word" and traveled on. David Osborn, Autobiography, cited in Stanley S. Ivins, Notebook No. 5, 111, Utah State Historical Society, Salt Lake City; photocopy in New York Public Library.

33. William Smith "Communications [to] D. C. Smith, Plymouth, Dec. 1st, 1840," *Times and Seasons* 2 (December 15, 1840): 252–53. William quotes the New Testament admonition "that he who will not provide for his own household is worse than an infidel and has denied the faith." William's wife, Caroline, seems to have appreciated his sincere desire to care for his family. Caroline, in a letter from Philadelphia to her brother Jedediah M. Grant, May 5, 1844, LDS Church Archives, asks him to "tell Wm he must keep up his spirits and do the best he can and not give himself trouble about my sufring for a want of means for I have been very well provided for so far last Sabath Br. Walton took up a colection for me and got two dolars and forty four cents. . . . I would like to see him [William] an hour or two mighty well about this time."

34. *The Prophet*, May 25, 1844, original in Newspaper Collection, New York City Public Library.

35. William Smith to Brigham Young, August 24, 1844, Brigham Young Collection, LDS Church Archives.

36. Joseph Smith, *History of the Church*, 7:300–301.

37. Brigham Young to William Smith, September 28, 1844, published in *The Prophet*, November 9, 1844, Newspaper Collection, New York City Public Library.

38. Wilford Woodruff to Brigham Young, Boston, October 9, 1844, Manuscript History of the Church, LDS Church Archives. Woodruff includes George Adams and Samuel Brannan in his complaint. Brannan had preferred a charge of slander against Elder John Hardy in Boston for saying they had been "engaged in the spiritual wife business." Woodruff advised them to let the matter alone. The secrecy surrounding the practice of plural marriage at that time led to many such problems. John Hardy, an anti-Mormon, wrote *History of the Trials of Elder John Hardy* (Boston: Conway, 1844); photocopy in authors' possession.

39. *Times and Seasons* 5 (December 1, 1844): 727.

40. As related in Clayton, Diary, December 19, 1844.

41. According to Cannon, Diary, April 9, 1890, Apostle F. D. Richards stated that "when some of the brethren in Nauvoo were sent out to collect funds for the building of the temple part of their collections stuck to their fingers. Because of this Joseph said he thought it best to put the brethren under bonds

to make correct return and this plan would be commenced with the apostles." Brigham Young objected to the lack of trust this signified and said he did not propose to be thus treated. Later he reached agreement with Joseph.

42. Parley P. Pratt, Editorial, *The Prophet,* January 18, 1845, Newspaper Collection, New York Public Library. Pratt wrote a similar laudatory comment about William Smith in the April 26, 1845, issue of *The Prophet.*

43. Parley P. Pratt, Editorial, *The Prophet,* January 4, 1845. This may be a veiled reference to William's performing plural marriages without authorization. Earlier, the *Warsaw Signal,* May 19, 1844, reported on the trial of John Hardy in Boston in which it was stated that William and George Adams "had preached the spiritual wife system and boldly proclaimed that a multiplicity of wives was a fact of their religion." Yet Willard Richards in a letter to Brigham Young from Nauvoo, June 30, 1844, Manuscript History of the Church, LDS Church Archives, wrote, "I heard Joseph tell Hyrum to let Adams alone, let Adams go back there and make all things right. That Parley has misapprehended some things and acted in the matter rather injudiciously."

44. William voiced his approval of Pratt's circular in a letter to *The Prophet* reproduced in the *Times and Seasons* 6 (February 15, 1845): 814: "Since the death of the prophet and patriarch the church has had to go through an entire revolution of things and those away from Nauvoo have had to guess their way . . . and if errors have been committed they have been of the head and not of the heart."

45. Quoted in Willard Richards, Diary, May 5, 1845, LDS Church Archives.

46. James Monroe, Diary, May 11, 1845, holograph in Coe Collection, Yale University Library, New Haven, Conn.; copy at the Huntington Library, San Marino. Monroe agreed with William that the Mormons were inviting persecution.

47. William and Caroline Grant Smith's children were Mary Jane, born January 1835 in Kirtland and married Andrew Scott; Caroline, born August 1836 in Kirtland and married James Quince. *Utah Genealogical Magazine* 26 (July 1935): 104–5.

48. Manuscript History of the Church, June 30, 1844, LDS Church Archives, cited in Linda King Newell and Valeen Tippetts Avery, *Mormon Enigma: Emma Hale Smith, Prophet's Wife, "Elect Lady," Polygamy's Foe* (Garden City, N.Y.: Doubleday, 1984), 215.

49. George A. Smith, Journal, May 24, 1845, George A. Smith Family Collection, Manuscripts Division, Special Collections, Marriott Library, University of Utah, Salt Lake City.

50. Joseph Smith, *History of the Church,* 7:418. See also Richards, Diary, May 24, 1845. Nine years later, William in a letter to Brigham Young, August 8, 1854, Brigham Young Collection, LDS Church Archives, complained that he never received a copy of his ordination.

51. Clayton, Diary, May 23, 1845. On May 29, 1845, Clayton recorded his prayer that "the Lord would over-rule the movements of Wm. Smith who is endeavoring to ride the Twelve down."

52. William Smith, "Patriarchal," *Times and Seasons* 6 (May 15, 1845): 904, followed by an untitled article signed "[Ed.]."

53. Monroe, Diary, May 27, 1845.

54. John Taylor, "Patriarchal," *Times and Seasons* 6 (June 1, 1845): 920–21. Again, the actual publication date probably followed the issue date by about three weeks. The text of the funeral service for Caroline, William's wife, also appeared in this issue. The handwritten text of Taylor's article is in his journal.

55. Joseph Smith, *History of the Church,* 7:418.

56. Ibid., 7:234, 301.

57. Ibid., 4:190.

58. Oliver Cowdery, Minutes, in Joseph Smith, Sr., Patriarchal Blessing Book, vol. 1, 1835, LDS Church Archives.

59. Joseph Smith, *History of the Church,* 4:189. See also B. H. Roberts, *A Comprehensive History of the Church of Jesus Christ of Latter-day Saints: Century I,* 6 vols. (Salt Lake City: Deseret News Press, 1930), 1:387: "The presiding patriarch over the patriarchs of the church, however, is not so limited, since his jurisdiction in the line of his calling extends throughout the church, and he presides over, instructs and directs the labors of all the patriarchs of the church."

60. See *Doctrine and Covenants of the Church of Jesus Christ of Latter-day Saints* (Salt Lake City: Deseret Book, 1955), 124:92.

61. Taylor, "Patriarchal," 921–22.

62. Oliver Cowdery, Minutes, in Joseph Smith, Sr. Patriarchal Blessing Book, LDS Church Archives.

63. Taylor, "Patriarchal," 922.

64. In emphasizing that William's calling would be subject to the Quorum of the Twelve in *the same way* as Hyrum's had been to the First Presidency, Taylor may have been counterproductive to some extent. After Hyrum was ordained Patriarch, he also stood to the First Presidency as associate president.

65. Taylor, "Patriarchal," 922.

66. Ibid.

67. Quoted in Taylor, Journal, June 25, 1845.

68. Clayton, Diary, June 27, 1845.

69. Ibid., June 24, 1845.

70. Taylor, Journal, June 25, 1845.

71. George A. Smith, Journal, June 25, 1845.

72. Taylor, Journal, June 25, 1845.

73. Ibid.

74. "October Conference Minutes, October 6, 1844," *Times and Seasons* 5 (October 15, 1844): 683.

75. George A. Smith, Journal, June 25, 1845.

76. Brigham Young to Wilford Woodruff, June 27, 1845, Wilford Woodruff Collection, LDS Church Archives.

77. Quoted in Taylor, Journal, June 27, 1845. The Mormonism that emerges in Mother Smith's *History* explains why William would claim that the Saints were dependent on the Smith family for the priesthood. Lucy's story makes

constant use of the pronouns "we" and "us" instead of simply referring to "Joseph." The martyrdom had caused a fundamental shift in perceptions of the right to church leadership. Jan Shipps, "The Prophet, His Mother, and Early Mormonism: Mother Smith's History as a Passageway to Understanding" (Paper presented at the Mormon History Association annual meeting, Logan, Utah, May 6, 1979), 17.

78. According to Taylor, Journal, June 30, 1845, "Elders Young, Kimball, O. Pratt, Page, Willard Richards, George A. Smith, and [John Taylor] of the Twelve together with Bishops Whitney and Miller, and Elder Cahoon one of the temple committee and some of her [Lucy's] own family were present" at the meeting.

79. George A. Smith, Journal, June 28, 1845.

80. Ibid., June 30, 1845. See also Clayton, Diary, June 30, 1845.

81. Taylor, Journal, June 30, 1845.

82. William Smith to Brigham Young, June 30, 1845, in Taylor, Journal, June 30, 1845.

83. Brigham Young to William Smith, June 30, 1845, LDS Church Archives. Also quoted in Benjamin F. Johnson, Letter to George S. Gibbs, 1903; and in Clayton, Diary, July 4, 1845; and copied by John Taylor into his journal for June 30, 1845.

84. George A. Smith, Journal, July 9, 1845.

85. "The Brethren" is a common term among church members to denote the "General Authorities." This group of hierarchical leaders form the highest echelon of the Mormon leadership. As of 1979 it was made up of the president of the church, his two counselors, the Council of the Twelve Apostles, the Presiding Patriarch (or Patriarch to the Church), the Seven Presidents of Seventy, the Quorum of the Seventy, and the Presiding Bishop and his two counselors (forming the Presiding Bishopric).

86. As quoted in Brigham Young to William Smith, August 10, 1845, Brigham Young Collection, LDS Church Archives.

87. Ibid. Brigham Young did, however, acknowledge what must have been a practice of giving patriarchal blessings for the dead during Hyrum's incumbency. At least one such blessing was given by William on July 16, 1845, when he gave a blessing in favor of Ann B. Peterson, deceased daughter of Edward and Mary Peterson, "on the head of Maryann Peterson sitting as proxy." No. 85 in the William Smith Patriarchal Blessing Book, June to September 1845, Theodore A. Schroeder Collection, State Historical Society of Wisconsin, Madison; copy in the Archives of the Reorganized Church of Jesus Christ of Latter Day Saints, Independence, Mo.

88. William Smith, Address, August 17, 1845, with remarks by John Taylor, LDS Church Archives. See also Richards, Diary, August 17, 1845; and Clayton, Diary, August 17, 1845. It should be noted that Brigham Young married William to at least one plural wife about this time, according to the deposition of Mary Ann Sheffield (West) taken in 1893. She testified that Young performed a marriage ceremony for her and William shortly after Caroline died and that Young thereafter sealed William to Mary Jones and Priscilla

Morgridge. Priscilla Staines also testified that she was married to William in Nauvoo. Temple Lot Suit, 380–8, Special Collections, University of Utah, Salt Lake City.

89. Clayton, Diary, August 17, 1845. Later William was allowed to be the Church's scapegoat in terms of plural marriage. Thomas L. Kane replied to President James Fillmore regarding the charge of polygamy among the Mormons: "The remaining charge connects itself with that unmixed outrage the spiritual wife story which was fastened on the Mormons by the ribald scamp . . . [William Smith] whom . . . they were literally forced to excommunicate for his licentiousness." Journal History, July 11, 1851.

90. William Smith to Brother Little, August 20, 1845, Journal History.

91. Noted in Clayton, Diary, August 27, 1845.

92. Richards, Diary, September 16, 1845.

93. William Smith to Brother [Lewis] Robbins, October 5, 1845, LDS Church Archives, cited in Rudd, "William Smith," 185.

94. Richard Morley, "The Life and Contributions of Isaac Morley" (M.A. thesis, Brigham Young University, 1965).

95. Elden Jay Watson, ed., The Orson Pratt Journals (Salt Lake City: E. J. Watson, 1975), 293. See also "Conference Minutes," Times and Seasons 6 (November 1, 1845): 1008; and Richards, Diary, October 6, 1845. Joseph Smith, History of the Church, 7:458, wrongly attributes the objection to Orson Pratt.

96. Quoted in Joseph Smith, History of the Church, 7:458–59.

97. Manuscript History and Journal History, LDS Church Archives, give the date of excommunication as October 19, 1845, as does Joseph Smith, History of the Church, 7:483.

98. See, for example, Deseret News 1989–1990 Church Almanac (Salt Lake City: Deseret News, 1988), which lists William but does not count him because he was not sustained.

99. Quinn, "The Mormon Succession Crisis of 1844," 193.

100. William Smith to Lewis Robbins, St. Louis, November 7, 1845, LDS Church Archives, cited in Rudd, "William Smith," 130.

101. James Kay letter, November 22, 1845, reproduced in the Millennial Star 7 (May 1, 1846): 134–35.

102. William Smith to Emma Smith, [month unclear] 21, 1845, LDS Church Archives.

103. D. Michael Quinn, "Comment on Patriarch Papers" (Response to papers given by E. Gary Smith and Irene M. Bates at the Mormon History Association annual meeting, Salt Lake City, May 2, 1986).

5

Patriarchal Bridge

Interregnum, 1845–47, and Uncle John Smith—
Fourth Patriarch, 1847–54

> We learned from President Young's teaching that it was necessary to
> keep up a full organization of the Church through all time as far as
> could be. At least the three first Presidency, quorum of the Twelve,
> Seventies, and Patriarch over the whole Church &c so that the devil
> could take no advantage of us.
>
> —Wilford Woodruff's Journal, December 27, 1847

At the time of William Smith's excommunication, the Quorum of the
Twelve was absorbed with the problem of surviving the persecutions of the
Illinois mobs. The mobs were burning members' homes and businesses,
making it virtually impossible for the Mormons to continue to live in Nauvoo. The Twelve began planning for a westward migration. Their efforts in-
tensified following the October General Conference, and the search for a
suitable replacement for William in the patriarchal office was put on hold.
Hyrum's oldest son, John, was still a boy of thirteen when the office was
vacated by William. The next nearest relatives were Asael and John Smith,
two brothers of Joseph Smith, Sr. Both had previously been ordained local
patriarchs.[1]

There are some indications that Asael was regarded as the unofficial
Church Patriarch between October 1845 and the fall of 1847. As a stake patriarch, ordained on October 7, 1844, and as the oldest of the Smith family in
the church, Asael occupied a de facto honorary position; but official records
are silent on the subject.[2] Asael was married to Elizabeth Schellinger, and he
had eight children. After a prolonged period of ill-health, he died on July 20,
1848, en route to the West.

Originally, the Saints planned to leave Illinois in April 1846; however, it was considered wise to send some westward before the winter was over to make advance preparations. On January 20, 1846, the Nauvoo Stake High Council issued a circular advising the Saints that "since grievances have alienated us from our country," some pioneers were to be sent to the "western country" as an advance guard. This first group would plant crops for those who would leave Nauvoo later.[3] The "advance group" soon became a mass exodus, however. By mid-May nearly twelve thousand Saints had crossed the Mississippi River, and by September 1846 they had established the temporary settlement of Winter Quarters near what is now Omaha, Nebraska.

The winter of 1846 was one of suffering and dying for many Saints as they struggled to make the cold and difficult journey. Despite the hardships, the Saints had completed building the temple in Nauvoo while making preparations to leave the country. Over five thousand members received ordinances in the temple by February 1846, and the temple continued to be used at least through the end of April as the Saints were leaving Nauvoo.

In the spring of 1847 Brigham Young led the first party of Saints on the epic journey to the valley of the Great Salt Lake, returning to Winter Quarters later that summer. By completing the initial trek to the new Zion of the Saints, Young had consolidated his position as uncontested leader of the church. This was apparent even in his relationship with the other apostles: apostles who would previously disagree with him in public were by late 1847 mentioning their differences only in private.[4] When Brigham Young returned to Winter Quarters, he likely already had in mind the idea of creating a new First Presidency, with himself as president. In spite of his secure position as the prime leader of the church, this was not to be an automatic accomplishment. The debate between Young and Sidney Rigdon three years earlier had left the clear impression that the apostles were temporary leaders and that they were not going to claim rights as a First Presidency but instead govern as the Quorum only. Most of the Twelve, carrying on in the absence of the Prophet Joseph Smith, understood their apostolic charge while remembering that the Prophet had indicated not many months before he was killed that possible succession rights might lie with his oldest son.[5]

There was another problem for the office of Patriarch in proposing a new First Presidency. If the senior member of the Twelve was to be the president, and thereafter each successor to the presidency would be the senior member of that quorum, it would be an "ascending," *seamless* flow of hierarchical authority from the Quorum of the Twelve up to the president. While the Prophet Joseph was alive, the Patriarch had been, in authority, above the Twelve but below the president. No member of the Twelve had any built-in right to become president of the church. In fact, the Quorum of the Twelve was only one of several quorums or levels of the hierarchy subject to the First

Presidency (such as the Quorum of the Seventy and the High Council). Once the Twelve becomes the First Presidency in embryo, there is no longer any place to fit the Patriarch in between the president and the Twelve. The Patriarch must either go above or below the Twelve.

Before 1844 the Presiding Patriarch had always been higher in stature and, for the last few years, higher in administrative authority than the Twelve; the Patriarch had *never* been subject to the Twelve. Indeed, when Hyrum held the office he was associate president at the same time, with indistinct lines, if any, separating the two callings. If a new president of the church was to come out of the Quorum of the Twelve, how would that affect the Church Patriarch's relationship with the remaining Quorum of the Twelve? Would the Patriarch be between the First Presidency and the Twelve, as he was previously?

On August 15, 1847, Brigham Young touched on this problem when he preached that the apostleship was the highest office of authority there was in the church. Wilford Woodruff quotes Young in his journal on August 15, 1847: "Some have had fears that we had not power to obtain revelations since the death of Joseph, but I want this subject from this time and forever to be set at rest. . . . An Apostle is the highest office and authority that there is in the Church and Kingdom of God on earth. Joseph Smith gave unto me and my brethren, the Twelve, the priesthood, power, and authority which he held, and these powers which belong to the Apostleship."[6]

With any reorganization of church leadership, the man who would become the Presiding Patriarch of the Church would be required to accept that statement. Young specifically emphasized that the apostles were senior to patriarchs—*all* patriarchs, including the "senior" patriarch:

> In Joseph's day we had to ordain patriarchs. Could we ordain men to authority greater than we held ourselves? No. But it is necessary to have patriarchs to bless the people that they may have blessings by the spirit of prophecy and revelation sealed upon the heads and their posterity and know what awaits their posterity. Father Smith was the senior patriarch in the Church and first patriarch in our day and afterwards Hyrum was the senior patriarch for his father sealed it upon his head but was their power and authority different from all patriarchs in the Church? No. They were all alike in their authority and blessings.[7]

Prior to 1844 there was a very real distinction between the Presiding (or "senior") Patriarch and those patriarchs "in all large branches of the church" with respect to whom the Twelve was given the responsibility of designating and ordaining. (See Doctrine and Covenants 107:39.) One way the Twelve had discerned hierarchical order was to look at who ordained whom, and the one doing the ordaining was then determined to be higher in authority than the one who was the recipient of the ordination. The Presiding Patriarch prior to 1844 was never ordained by the Twelve. Joseph Sr. was ordained by the Prophet, and Hyrum was ordained by his predecessor in office, Joseph Smith, Sr. Brigham Young was countering the argument for a patriarchal authority higher than the Twelve by pointing out that both the presiding and the local patriarchs gave blessings of equal authority and that the "senior" patriarch must therefore be "ordainable" by the Twelve in the same way that local patriarchs were. By eliminating the distinctions between the Presiding Patriarch and the local patriarchs, Young was placing the Church Patriarch *below* the Twelve within the hierarchical structure that he was about to propose.

Later, at Winter Quarters, Brigham Young began individually lobbying the Quorum of the Twelve for the creation of a First Presidency. Several of the Twelve were apprehensive. George A. Smith, Amasa Lyman, and Wilford Woodruff wanted to continue as it had been rather than sever the Quorum by taking three apostles out to form another quorum. Wilford Woodruff and Orson Pratt claimed that a revelation was required. Woodruff also maintained "that by appointing a presidency it is robing [*sic*] some of the rising generation or taking someone's rights." Some apostles not present at Winter Quarters wrote letters suggesting a delay to avoid preempting the rights of Joseph's posterity.[8] Orson Pratt opposed the reestablishment of a First Presidency on constitutional grounds, in other words, that there is no authority higher than a majority vote of the Twelve. Brigham Young had a de facto authority that already exceeded one twelfth of the Quorum; this was undoubtedly the reason he wanted to create a de jure office of president. In arguing against the First Presidency, Orson Pratt used the very principle of hierarchy by right of ordination that Brigham Young had used to place the office of Church Patriarch below the Twelve. Pratt asked, "The three men [in the First Presidency] need an ordination to be appointed presidents. Who will ordain them?"[9]

One of the arguments Brigham Young used for the establishment of the First Presidency was that "it was necessary to keep up a full organization of the Church through all time as far as could be. At least the three first Presidency quorum of the Twelve, Seventies, and Patriarch over the whole Church &c so that the devil could take no Advantage of us."[10] The reorganization was to include a permanent calling of "Patriarch over the whole Church," as well as that of president. On December 5, 1847, at Orson Hyde's home, eight of the apostles "elected" Brigham Young president and Heber C. Kimball and Willard Richards as first and second counselors.[11] The next day the apostles again met at Hyde's home and "voted that John Smith be the Patriarch to the whole church."[12] "Uncle" John was the uncle of the Prophet and the brother of Joseph Smith, Sr. Although Asael was older and did not die until July of 1848, he was infirm at that time, while John was a vigorous fifty-two-year-old.

On December 23 the Twelve sent a "general epistle" to the church: "we now, having it in contemplation soon to reorganize the church according to the original pattern, with a First Presidency and Patriarch. . . ."[13] Then on December 24 a conference began in the log tabernacle in Winter Quarters, at which time Brigham Young was sustained as president, with Heber C. Kimball and Willard Richards as first and second counselors. John Smith was voted to be Patriarch to the whole Church, "in the same capacity as Father Smith was and also Brother Hyrum."[14] (In fact, however, the position of the proposed office was significantly different from the one held by Joseph Sr. and Hyrum with respect to its relative position in the hierarchy.) The proposals were seconded and carried without a dissenting vote. In Brigham Young's acceptance remarks he maintained that "the Kingdom is set up and you have the perfect pattern and you can lead the Kingdom in at the gate."[15]

It should be noted that the Patriarch was sustained immediately after the First Presidency, a point of procedure that would later become a source of contention. That order of sustaining was inconsistent with placing the rank of Patriarch below that of the apostles, which was the de facto order after the martyrdom, and was even more at variance with Doctrine and Covenants 124, which mandated that the Patriarch be sustained even before the president.

Although Uncle John was sustained with regularity following the initial vote in Winter Quarters, he was not actually ordained to the office until January 1, 1849. Uncle John was in the Salt Lake Valley acting as stake president during the time of reorganization at Winter Quarters, and logistics delayed the actual ordination.

With the reorganization finally completed, the machinery was put in motion for the formal transformation of the original charismatic movement into a rationalized institution. A mediated "office charisma" would play its part in taking care of the continuation of a church that rested on a foundation of latter-day revelation. This transformation from "familial charisma" to "office charisma" was accomplished without relinquishing all ties to the Smith family. The wives and children of Hyrum Smith and Samuel Smith went West with Brigham Young and the Twelve, as did the family of Uncle John, brother of Joseph Smith, Sr. The immediate family of the Prophet Joseph, including his widow, William Smith's family, and Joseph's sisters, Sophronia, Catherine, and Lucy, all chose to stay in Nauvoo, as did Mother Lucy Mack Smith.

Although the new patriarch, Uncle John Smith, was of the founding family, he was certainly no threat to the church leadership. He was content to follow Brigham Young as the ultimate authority—a leader whose will, as far as Uncle John was concerned, was in accord with the will of God. Just as William Smith had made manifest the tension inherent in trying to combine lineal authority rights with institutional requirements, so Uncle John provided the necessary accommodation by never asserting the heritage of primacy.

Chapter 4 described the watershed that the 1844 succession crisis represented for the church and the office of Presiding Patriarch. Uncle John Smith was the Patriarch following that crisis and the short and turbulent incumbency of William Smith. The specters that loomed during the crisis were not finally laid to rest, however. Even though the existence of a hereditary office of primacy was the inherent problem, William's example remained a dark lens of uncertainty through which the office would be viewed in subsequent years. Uncle John's tenure, however, provided a breathing space in which the church leadership was able to consolidate power during the years of settlement in the Salt Lake Valley. Uncle John, who served from 1847 to 1854, was devoted, dedicated, and obedient.[16] As the fourth patriarch, he provided continuity and much-needed stability. He thus alleviated for a time the anxiety surrounding the office and was much appreciated by the rest of the church hierarchy.

Uncle John Smith, brother of Joseph Smith, Sr., was born in Derryfield, New Hampshire, on July 16, 1781, the eighth of eleven children of Asael and Mary Duty Smith. He married Clarissa Lyman on September 11, 1815, and they became the parents of three children, George Albert, Caroline, and John Lyman Smith. They were members of the First Congregational church until they embraced the Mormon faith and were baptized at Potsdam, New York, in January 1832. According to Lucy Mack Smith, John's sister-in-law, he was dying of consumption when he was baptized.[17] His son George A. told of breaking the ice for the baptism, while "the neighbors looked on with astonishment expecting to see him die in the water, but his health continued improving from that moment."[18]

Uncle John was ordained a high priest on June 3, 1833, became chairman of the Kirtland High Council in 1836, accompanied Patriarch Joseph Smith, Sr., on a mission to bless the Saints that same year, and was appointed assistant counselor to the Prophet, along with his brother Joseph Sr., his nephew Hyrum, and Oliver Cowdery, in 1837. He was included in Joseph Smith's statement that "these last four, together with the first three [First Presidency] are to be considered the heads of the church."[19]

Uncle John was indeed the antithesis of his spectacular, unstable nephew William Smith. He displayed a deep sense of gratitude for being restored to health following his baptism. The recovery must have seemed miraculous to John, and this might account for his lifetime of quiet devotion, obedience, and sacrifice. His letters and journals display unusual literacy for his time and education, and it is through his diligence in keeping a journal that we have some knowledge of the experiences of his brother, the first patriarch, with whom he traveled for the purpose of giving patriarchal blessings.

(Uncle) John Smith, 1781-1854. Fourth presiding patriarch, 1847-54. Courtesy of Special Collections, J. Willard Marriott Library, University of Utah.

The darker side of Uncle John's devotion, however, was his constant pre-occupation with his own shortcomings. His journal is replete with such entries as "O Lord keep back thy servant from presumptuous sins, cleans me from secret faults for Jesus sake" or "Lord forgive what thou hast seen amiss in poor unworthy me this day and give wisdom."[20] He was equally concerned about the unworthiness of others. Uncle John had no tolerance for anyone who might pollute or dilute the sacred mission of the church. At least twice at high council trials he insisted that the guilty parties make full public confession in church periodicals, until Sidney Rigdon suggested Uncle John would "spread darkness rather than light upon the subject." The Prophet Joseph later labored with his uncle, who admitted his error of judgment.[21] When things were not going well for the Saints, Uncle John always attributed their trials to a lack of valiancy, to sinful behavior, to a weakness of faith, or merely to the discipline of a loving God. When his young nephew Jesse Smith died on July 1, 1834, while on a mission, John wrote to his brother Asael, Jesse's father, referring to the "chastening which our Heavenly Father has seen fit in his wisdom to put upon you . . . therefore I feel a secret joy diffusing through my breast for the testimony my Heavenly Father has given that he loves you."[22]

An 1834 letter written to his nephew Elias Smith, who had expressed some resentment toward the church, displays John's faith and enthusiasm:

> You say the things that you have seen and heard of late look like absurdities to you. Suppose you mean the Gospel which I have embraced of late . . . I tell you in the fear of God that these things are true as the Lord lives, and I would that you would search out these things for yourself, for I know that it [is] within your reach if you are willing to humble yourself before the Lord, as you must . . . or you cannot enter in the kingdom of God. . . . If you will give heed to the council which you have heard you will have peace like a river and righteousness like an overflowing stream. Tell Amos the Lord prospers the church here and it increases in numbers. I repeat it—the Church of the Latter Day Saints will prosper in spite of wicked men and devils until it fills the whole earth.[23]

In 1836 John accompanied his brother Joseph Sr. on a mission to the branches of the eastern states "to set them in order and confer on the brethren their patriarchal blessings."[24] This might well have served as an apprenticeship for John's future calling as Patriarch. The two were gone three months and traveled twenty-four hundred miles, visiting the branches of the church in New York, Vermont, New Hampshire, and Pennsylvania, as well as collecting money for the proposed Kirtland Temple. John reported in his journal that Joseph Sr. pronounced patriarchal blessings on the heads of several nonmembers, some of whom were baptized two days later.[25]

John sometimes saw himself as God's instrument for cleansing the church. During the troubled years in Kirtland, 1837 and 1838, John's letters to his son George A. reveal his concern for the purity of the church. On January 1, 1838, he wrote, "I called the High Council together last week and laid before them the case of dissenters, 28 persons were, upon mature discussion cut off from the Church. . . . We have cut off between 40 and 50 from the Church since you left. Thus you will see the Church has taken a mighty pruning and we think she will rise in the greatness of her strength, and I rejoice, for the Lord is good and He will cut his work short in righteousness. . . . I will rejoice for the Lord will purify His Church."[26]

Two weeks later in a letter to George A., Uncle John referred to "a time of Jacob's trouble, troublous times among us as a Church," and went on to explain: "The scarcity of money causes disappointment which perplexes the people. . . . I mentioned to you in my last that many had deserted from the Church and they are striving to destroy with a great deal more zeal than they ever did to build up . . . and they cause law suits by scores by joining the enemy, as did the dissenting Nephites of old . . . for you know that a lying spirit is gone out into the world and the inhabitants thereof are stirred up to anger one with another."[27]

When mobs forced the Saints to leave Kirtland early in 1838, Uncle John and his family left with few possessions. They had forty dollars to see them through what was to be a horrendous journey to Far West, Missouri. Lame horses, inclement weather, bad roads, and the scarcity of food and shelter only brought from John such comments as "What the Lord will do with us I know not, altho he slay me I will trust in him" and "We neglect prayer and trust too much in our own wisdom."[28] Later he wrote, "At evening heavy thunder with a powerful rain wet our clothing [and] bedding . . . but the Lord has preserved our health thus far."[29] The persecution endured by the Saints persisted in Missouri and resulted in the formation of a Mormon secret society, the Danites, for the purpose of defending the Saints and their property. There has been considerable debate about the extent of official church involvement in this society. Whether in an official position or not, Uncle John attended some of their meetings.[30] Difficulties escalated, and Governor Lilburn W. Boggs of Missouri issued an "Extermination Order" on October 27, 1838, stating, "[I] have received . . . information of the most appalling character, which changes the whole face of things, and places the Mormons in the attitude of open and avowed defiance of the laws, and of having made open war upon the people of this state. . . . The Mormons must be treated as enemies and must be exterminated or driven from the state."[31]

The citizens of Caldwell County had already appointed a committee of seven, including Uncle John Smith, to draft resolutions requiring the Mormons' removal from the state according to the governor's orders and to devise means of removing the destitute.[32] Most, including Uncle John, were destitute. More than fifty Mormons were arrested and put in jail on November 11, 1838, for crimes of "high treason against the state, murder, burglary, arson, robbery, and larceny."[33] Subsequently all but eleven were released for want of evidence. Joseph Smith, Jr., and Hyrum Smith were among those detained, but they escaped in April 1839.[34]

In the meantime Uncle John and the rest of the Saints were once more out in the cold. Uncle John recorded that "200 families, many of them without means to help themselves, then were turned out of their houses and such scenes of suffering is not recorded in any land as were endured by the saints."[35] Uncle John himself was forced to sleep in the open and suffered frostbitten feet, which caused him trouble for several years. The Saints, bereft of their leader, moved to Illinois and for a while rested in the kindness they received at the hands of the people of Quincy.

When the Saints moved on to Commerce (later named Nauvoo), Illinois, they encountered troubles once more, but at first these woes were of a different kind. Summer on the banks of the Mississippi brought severe sickness, and in September 1839 Uncle John referred to "being given into the hands of Satan as much as was Job to be tried and I was very low." He recalled that Joseph Jr., Hyrum, and Bishop Knight came to see him: "One thing is worthy of note and will never be forgotten by me. Joseph took the shoes from his feet and gave [them] to me [and] rode home without any seeing our unhappy condition."[36]

It was during this period that Uncle John, for the first and perhaps the only time, questioned a decision of church leaders. His journal reflects his concerns:

> Pres. [Hyrum] Smith delivered a lengthy speech showing the folly of trying to keep the law of the Lord until Zion is redeemed. Returned home the next day, December 16, thinking that I would search prayerfully the Doctrine and Covenants and learn the will of the Lord concerning the consecration of property & taking care of the poor and needy, the widow etc. spend my time from this to the next meeting of the High Council to know my duty to the Church, how to organize in that oneness and equality that the Law of God requires that we may be the Lord's people and for the life of me I can see no other way only in the honest consecration of property that we may be Stewards of the Lord according to his law.[37]

Three weeks later he reported meeting with President Hyrum Smith and Oliver Granger and said they were "pleased with our resolution to observe the law of consecration but since that time they have seemed to operate against all our proceedings."[38]

In later journal entries Uncle John Smith suggested that the pervasive sickness among the Saints was brought on by a lack of righteousness. On November 29, 1840, he observed, "There is a spirit of jealousy and evil surmissing [sic] creeping in among the brethren which I greatly fear will be injurious to the cause of truth. O Lord lead thy people in the paths of peace." On December 20 he pleaded, "O Lord help them to repent and so indeed that thou mayest love them."[39] In a letter to his son George A., he said, "It requires the patience of a Job and the wisdom of a Solomon and the perseverance and faithfulness of an Abraham to keep such order as ought to be in the Church of Christ."[40] In his journal he reported, "Did something towards stoping drinking and dancing which has been practiced by certain ones in the Church to the shame of the Saints."[41]

During these years Uncle John served as president of the Zarahemla Stake in Nauvoo. On January 10, 1844, however, the Prophet Joseph ordained him to be a stake patriarch. Five months later, one day before the assassination of Joseph and Hyrum, Uncle John visited them in the Carthage jail, an indication of his devotion to his nephew the Prophet.[42] Although deeply grieved by the deaths of the Prophet and Hyrum, his dedication to the church meant that he had little difficulty in transferring his allegiance to Brigham Young as the new leader.

Brigham Young apparently recognized Uncle John's single-mindedness in furthering the cause of Mormonism and twice suggested that he might legitimately be called as Church Patriarch following Hyrum's death, because "the right is in the family of Joseph Smith, his brothers, his sons, or some one of his relations."[43] One could infer from this that Young would have preferred Uncle John to William Smith as the Patriarch. Later, when W. W. Phelps moved that Brigham Young be upheld as "President of the Quorum of the Twelve and First Presidency of the Church," Uncle John seconded and put the motion to the church. It carried unanimously.[44]

Despite advancing years, Uncle John took several plural wives. On January 15, 1846, he was "sealed for time" to his brother's widow, Mary Aikin Smith, as well as to Ann Carr, Miranda Jones, and Sarah Kinsley. Marriage in this mortal life still allowed women to be sealed in "celestial" or "eternal" marriages with previous husbands.[45] For example, John acted as proxy for his brother when Mary Aikin was sealed to the deceased Silas Smith "for eternity." On January 24 John was sealed to Aseneth Hubert, Rebecca Smith, and Julia Hills for eternity.[46] All of these women were between fifty and sixty years of age, and it seems John might have married them to care for them during the removal from Illinois and on the journey to Salt Lake. It is also possible that the women requested marriage to Uncle John. Marrying a church leader, it was thought, brought the promise of glory in the hereafter, and certainly plural marriage was deemed by many to be an essential ingredient in the celestial destiny of men. Two months later, on March 27, 1846, John and his wives and their families departed Nauvoo, with Uncle John acting as captain of the first group of fifty.[47]

During the trek West Uncle John was still a stickler for correct procedures. Hosea Stout tells of Brigham Young's humor in dealing with Uncle John's persistent attention to detail. Stout writes on February 4, 1847, that "the subject of the beef committee was taken up on the complaint of Father John Smith who was not satisfied with some things about it. The thing was talked out of 'countenance' and finally Prest Brigham Young moved to have the whole matter laid over till the first resurrection & them [*sic*] burn the papers the day before."[48]

Brigham Young nevertheless trusted Uncle John. On August 22, 1847, upon the arrival of the first company of Saints in the valley, Young called him to serve as the first stake president of the Salt Lake Stake. On December 23, 1847, at Winter Quarters, Young proposed Uncle John as Patriarch over all the Church. A "General Epistle from the Council of the Twelve Apostles to the Church of Jesus Christ of Latter-day Saints, abroad, dispersed throughout the earth" was issued:

> Since the murder of President Joseph Smith, many false prophets and false teachers have arisen, and tried to deceive many, during which time we have mostly tarried with the body of the Church, or been seeking a new location, leaving those prophets and teachers to run their race undisturbed, who have died natural deaths, or committed suicides; and we now, having it in contemplation soon to reorganize the Church according to the original pattern, with a First Presidency and Patriarch, feel that it will be the privilege of the Twelve, ere long, to spread abroad among the nations, not to hinder the gathering, but to preach the gospel and push the people, the honest in heart, together from the four quarters of the earth.[49]

At the 1848 October General Conference in Salt Lake Valley Uncle John was released as stake president and sustained, immediately after the First Presidency, as "Patriarch over the whole Church of Jesus Christ of Latter Day Saints."[50] Uncle John expressed his feelings in his journal as follows: "I was released from my Presidency [of the Salt Lake Stake] and appointed Patriarch over the Church and President over the Patriarchal Priesthood. Since that time my burden has been lighter and I have been regaining my health since but I find that I am about worn out with excessive labour. Although I have been faulted in some things while presiding in the valley my conscience is clear & I have done the best I knew & I ask no man's forgiveness."[51] Brigham Young ordained Uncle John on January 1, 1849, saying:

> It is thy right by lineage & by birth & inasmuch as those who have been ordained to hold the keys of this Priesthood have fallen asleep in testimo-

ny of the truth & some have left the church & forsaken the paths of truth
& righteousness . . . thou hast the privaledge to rise up & magnify this calling & to hold the keys of the Priesthood as thy brother Joseph did & thy
nephew Hyrum did & as William did who has turned aside from the ways
of the Lord & forfeited his rights & privaledges & treated all his blessings
with lightness and esteemd the ordinances of the Holy Priesthood as a
thing of nought . . . & we say unto thee receive all the keys and authority
pertaining to this calling that thou mayest be a Presiding Officer over this
Priesthood.[52]

Brigham Young's confidence in the loyalty of this new patriarch was not
misplaced. One incident provides a dramatic illustration of both Uncle John's
intolerance for what he deemed unrighteous behavior and his unquestion-
ing obedience to an authority who, because he was called by the Lord to preside, would never lead him astray. In a letter written to a D. H. Miller in Iowa
on July 13, 1849, Uncle John painted a rosy picture of Salt Lake Valley and then
referred to the "wild confusion which reigns among the inhabitants of the
earth. we have a small taste of it in our midst as the gold was first discovered
by 2 of our Bretheren." He went on to tell Miller that "some of our people
have catched the fever & have gone to the gold diggings & it is said here probably not many of them will ever return which we hope may be the case."[53]
Yet only three months later we learn from Henry Bigler, one of the discover-
ers of gold at Sutters Mill, that

President Young had told Father John Smith that as he had been kicked
and cuffed about and driven out of the United States because of his Religion and had become poor, it was his council that Father Smith fit out some
person and send him to California or to the gold mines and get some trea-
sures of the earth to make himself comfortable in his old age and the old
gentleman has called on me to go. . . . This intelligence was unexpectedly
received by me. I was not looking for any such mission. Indeed it had been
the President's council not to go to the gold mines and those who went after
such council had been given was looked upon as Jack Mormons as they
were called.[54]

In Bigler's diary there follows a heartrending account of his feelings about
leaving his little home and suffering the injustice of being looked upon as a
renegade "Jack Mormon." The mission was not fruitful, and Bigler had to
repay Uncle John the advances he had made to fit out Bigler for the journey.
     Patriarch Smith did have many family obligations to meet. He continued
to feel financially responsible for Mary Aikin Smith's family. Jesse N. Smith,
son of Silas and Mary, tells of being called on a mission to Parowan, along
with his brother Silas:

We were soon under way and stopped for the night in Salt Lake City at Uncle John's. He remarked that himself and brothers had always desired that one of their family should be educated. . . . He wished me to remain and go to school at his expense here; he would see Pres. Young and have me excused from the mission to the south. Although I greatly desired to get an education I preferred to go upon the mission, fearing also that the expense would be burdensome to him. When I acquainted him with my resolution he blessed each of us with a Patriarchal blessing.[55]

John Smith believed that the Smith family was of vital importance. In a blessing to his eldest son, George A., on September 20, 1853, he promised that "all the inhabitants of the earth shall know that the Lord did choose the Smith family to build up Zion & did by them lay the foundation of this Church which shall never be overthrown neither shall the name of the Smith family be blotted out under Heaven."[56]

Earlier, in 1851, he had said, "In Kirtland, Ohio, four brothers sat in the patriarchal seat in the temple of God, and I only of that number am left to tell the tale."[57] Uncle John's own patriarchal blessing, received from the stake patriarch Isaac Morley on September 25, 1851, promised that "thy name shall be equal with the Patriarchs, even Abraham, Isaac, and Jacob."[58] Despite his feelings about the special role to be played by the Smith family, Uncle John never represented a threat to the presiding officers of the church.

On April 4, 1854, following the death of his wife Clarissa and just seven weeks prior to his own death, Uncle John was married to Mary Franky. Six weeks later, on May 15, 1854, Uncle John's son, John Lyman Smith, sent the following request to the church leaders: "Father John Smith Patriarch does not wish the bretheren who meet in the Council house to pray for him to live for I know it is the will of the Lord to take me to himself when he pleases & I want him to do it in the best possible manner for my ease and comfort."[59] Ten days later he died. His *Deseret News* obituary noted that when he moved out of the fort onto his own city lot in February 1849, he was able "for the first time in twenty-three years, to cultivate a garden two years in succession."[60] He had given 5,560 blessings in ten years of service as local and Church Patriarch.

Stolid and reliable man that Uncle John was, it is perhaps through the blessings he gave that we are able to catch a glimpse of a more dramatic side of the Patriarch. He told some women they would be given the priesthood. In 1846 Catherine Campbell Steele, for example, was told she would be given

all the blessings of the holy priesthood which were sealed upon the fathers and continueth upon the heads of their children from generation to generations I now place the same upon thee and upon thy posterity which shall

be exceeding numerous and continually increase in common with thy husband thou art of the same blood & lineage with him and shall partake of
all the blessings power & priesthood that it sealed upon him the sick shall
be heald at thy rebuke the destroyer shall flee away thy house shall be a
healthy habitation the angel of peace shall dwell there thy Store house shall
be well filled & thy table well supplied & no power on Earth shall disturb
thy peace for thou shalt be filled with wisdom & patience to know how to
baffle the schemes of the Enemy thou shalt live to see the closing scene of
this generation if you desire it with a perfect heart and enjoy all the blessings beauties and glories of Zion.[61]

Three poems, written in Uncle John's honor, reflect the comfort people
received from his patriarchal blessings. One of them by Eliza R. Snow, a
Mormon poet and hymn writer, who later headed the women's Relief Society, said:

> Thou art greatly belov'd by the saints that surround thee
> They have tasted thy blessings & greatly rejoice
> The pow'r of the Priesthood is felt thro' thy presence
> The weak become strong at the sound of thy voice. . .
> I have oft felt the pow'r of thy blessing upon me
> And my heart feels to bless thee, thou servant of God.[62]

Upon the death of Uncle John, a eulogy was written by John Lyon, which
said in part:

> And oft when the storm-cloud of vengeance rolled high
> And no hope for the Saints, but in heaven
> His words in their blessings to them ever nigh
> Cheered their souls, tho' maltreated, and driven.[63]

As far as Uncle John's relationship with the rest of the hierarchy was concerned, the challenges of the exodus from Nauvoo and the resettlement in
Utah might well have rendered concerns about the patriarchate less significant. Certainly Uncle John's gratitude and devotion inhibited him from questioning his position. That he was valiant and dedicated is beyond question.
Uncle John was the kind of man both Brigham Young and the church needed during this crucial period of transition. By acknowledging and accepting
direction from Brigham Young, Uncle John laid to rest for the time being the
specter of patriarchal autonomy that William had raised during the succession crisis. William's stubbornness might have saved the office of Presiding
Patriarch from an early extinction, but Uncle John assured it a more comfortable, though diminished, role in the Mormon hierarchy. He provided a
season of peace and the predictability that was essential to the growing in-

stitution. For Brigham Young, John Smith had indeed been the right man at the right time. The years that followed, beginning with young John Smith's incumbency, would see a reemergence of the tensions and uncertainties that continued to plague this initially important office.

Notes

1. Jesse, the oldest brother, was antagonistic toward the new religion founded by his nephew and never joined the church. The other brothers were Joseph Sr., Asael, Samuel (died in 1830), Silas, John, and Stephen. Four sisters, Priscilla, Mary, Susannah, and Sarah, brought the number of siblings to eleven.

2. References to Asael acting in a de facto capacity include a list of those in office Hyrum G. Smith gave in "Patriarchs and Patriarchal Blessings," *Improvement Era* 33 (May 1930): 465–66; and Andrew Jensen, *Latter-day Saints Biographical Encyclopedia,* 4 vols. (Salt Lake City: Andrew Jensen Historical Co., 1901), 1:182.

3. Joseph Smith, *History of the Church of Jesus Christ of Latter-day Saints,* 2d rev. ed., ed. B. H. Roberts, 7 vols. (Salt Lake City: Deseret Book, 1978), 7:570.

4. Richard E. Bennett, *Mormons at the Missouri, 1846–1852: "And Should We Die. . . ."* (Norman: University of Oklahoma Press, 1987), 202.

5. See discussion of evidence for a succession blessing in Linda King Newell and Valeen Tippetts Avery, *Mormon Enigma: Emma Hale Smith, Prophet's Wife, "Elect Lady," Polygamy's Foe* (New York: Doubleday, 1984), 169. Although the quoted blessing has been found to be a forgery, the balance of the discussion is valid. For details of the several possible successors named by the Prophet, see D. Michael Quinn, "The Mormon Succession Crisis of 1844," *Brigham Young University Studies* 16 (Winter 1976): 187–233.

6. Wilford Woodruff quoting Brigham Young in Scott G. Kenney, ed., *Wilford Woodruff's Journal, 1833–1898,* 9 vols. (Midvale, Utah: Signature Books, 1983–85), 3:257.

7. Ibid.

8. Quoted in Bennett, *Mormons at the Missouri,* 202–3.

9. Minutes of a Meeting of the Twelve and Seventy, November 30, 1847, as quoted in Bennett, *Mormons at the Missouri,* 202–3. With Orson Pratt's question in mind, the Twelve not surprisingly reacted with some concern when Joseph F. Smith, early in the twentieth century, had his half-brother, Presiding Patriarch John Smith, ordain him as president of the church.

10. Quoted in Wilford Woodruff, Journal, December 27, 1847, Archives of the Church of Jesus Christ of Latter-day Saints, Salt Lake City (hereafter LDS Church Archives).

11. Joseph Smith, *History of the Church,* 7:621.

12. Ibid., 7:622.

13. General Epistle from the Council of the Twelve Apostles to the Church of Jesus Christ of Latter-day Saints abroad, dispersed throughout the earth, *Millennial Star* 10 (March 15, 1848): 114–15. Also found in Historian's Office Journal, September 1, 1861, and manuscript of sermon, October 7, 1866, as cited in Quinn,

"The Mormon Succession Crisis of 1844," 229–30. Cited also in J. Max Anderson, "Succession in the Patriarchal Priesthood," undated typescript, LDS Church Archives.

14. Ibid.

15. Minutes of the Conferences in the Log Tabernacle, December 27, 1847, quoted in Bennett, *Mormons at the Missouri*, 214.

16. John Smith, brother of Joseph Smith, Sr., who became the fourth patriarch, is referred to as "Uncle John" throughout this study in order to avoid confusion with the fifth patriarch John Smith, son of Hyrum Smith.

17. Lucy Mack Smith, *Biographical Sketches of Joseph Smith the Prophet and His Progenitors for Many Generations* (Liverpool, England: Published for Orson Pratt by S. W. Richards, 1853; New York: Arno Press and New York Times, 1969), 204.

18. George A. Smith, Journal, January 9, 1832, George A. Smith Family Collection, Manuscripts Division, Special Collections, Marriott Library, University of Utah, Salt Lake City.

19. Joseph Smith, *History of the Church*, 2:509.

20. John Smith, Journal, February 25 and March 10, 1833, LDS Archives; copy in George A. Smith Family Collection.

21. Joseph Smith, *History of the Church*, 2:303 (quote); trial of Sylvester Smith, who had accused Joseph Smith of "prophesying lies in the name of the Lord," August 23, 1834, Journal History, LDS Church Archives; trial of Isaac Hill, who was excommunicated for "lying, and an attempt to seduce a female," November 8, 1835, Joseph Smith, *History of the Church*, 2:303.

22. John Smith to Asael Smith, August 12, 1834, George A. Smith Family Collection.

23. John Smith to Elias Smith, October 19, 1834, copied by Zora Smith Jarvis from original, Emily Smith Stewart Collection, Special Collections, Marriott Library, University of Utah, Salt Lake City.

24. Joseph Smith, *History of the Church*, 2:446.

25. John Smith, Journal, May 12, 1836.

26. John Smith to George A. Smith, January 1, 1838, LDS Church Archives.

27. John Smith to George A. Smith, January 15, 1838, Journal History, LDS Church Archives.

28. John Smith, Journal, April 23 and May 9, 1838.

29. Ibid., May 16, 1838. For further details of John Smith's life in the church, see Irene M. Bates, "Uncle John Smith, 1781–1854: Patriarchal Bridge," *Dialogue: A Journal of Mormon Thought* 20 (Fall 1987): 79–89.

30. John E. Thompson, "A Chronology of Danite Meetings in Adam-Ondi-Ahman, Missouri, July to September 1838," *Restoration* 4 (January 1985): 12. Thompson quotes from John Smith's diary, August 14, 1838.

31. Quoted in Joseph Smith, *History of the Church*, 3:175.

32. Joseph Smith III and Heman C. Smith, *History of the Reorganized Church of Jesus Christ of Latter Day Saints*, 7 vols. (Lamoni, Iowa: Herald Publishing, 1896–1903), 2:171.

33. Joseph Smith, *History of the Church*, 3:209, gives a list of those arrested.

34. Ibid., 3:320–21.
35. John Smith, Journal, October 24, 1838.
36. Ibid., September 21, 1839.
37. Ibid., December 15, 1839.
38. Ibid., January 4, 1840.
39. Ibid., November 29 and December 20, 1840.
40. John Smith to George A. Smith, January 7, 1841, Journal History, LDS Church Archives.
41. John Smith, Journal, January 15, 1841.
42. Joseph Smith, *History of the Church*, 6:597–98.
43. Ibid., 7:241, also 234 and 242. This statement itself established a precedent in ignoring the tradition of primogeniture. It was a precedent that would resurface nearly one hundred years later.
44. Brigham Young, "Conference Minutes, October 7th, 1844," *Times and Seasons* 5 (October 15, 1844): 692.
45. "For time" meant for this life only, as distinct from "for eternity." John's marriage to his brother Silas's widow was reminiscent of Old Testament practices. LDS children born to the second husband would belong to the deceased brother "for eternity," as was true in biblical times.
46. Nauvoo Temple Record, Special Collections, Genealogical Library, Salt Lake City.
47. Patty Sessions, "History of Patty Bartlett Sessions: Mother of Mormon Midwifery, 1795–1893," typescript, Huntington Library, San Marino, Calif., mentions being in the company of "Father John Smith" and his "wives" after the exodus from Nauvoo, but it is not clear how many of his plural wives accompanied him to Utah. See also Juanita Brooks, ed., *On the Mormon Frontier: The Diary of Hosea Stout*, 2 vols. (Salt Lake City: University of Utah Press, 1964), 1:144, 171.
48. Brooks, ed., *On the Mormon Frontier*, 1:235.
49. *Millennial Star* 10 (March 15, 1848): 86.
50. Manuscript History of the Church, LDS Church Archives. The order of sustaining, with the Patriarch preceding the Twelve Apostles, would become a cause of debate in later years.
51. John Smith, Journal, n.d. 1848.
52. Typescript of ordination of Patriarch [Uncle] John Smith, January 1, 1849, LDS Church Archives; copy in Eldred G. Smith Personal Records, Salt Lake City.
53. John Smith to D. H. Miller, July 13, 1849, George A. Smith Family Collection.
54. Henry W. Bigler, Diary, October 7, 1849, Book A, holograph, Huntington Library, San Marino, Calif.
55. Jesse N. Smith, *The Journal of Jesse Nathaniel Smith, 1834–1906* (Salt Lake City: Jesse N. Smith Family Association, 1953), 17.
56. Patriarchal blessing given to George A. Smith by John Smith, September 20, 1853, George A. Smith Family Collection.
57. George Albert Smith, Uncle John's grandson, quoted from this earlier *Deseret News* statement in *Conference Reports of the Church of Jesus Christ of Latter-day Saints* (Salt Lake City: Church of Jesus Christ of Latter-day Saints, April

1927), 85.

58. Patriarchal blessing given to Church Patriarch Uncle John Smith by Isaac Morley, September 25, 1851, Eldred G. Smith Personal Records.

59. John Lyman Smith, Journal, May 15, 1854, LDS Church Archives.

60. This obituary, appearing in the *Deseret News* on May 25, 1854, was reprinted as "Death of the Patriarch John Smith" in the *Millennial Star* 16 (August 1854): 493.

61. Blessing given to Catherine Campbell Steele by Patriarch Uncle John Smith, January 26, 1846, when he was a stake patriarch, LDS Church Archives; copy in authors' possession.

62. Eliza R. Snow, Diary, between October 2 and 28, 1846, holograph, Huntington Library, San Marino, Calif. Maureen Ursenbach Beecher provided a copy of Snow's entire poem eulogizing the Patriarch.

63. John Lyon, "Sacred to the Memory of John Smith, Patriarch," July 20, 1854, holograph, LDS Church Archives. The other poem, written by E. Howard after John Smith's death, is in the LDS Church Archives.

6

Continuing the Tradition

John Smith—Fifth Patriarch, 1855–1911

> In the name of the Lord Jesus Christ of Nazareth, we his servants
> lay our hands on your head and ordain and set you apart to your
> office and calling which falleth unto thee through the lineage of
> your forefathers . . . and we confirm thee [John] to be the first
> in the Church of Jesus Christ among the Patriarchs, to set apart
> and confirm other Patriarchs . . . and we bless thee with all the
> keys belonging unto you from your Father.
>
> —Brigham Young's ordination blessing of John Smith,
> February 18, 1855

Following the death of Uncle John Smith, the tradition of primogeniture brought the office back to the eldest son of the eldest son of the original patriarch. On February 18, 1855, young John Smith, the eldest son of
the second patriarch, Hyrum Smith, was called as Presiding Patriarch. He
was twenty-two years old. Although Uncle John's successor would not
present the kind of challenge to the hierarchy William Smith presented,
young John would begin to disturb the complacency characteristic of his
great-uncle.

Brigham Young took steps immediately after the call to neutralize any
assertiveness the new presiding patriarch might evidence. Young changed
the order in which the General Authorities were sustained in General
Conference. During Uncle John's tenure, the Patriarch had continued to
be sustained immediately following the First Presidency and before the
Quorum of the Twelve.[1] When young John Smith was appointed Church
Patriarch, he was sustained *after* the Twelve.

Brigham Young's fears never materialized. John Smith did not aspire
to position or power. While not as rigid in his religious observance as his
predecessor, young John was also neither as ambitious nor as volatile as
William. His letters and journal reveal him to be a charismatic, compas-

sionate individual, who cared more about people than about institutional requirements.

From an early age John began to assume responsibility for family and friends—perhaps because he was so young when his parents died. John Smith's mother, Jerusha Barden, died when he was five years old; his father was killed when he was eleven. He was baptized in the spring of 1843 and was ordained an elder in the Nauvoo Temple on January 24, 1846, when he was just thirteen. When he was fifteen, he left Nauvoo with Heber C. Kimball in February 1847, but, after hearing that his stepmother, Mary Fielding Smith, was on the road with her family, he went back 150 miles to help them. They arrived at Winter Quarters and spent two winters there. John built a log cabin for Mary Fielding, constructed fences, tilled soil, and did the work of a man in the fields.

It was at Winter Quarters that John received a letter from Joseph III, eldest son of the Prophet Joseph Smith. The two cousins had been close companions in childhood. Joseph III was just six weeks younger than John, both boys were eleven when their fathers were murdered, and both were fifteen when separated by the westward migration of the church. Joseph III remained in the Midwest with his mother and eventually became president of the rival denomination, the Reorganized Church of Jesus Christ of Latter Day Saints. Despite their religious differences, Joseph III and John remained friends throughout their lives. Joseph III's letter of March 21, 1848, evidences both their friendship and their differences:

> Cousin, You know me better than to suppose for a moment that I will or would condescend to be dictated by any person what I shall write & what I shall not write. . . . You expiate [sic] largely upon helping to roll on the great work in the track of our father but if you mean by this I must support [here a word is scribbled out] spiritual wifery & the other institutions which have been instituted since their deaths (for you very well know that they never upheld such doctrines in public or practised them in private) I most assuredly shall be your most inveterate adversary. I do not now nor shall I ever countenance such iniquity so help me heaven. . . . You perhaps do not want to change your situation at present but time will show and the Lord judge between you and me.[2]

Whether John replied to this particular letter is not known, but it made little difference to their friendship. Although Brigham Young frowned on John's continued friendship with his Reorganized Church cousins, the friendship did not alter John's commitment to the Utah church. John's life was one of tireless service to the church and to the less fortunate.

In April 1848 he started out for Salt Lake. On his sixteenth birthday, September 22, he drove not just one wagon but five down the "big mountain" east of Salt Lake. In 1850 he joined the "Battalion of Life Guards" to help protect the Saints from Indians, and he later served in at least three military expeditions.[3] When Mary Fielding died on September 21, 1852, John was supporting the family of eight, three members of which were over sixty years old. On December 23, 1853, he married Hellen Fisher and built a two-room adobe cottage just a few yards from the family home.[4]

Brigham Young's ordination of John as Patriarch to the Church in 1855 stated in part:

> In the name of the Lord Jesus Christ of Nazareth, we his servants lay our hands on your head and ordain and set you apart to your office and calling which falleth unto thee through the lineage of your forefathers, and ordain thee to the High Priesthood of Almighty God, conferring on thee all the powers and blessing and authority of the Priesthood, with the keys as thy Grandfather Joseph Smith held them, who conferred them on your father Hyrum Smith, *so we confer them instead of thy father, who would have conferred them on thee if he had been alive;* and we confirm thee to be the first in the Church of Jesus Christ among the Patriarchs, to *set apart and confirm other patriarchs* . . . and we bless thee with all the keys belonging unto you from your Father.[5]

This ordination by Brigham Young is interesting in several respects. First, it shows that Young accepted the principle of an incumbent patriarch's ordaining his successor. Before Joseph Smith, Sr., died, he ordained Hyrum to the office, but even though the practice was established early, acknowledged by Young, and believed in by later incumbents of the office, Joseph Sr.'s ordination of his son was the first and last time it actually took place. Second, the ordination empowered John, as Patriarch, to "set apart and confirm" other patriarchs. This was particularly curious since the Quorum of the Twelve's exclusive right to ordain local patriarchs, as set forth in Doctrine and Covenants 107:39, was a jealously guarded prerogative when distinctions were being made between the authority of the Twelve and that of the Patriarch.

The tone of the blessing, as well as later announcements, confirmed that young John, like Uncle John, was to have authority to be the "Presiding Patriarch over this Priesthood." At the April 1855 General Conference, John Smith was sustained as "Presiding Patriarch of the Church," and during an area conference in Switzerland in 1856, he was sustained as "Patriarch of the Whole Church and president of the patriarchal priesthood."[6]

A year later John still had not commenced his duties, however. He wrote to his half-brother, Joseph F. Smith, who was on a mission in the Pacific Islands, "As to my office I have not done anything in that line as yet and I do not know how soon I shall, but I am not afraid to say that

Hellen Fisher Smith, 1835–1907. Wife of the fifth presiding patriarch, John Smith. The twins in her arms were born August 13, 1867, the sixth and seventh of nine children; Evaline died in 1878, and Alvin Fisher died 1955. Courtesy of E. Gary Smith.

John Smith, 1832–1911. Fifth presiding patriarch, 1855–1911. Taken when John was twenty-one or twenty-two years old, shortly after being ordained Patriarch. Courtesy of E. Gary Smith.

when you return that I will give you a good blessing the Lord being my helper."[7] Four months later, on August 17, 1856, he gave his first patriarchal blessing to Samuel Knight.

There are several early indications that John's relationship with the rest of the church hierarchy would be an uneasy one. In a letter to Joseph F. Smith on January 31, 1856, John shared his annoyance that Brother William Pierce had married John's sister, Jerusha Smith, without his permission. Brigham Young had appointed John guardian of the family after Mary Fielding died. In his letter John referred to the nineteenth-century Mormon practice of adoption, the sealing of members to church leaders "for eternity."[8] He commented, "I know the Pierce family belongs in Brother Brigham's family, and he would like it first rate to get one of Father's daughters into his family and leave Father without any kingdom. . . . I do not believe that Bill married Jerusha because he loved her . . . it was the name more than anything else."[9] John was also uncomfortable with some of his more public responsibilities. On May 31, 1856, John wrote Joseph F. of being scared "most to death" of public speaking. He said, "I have refused allmost every time Brother Brigham called on me to dismiss the conference."[10]

In later correspondence with Joseph F., still serving a mission in the Sandwich Islands, both John and his wife, Hellen, referred to a "refermation" going on in the Salt Lake Valley. Hellen told Joseph, "We have all got to repente of our sins and be baptized and do awer first work over again." In the same letter she informed her brother-in-law that "Bro. Young told John to get another wife."[11]

Neither John nor Hellen was enthusiastic about plural marriage, and when John did marry a second wife, twenty-three-year-old Nancy Melissa Lemmon, on February 18, 1857, Hellen made her feelings known to her brother-in-law: "Well, John has got another wife, perhaps you know her, her name is Milisa Lemins. Dear Joseph it was a trial to me but thank the Lord it is over with. . . . I care not how many he gits now, the ice is broke as the old saing is, the more the greater glory. . . . All of the girls is a giting maried from 10 to 18. If there is any left till theyre are 18 they are on the oald maids list."[12]

Hellen wrote to John in May, "Talk about me apostizing, God forgive me for I am a later day saint, but the Lord knows that I am know poligamist, and with the help of the Lord I will have nothing to do with it, can you understand that." Hellen reminded John that he wanted to know her mind so he must not complain if she told him. She added a caution: "Report is that you are bringing a lady-wife with you. I wood advise her to leave a portion of her refinement on the plains and it will not go so hard with her when she gets here. . . . May the Lord bless you and bring you home in safty is the prare of your wife as ever."[13] Later, when John was visiting relatives in Nauvoo, he received a letter from his wife, warning him, "John when you left you said you wood gow away and when you came back I wood bee a betar girl, for beter or for worse you will find me changed from a weeke girl to a stronge minded woman that will have her writes if there are writes for a woman."[14] Perhaps John's reluctance and Hellen's outspoken distaste for polygamy estranged Brigham Young and John further. Although Hellen's opinion of polygamy never changed, she remained a loyal and loving wife.

John's continuing friendship with his "apostate" cousins in the Midwest was also some cause for concern. On John's return home from Nauvoo on April 18, 1860, he wrote to Joseph F., "Nauvoo is a desolate looking place, the front or west end of the temple is standing yet. . . . I had a tolerable plesent visit with the folks . . . I was very well treated they all appeared very glad to see me . . . they all profess Mormonism except poligamy. there is considerable excitement . . . about Joseph they are expecting him to come out there and take the leadership of a branch of the church. I do not know whether he will come or not."[15]

It is possible that John's friendship with his relatives in the Reorganized Church was the reason he was called in April 1862 to serve a mission in Scandinavia. The reason given, however, was that John was young and needed experience. Earlier, however, Brigham Young appears to have thought otherwise. In April 1854 he had said of the young patriarch-to-be, "Some say he is too young, but he can seal up a Patriarchal blessing upon the heads of the people better than any old man in this church. His mind has never been tramelled with the unhallowed doctrines of sectarianism, nor suffered the withering blight of vice, but it is free, active and noble, and it expands and is still calculated to expand to understand all things."[16]

On June 28, 1854, Jedediah M. Grant of the First Presidency expressed similar feelings. He declared, "I would rather have a young man to fill this office than an old man who is filled with the leaven of sectarianism. Give me a man who was raised by a Mormon father, and a Mormon mother, and raised up in the faith from his childhood."[17] Yet eight years later John was asked to leave behind his patriarchal responsibilities to go on this mission.

John left Salt Lake on May 17, 1862, and arrived in Denmark on September 6, 1862.[18] Four months later he recorded in his journal, "I will here state that nothing of importance has transpired during my stay in Copenhagen . . . except my studying the language which is weariness etc."[19] John's missionary journal reveals his compassionate nature. He was constantly concerned about the welfare of his fellow missionaries and often cared for the sick or injured elders.[20]

John's missionary journal also suggests the lack of emphasis given to the Word of Wisdom health law at the time. Quite matter-of-factly John revealed that the elders drank coffee regularly and that occasionally he and his companions partook of tea, beer, and wine. Yet he mentioned lecturing the boys on the use of tobacco. In July 1863 he said, "In the evening I had a long walk with Carl . . . and talked with him about his slackness in his work and his using tobacco and spending money instead of saving it etc." Three weeks later he "talked with the boys about using tobacco. Julius promised me he would leave it off and not smoke any more cigars."[21]

Probably out of curiosity, John on one occasion attended High Mass at the Catholic church. Although not a philosopher by nature, his missionary letters suggest an active interest in studying his religion. In a letter to Hellen on September 23, 1863, he replied to some statement she had made about his faith: "I believe if I remember right you said in your last letter that I had religion enough for you and me both. I wish I had but I am afraid I have not. I do not think that I am any more religious now than I was when I left home but I will say that I feel more of the necessity of [unclear] in the religion which I acknowledge to believe. If we stay away from meeting so that we do not hear what is preached . . . nor take any panes to learn, how do we know whether our religion is true or not?"[22]

John's letters reveal a forthright, caring relationship with his first wife, who remained his first love. In his journal he mentions writing to Melissa, his plural wife, and receiving a letter from her, and in each case he refers to her simply as "Melissa," never as "my wife."[23] One undated letter to Hellen reveals some lingering feelings about his capitulation to the practice of polygamy:

Well, Hellen, one thing more, you say that I must write to my wife if I beleave in wives . . . have I not written to you enough, I think I have written to you about twenty times since I left home and I intend to write again every time that I feel like it . . . as to Melissa, I have only written two or three times but I intend to write again when I get ready and feel like it. You again advise me to get two more wives when I get home, again what do you mean? . . .You say also that if I do get more wives I will take them on your terms . . . if I am to understand it as this reads I would suppose that you was a going to hunt up two wives for me . . . and to do all in your power for my good and for my comfort with out a word of complaint, for this kind offer my thanks, for your kindness. I know that your generous hart is ever ready to do me good but for the present allow me to say that I have wives enough.[24]

On January 19, 1863, John felt it necessary to reassure his wife. He told her, "Dear Hellen, be not afraid to trust me. I think that I can look at a woman without lusting after her if you think otherwise you do not know me."[25]

Evidently things were not easy for his family back in Utah. John recorded in his journal on November 17, 1863, "Received a letter from home and my wife had received the things I sent her. She inquired if she could sell some land to buy something to eat as she could not get anything from it." In a letter to Hellen, who had been having difficulties with "Minor," a man who had been left in charge of their farm in John's absence, John told her that he had asked Brigham Young, Jr., and Joseph F. Smith to look into the matter. Even from Denmark, John took great interest in the details of family life back home. This counsel to Hellen shows his tenderness and sensitivity:

> what can't be cured must be endured so let us be as contented as posible with our lot and let me say as I have said before, be a good Girl do the best you can . . . and all will come out right some time. to know that one is right is worth more than money (at least I think so) take care of your health and that of the children the best that you can be sure to keep Hyrum with warm clothes on . . . and his feet warm and dry and tell the School teacher that Hyrum must not be whiped let him do what he will, I say he must not be whiped, the old proverb says spair the rod and spoil the child but in this case I do not beleave it. Hyrum is the same . . . that I was and I was whiped untill I was case hardened and it made me worse than I otherwise would have been. Study his disposition and govern him with kindness.[26]

While on his mission John corresponded a great deal with his relatives in Nauvoo, and his friendly association with his family in the Reorganized Church was evidently a topic of conversation back in Utah. On January 2, 1864, John wrote from Copenhagen to Joseph F. Smith:

> I am glad you mentioned that it had been said that I was a Josephite although it is no new thing to me for Hellen wrote the same as early as June 14, but she did not mention any name. . . . If you hear anything more please inform me for it will be interesting to know what folks think of one (so far away). . . . As to what people choose to say about me I will say (in Danish) det er mig lige what they say it will not make one hair neither white or black, if when I am released here I should stop in Illinois that is my own affair if I come home like an honest man it will not change the case by madam rumors talking about it.[27]

John had written to his brother asking him to purchase three or four copies of Lucy Mack Smith's *History* to give to relatives in Nauvoo.[28] It seems unlikely that Joseph F. ever did manage to get copies of the book.

Earlier John had asked his cousin Jesse to get some while he was in Liverpool (where it was printed and published originally by Orson Pratt "without saying a word to the First Presidency or the Twelve"), but Jesse was told copies would not be allowed out of the office. The book was condemned by Brigham Young as being "utterly unreliable as a history as it contains many falsehoods and mistakes." Young said, "We do not wish such a book to be lying on our shelves to be taken up in after years, and read by our children as true history. . . . It is transmitting lies to posterity . . . and we know that the curse of God will rest upon every one . . . who keeps these books for his children to learn and believe in lies."[29]

A revised version of the book was later approved by a softened Brigham Young, even though it contained few substantive changes. Martha Coray, Lucy's amanuensis, refused to sanction the changes, and it was not until 1902 that this edition was finally published, under the title *History of the Prophet Joseph Smith.*[30] It has been suggested by Jan Shipps that the earlier recall of the book might have been motivated by the fact that the sons of Joseph Smith, Jr., were in Salt Lake City at the time doing missionary work and advancing the claims of the Reorganized Church. It did not help that Lucy Mack Smith emphasized the role of the entire Smith family in the book.[31]

In the spring of 1864 John was getting ready to leave Copenhagen. A month before he left he comforted his wife once more about her financial situation: "Well, Hellen, I am sorry that you have to call on the missionary fund but that is better than to do worse."[32] At a meeting preparing for the journey home, held on board the *Monarch of the Sea* on April 13, 1864, Patriarch John Smith was appointed president of the immigrant ship taking charge of 973 Saints from Britain, Scandinavia, and Germany. After forty days at sea, with John taking care of the sick even though unwell himself, they arrived in New York on June 3, 1864. John then took charge of thirty wagons (later increasing to sixty) across the plains, arriving in Salt Lake City on October 1, 1864.[33]

Back in Salt Lake, John continued his association with his relatives in the fledgling Reorganized Church, despite the displeasure of some Utah Mormons, who probably read this as giving comfort and aid to the enemy. John wrote to Emma Smith, the Prophet's widow, on December 2, 1866, expressing his pleasure in having her son Alexander stay with him during a visit to Salt Lake City. He assured Emma that he had not forgotten her or any relatives in that part of the country: "It was a very good visit with Alexander, with one exception, that is his stay was too short. He made his home at my house while he was in this city. He had his likeness taken here by Edward Martin and I have two or three of them, and I wish I had yours and all of the relatives who are in Illinois. I would also

Hellen Fisher Smith, taken in 1888. Courtesy of E. Gary Smith.

John Smith, taken in 1877, when John was forty-five years old. Courtesy of E. Gary Smith.

John Smith's home at 260 South First West in about 1879. John is at the far left, and Hellen, his wife, is seventh from the left. Courtesy of E. Gary Smith.

like Uncle William's and I will ask where Uncle William is and what is he doing & I wish I could see him."[34]

John continued religious debates with Alexander and Joseph Smith III and used his friendship and love in carrying on missionary work with members of the Reorganized Church. The cousins, for their part, were equally determined to assert the Reorganites' position. Alexander wrote to John:

> I am well aware that your position is such that you must needs act with great care, caution and forethought, more particularly if you do not agree with those in more exalted position in that organization. John, I do not know how strongly you may be bonded in those secrets, oaths, and combinations that have been established in that organization to bind the members together, in the absence of the true love and power of God, which should bind the children of God more firmly together than any covenants or oaths that man can invent. I do not wish to begin a tirade of abuse against any person or persons but wish to carefully investigate the Principles of the respective Churches. . . . In the name of Israel's God I ask you to give heed to the dictates of the spirit of Almighty God and seek your true position ere it be too late. . . . And in this investigation I will try to show you plainly wherein it is in your interest to come out of that Modern Sodom.[35]

Perhaps John's own discomfort with polygamy, together with this intimacy with his cousins, underlay some of the displeasure expressed by church leaders about John during his tenure as Presiding Patriarch. Official reasons for the disapproval are never made clear. Wilford Woodruff wrote in his journal on October 9, 1875, about a meeting of the Twelve with President Brigham Young and reported that after discussion "the Presidency & Twelve voted to drop John Smith from the Patriarchal office & put in his place Joseph F. Smith, but during the day John and Joseph F. Smith had seen President Brigham and pled very hard to try John another six months to see if he would magnify his calling any better than he had done in the past."[36] It is difficult for us to know what was meant by this criticism, but some light may be shed by what transpired at a meeting of the First Presidency, the Twelve Apostles, and presidents of stakes eight years later, on October 12, 1883. Those assembled were members of the School of the Prophets. Joseph F. Smith, then a counselor in the First Presidency, spoke on the importance of being an example in living the law of plural marriage and the Word of Wisdom. The minutes record:

> He [Joseph F. Smith] referred to John Smith's absence. Said it was because as he thought John had not lived his religion therefore he (Jos.

F. Smith) had not asked that he (John Smith) be admitted, though he held the position of Patriarch to the Church. He smoked and, though having two wives, he lived entirely with one. It became a question to his mind, if under the circumstances, he was not mostly to belong to this School, was he worthy to be a Patriarch? He asked the brethren to use their influence that Bro. John might become a man.[37]

Others at the meeting renewed their commitment to avoid the temptation to break the Word of Wisdom and to engage in sins of the flesh. The president of the church, John Taylor, referred to the power of the priesthood and then added, "We have no right to present any of our relations, children, or friends to any of these plans or to receive any ordinances of the church who are not worthy from their acts. Just the same as Bro. Joseph F. expressed himself in regard to his brother John, who does not and has not lived to the privilege he might enjoy."[38]

Pressure to enter into plural marriage continued. On April 6, 1884, just six years before President Wilford Woodruff's Manifesto outlawed the practice, Apostle Abraham Cannon noted in his diary, "At a priesthood meeting held in the evening (after the Hall was cleared of all those who were not worthy of being present) the strongest language in regard to Plural Marriage was used that I ever heard, and among other things it was stated that all men in positions who would not observe and fulfil that law should be removed from their places."[39]

Insofar as the Word of Wisdom was concerned, John was caught in the changing values of the institution. His grandson Ralph Smith remembered John's saying that it was Heber C. Kimball, counselor in the First Presidency, who taught him how to chew tobacco.[40] When the Word of Wisdom became more strictly regarded, John had difficulty changing as quickly.

Nevertheless, and despite criticism from some quarters, John's patriarchal blessings reflect a deep spirituality. Even though he lacked confidence in terms of public speaking, John's blessings are often eloquent. For example, he said to Nancy Naomi Tracy in 1869, "I ask God, the eternal Father, to smile in mercy upon thee and give unto thee of the influence of his holy spirit and open the visions of eternity unto thy view. for thou hast passed through many trials and seen many changes, and I say unto thee verily thou shalt receive thy reward, for thou hast withstood the test and been faithful. . . . Thy name shall be written in the Lamb's Book of Life, and thou shalt be crowned hereafter among the faithful mothers in Israel."[41]

John gave over twenty thousand blessings during his tenure and traveled hundreds of miles in all weather, mostly on horseback, to bestow these blessings. The suggestion that John could have done more to "magnify" his church calling was doubtless not referring to the blessings themselves or to John's willingness and ability to give them.

Local patriarchs were also causing some concern to the Brethren at about this same time. On November 7, 1877, Apostle John Taylor wrote to George Q. Cannon: "The subject of the present condition of the patriarchs has lately been considered by us. It has appeared to several of the members of the Quorum that they have noticed a spirit amongst some of the brethren ordained to this office, to degrade it to a mere means of obtaining a livelihood, and to obtain more business they had been travelling from door to door and underbidding each other in the price of blessings. This, we all considered, an evil that should be remedied as soon as possible."[42]

The solution, suggested Elder Taylor, was to organize a quorum of patriarchs, over which "Bro. John Smith, by virtue of his calling, will preside, and the members of which quorum he will direct their labors and operations, as he shall be instructed by the Council of the Apostles." John Taylor then added, "If Bro. John will do this, as it should be done, I feel that the calling of the patriarchs will arise to the dignity that naturally and properly belongs to it and as such be respected in the midst of Israel."[43] It is not known exactly how, or if, John proceeded to preside over the local patriarchs. It was probably initiated informally as John traveled around the church.

False rumors lingered about John's loyalty to the church. In a letter to Joseph F. Smith on June 6, 1887, the Patriarch said, "In regard to my being debared the priveledges of the Temple I had never heard of it. . . . It is evident that all mischief makers are not dead yet."[44] In another letter to his "Brother in Exile" (Joseph F. Smith was a polygamist, apparently living "underground" at the time), John defended himself from suggestions that he might give his brother away to those who were hunting the Brethren still practicing polygamy. He told Joseph F., "I have heard other reports which gives me to understand that I have enemies somewhere, but my informant will not tell me where they got there news. I am satisfied that there has been an evil influence working against me for sometime, and why this should be I am unable to discern as yet." What hurt John most of all was "to be accused harshly by my brother to whom I have ever been true as my Heavenly Father knows if he knows anything."[45]

The Patriarch was having financial problems, too. On January 20, 1888, President Wilford Woodruff wrote to John Smith refusing his request for financial assistance. Woodruff pointed out that the Patriarch was drawing a thousand dollars a year from the church, "not mentioning the amount that is paid to Sister Lemon [John's plural wife]."[46] What Presi-

John Smith and his son Hyrum Fisher Smith, with their families on an outing in Chalk Creek Canyon around 1896. John is seated on the wagon, Hyrum F. is sitting with his hat on in front of the tent, and Hannah, Hyrum F.'s wife, is the second woman to his left. Courtesy of E. Gary Smith.

John Smith dressed for the July 24 parade around 1909 or 1910. He is wearing his father's (Hyrum's) dress sword. Courtesy of E. Gary Smith.

John Smith, taken in the latter part of his life. John was proud of his full white beard. Courtesy of Eldred G. Smith.

dent Woodruff failed to acknowledge, however, was the fact that other general authorities were drawing twice that amount. Michael Quinn's study of the Mormon hierarchy reveals that the Patriarch's pay was always the lowest of any paid church leader's and that he did not have access to the personal income that other general authorities derived from appointments in church business corporations.[47]

Not content with private reproval of John, President Woodruff reprimanded the Patriarch publicly at the October 1894 General Conference for John's failure to keep the Word of Wisdom:

> I have many good sisters come to me and say I have been raised on Tea and coffee and if I do not have it I will be sick. I cannot get along without it or I will die. And what have I said to them, Better die and keep the commandments of the Lord than to live and break them and here I see the Presiding Patriarch of the Church close to me, if he can not keep the Word of Wisdom and the commandments of God, we will have to get another Patriarch of the church. If he can not put away his tobacco and smoking he better resign. If he thinks those things are of greater value then the Holy Spirit, Brother John Smith you better resign, and we will get some one who will keep the commandments of the Lord. You better throw away your pipe and liquor habits and keep the commandments of the Lord [or] give way to someone who will honor that calling. . . . We want men who honor their calling . . . to occupy positions of trust and not those who do not live worthy of the blessings of the Almighty.[48]

With respect to the Word of Wisdom, John was not unlike the beloved J. Golden Kimball and B. H. Roberts, who, as general authorities, struggled with the same problem. Many of the Brethren of this generation were challenged by the changed emphasis. Wilford Woodruff himself, fifty years earlier, had considered the Word of Wisdom in a far less rigid light. Quoting Brigham Young, he wrote in his journal in 1841, "Shall I break the word of wisdom if I go home and drink a cup of tea? No, wisdom is justified of her children. . . . All concluded that . . . a forced abstainance was not making us free but we should be under bondage with a yoak upon our necks."[49]

In keeping with the changed emphasis of the late nineteenth century, Apostle Heber J. Grant also made veiled allusions to John Smith's habits at the 1894 General Conference:

> I remember going to another Stake of Zion and preaching to the people about the necessity of refraining from tea and coffee . . . and the president of the stake remarked . . . that he thought the Lord would for-

give them if they did drink their coffee because the water in that stake of Zion was bad. . . . I had to pray to the Lord to bite my tongue to keep from getting up and doing something that I never have done in my life, and that is, to pick out a man and thrash him from the public stand. . . . I have become so discouraged, so disheartened, so humiliated in my feelings, after preaching year after year both by precept and example, to realize there are Bishops, Bishops' Counselors, Presidents of Stakes, and Patriarchs among the Church of God whose hearts I have not been able to touch. . . . I felt that it was like pouring water on a duck's back.[50]

Even though John was not alone in his indulgences, the accusations were certainly not without foundation. John's nephew Samuel S. Smith remembered that he had heard it said that John would smoke cigarettes in his office while people were there receiving blessings. Disapproving of this, Apostle Grant went to President Joseph F. Smith and pushed very hard to have John removed from office. President Joseph F. Smith refused.[51] Despite the earlier criticism Joseph F. Smith voiced regarding John Smith's Word of Wisdom problem, complaints about the Church Patriarch declined in the following years. Whether John Smith modified his behavior as a result of these criticisms is not apparent, although his grandson Ralph Smith claimed that he did. Indeed, by 1900 Apostle John W. Taylor spoke well of him from the pulpit at the General Conference:

We have a man who stands at the head of the patriarchal order in our Church. That man is Brother John Smith. He always sits here with the First Presidency of the Church. Why is it that he occupies this exalted position when sitting before the people in their general conferences? It is because the Lord acknowledges a Patriarch as a man who is endowed with a very high office in the Church and kingdom of God, and who has a special endowment given unto him for a special purpose. If there is any man in this Church who has a special calling for life it is a Patriarch. I have sometimes thought, however, from remarks which I have heard from men bearing the holy Priesthood, that the ignorance regarding the Patriarchal order is extremely dense among the Latter-day Saints.[52]

By 1902 John's half-brother Joseph F. Smith was president of the church. For the second time in the church's history two brothers occupied the positions of president and patriarch. It was inevitable that comparisons would be made and that there would be those who hoped for the past to repeat itself and those who feared the reemergence of the primacy dimensions of the patriarchal office.

Patriarch John Smith and President Joseph F. Smith. Courtesy of E. Gary Smith.

Joseph F. Smith unsettled the other apostles at the very beginning of his tenure as president by requesting that his brother, the Patriarch, ordain him.[53] President Smith commented, "And we did it strictly in accordance with the pattern the Lord has established in this Church."[54] This official act must have concerned the Twelve, given the memory of the metaphor used by John Taylor in his *Times and Seasons* article regarding William Smith's ordination to the patriarchal office. Taylor had asked, rhetorically, "Can a stream rise higher than its fountain? No. Says Paul, 'The less is blessed of the better.'"[55] John's ordaining Joseph F. placed the "less" (the Patriarch) above the "better" (the president and the Quorum of the Twelve) within the hierarchy. The stream was rising higher than the fountain. Paranoia, if not legitimate fears, arose about the impact this could have on presidential rights.

The Smiths were well represented in the ranks of church leaders at this time but as members who held office at the invitation and consent of the institution, not by reason of hereditary or familial rights. Their very presence, however, suggested to some a threat that the Smith family might regain the original familial primal rights to preside over the church. Frank Cannon, son of George Q. Cannon of the First Presidency, commented, "There may yet be a quorum of Smiths to succeed endlessly to the Presidency and make the Smith family a perpetual dynasty in Utah."[56]

It was not long before President Joseph F. Smith attempted to restore another problematic prerogative of the patriarchal office, but this time he would be stopped by the Twelve. In his first conference address, in November 1901, President Smith announced that the Patriarch should be sustained in conference *before* the president: "We have not always carried out strictly the order of the priesthood; we have varied it to some extent, but we hope in due time that by the promptings of the Holy Spirit, we will be led up into the exact channel and course the Lord has marked out for us to pursue."[57]

President Smith read from Doctrine and Covenants 124, where Hyrum Smith, as Patriarch, was to be sustained first, then Joseph as presiding elder, then the counselors to Joseph, then the president of the Twelve, then the Twelve, and so forth. President Smith continued, "It may be considered strange that the Lord should give first of all the Patriarch; yet I do not know any law . . . from God to the contrary, that has ever been given through any of the Prophets or Presidents of the Church. At the same time we well know that this order has not been strictly followed from the day we came into these valleys until now."[58]

The president, who owed his position to a policy of apostolic succession, was suggesting a return to the pre–1844 status of the patriarchal office. According to Apostle John Henry Smith, during the noon hour between sessions of the April 6, 1902, General Conference, the First Presidency, Twelve Apostles, and Patriarch debated about when the Patriarch of the Church should be sustained—before or after the Quorum of the Twelve. It was determined "to leave it over for the present."[59] In a journal entry on April 6 Brigham Young, Jr., also mentioned some discomfort on the part of the Twelve during this meeting: "This question of Patriarch John Smith standing next to the President, preceding the President of the Twelve. Brother John H. S. [Smith] said might change succession of President of Twelve to the Presidency. I thought him unnecessarily exercised."[60] It was again debated June 25, 1902, but there is no evidence to suggest that any change was made in the order of sustaining.[61]

In other ways, President Smith was more successful in promoting the status of the patriarchal office. James Allen and Glen Leonard reported some of these changes:

> Despite his interest in relieving General Authorities of peripheral responsibilities, President Joseph F. Smith considered the Patriarch to the Church an exception. In order to enhance the prestige and importance of that position, beginning in 1902, Patriarch John Smith was invited to address the general conference. In addition, his name was added to the fifteen General Authorities customarily sustained as "prophets, seers, and revelators." President Smith encouraged the Patriarch to travel among the Saints and believed such action was necessary to give the office the primal position outlined in the Doctrine and Covenants.[62]

John's wife, Hellen, died in 1909, but John continued to fulfill his obligations as the Patriarch. He also kept in touch with his cousin Joseph Smith III, head of the Reorganized Church. He received a letter from Joseph dated December 20, 1909, in which his cousin said he was not surprised that John had not remarried, because "your life with Cousin Helen was so long continued that it would seem difficult to assimilate with another, and take up association under new conditions." In the letter Joseph recalls some of their shared childhood experiences and fondly remembers mutual relatives and friends. John replied to his cousin, saying he was keeping well "but lonesome at times, and the Idea of remarrying I dont know what to say for the one to fill Hellen's place dont come along as yet, and to get a substitute would be difficult. We had been married 54 years, less 3 months, 22 days."[63] John did not mention Melissa, his plural wife, who was still alive. On July 7, 1911, he received a letter from Joseph III:

> Dear Cousin, I would have liked in the past to have had a heart to heart talk with you in regard to polygamy, or plural marriage, but I steadily refused to urge the matter upon your attention while visiting with you

in Salt Lake City, because I did not wish in any wise to compromise you with your brethren by indulging in such conversation, echoes of which might have reached other ears than those for whom it was intended. . . . I had known, by rumor, that you had taken a polygamous wife, but that upon returning home from Illinois upon one of the trips you made East, you at once severed the connection, refusing to acknowledge it any longer. . . . I was satisfied that it was what you heard upon that trip East that you based your action in regard to putting the polygamous wife away. . . . In view of what has taken place in the abandonment of the dogma and practice of plural marriage, I sincerely congratulate you upon the wise, prompt, and decided course you pursued in freeing yourself from the entanglement of a polygamous marriage. I commend you still. . . . You could have made no appreciable headway against the dogma. . . . It would only have involved you in an interminable quarrel with the church authorities, with no possible good results.[64]

John corresponded with several other members of the Smith family who were disaffected from the Utah church, maintaining affectionate relations with them all.[65] His bonds with his own immediate family were also very strong. Just five months before he died, John received a postcard from his grandson Hyrum G. Smith, telling him that Hyrum had passed the state board examination in dentistry in Los Angeles.

John served fifty-six years as Church Patriarch. During that time he gave 20,659 blessings. Extravagant promises were rare in John's blessings, although he did promise several women that they would be able to heal the sick.[66] Charlotte Cornwall, for example was told, "Thy mind shall expand, wisdom shall be given thee, thou shalt counsel in righteousness among thy sex and in thy habitation. Thou shalt be enabled through prayer and faith to heal the sick of thy family and hold the adversary at bay that health and peace may reign in thy dwelling."[67]

Most of the blessings were more concerned with the challenges of this life than with the life to come. The Patriarch gave his last blessing just one week before he died. He became ill with pneumonia and died on November 6, 1911, after only a six-day illness. The obituary in the *Deseret News* was headed "Patriarch Smith summoned home," and it noted, "Besides the five children, Patriarch Smith is survived by his wife, Mrs. Melissa L. Smith, 27 grandchildren, and 27 great-grandchildren. He was 79 years old."[68]

The day after John died, his eldest son, Hyrum Fisher Smith, received a letter from a John McDonald. The tribute summarizes John Smith's life:

John Smith with his granddaughter-in-law, Martha Gee Smith, wife of Hyrum G. Smith. Taken on a trip to Catalina in 1911, shortly before John's death. Hyrum G. and Martha were living in Los Angeles at the time. Courtesy of E. Gary Smith.

Tongue cannot tell how I feel on the passing of your Father, as you know he was one of the best friends I ever had. I learned to love him from my boyhood. . . . I found him to be one of the greatest men that ever lived; in this way, he had a good word for man, woman & child, and even those that persecuted us he spoke well of. He had flowing in his veins some of that noble blood that his Master had when He said Father forgive them for they know not what they do. How often has he, when people complained, turned and given them a blessing. We all love him, we shall all miss him. There was nothing boasting about him, he was simply Patriarch John Smith. It seems to me it took his departure to have his name or picture in a paper, yet he held one of the greatest offices in the Church.

John McDonald continues by assuming that Hyrum F. will become the new patriarch, and he asks to be the recipient of his first patriarchal blessing. He encourages Hyrum to magnify his calling and refers to him as "an unpolished gem."[69] But it was not to be. Hyrum Fisher Smith was not called as Presiding Patriarch, and no official explanation was ever offered as to why John's eldest son was passed over in favor of Hyrum Fisher's eldest son, John's grandson, Hyrum Gibbs Smith.

Notes

1. Journal History, Archives of the Church of Jesus Christ of Latter-day Saints, Salt Lake City (hereafter LDS Church Archives). Also issues of *Millennial Star*, 1849–54.

2. Joseph Smith III, in Nauvoo, to John Smith, "care of Henry Phelps" at Council Bluffs, Winter Quarters, March 21, 1848, Eldred G. Smith Personal Records, Salt Lake City; photocopy of holograph in authors' possession.

3. John Smith served seven days, from April 26, 1853, to May 2, 1853, as a private in Major James Ferguson's Companies of Cavalry in an expedition sent to strengthen the settlements in the southeast part of the territory against hostile Utes. He also served seven days with George Woods's detachment in August 1853 and eleven days with Major Robert Burton against the Shoshone Indians in October 1855.

4. John and his wife always spelled her name "Hellen," but others in the family, as well as official records, refer to her as "Helen."

5. Brigham Young ordination blessing of John Smith, February 18, 1855, Eldred G. Smith Personal Records (emphasis added).

6. John Lyman Smith, Journal, Geneva, Switzerland, September 28, 1856, BYU Archives.

7. John Smith, in Salt Lake City, to Joseph F. Smith, in Hawaii, April 30, 1856, Eldred G. Smith Personal Records.

8. John Smith to Joseph F. Smith, January 31, 1856, Eldred G. Smith Per-

sonal Records. Some of the Saints would request adoption into a church leader's "kingdom." The practice was discontinued in May 1894, when President Wilford Woodruff canceled many of the existing sealings, saying church members should stay within their own families. The Nauvoo Temple Record in the Genealogical Library in Salt Lake City contains notes of cancellations.

9. John Smith to Joseph F. Smith, January 31, 1856, Eldred G. Smith Personal Records.

10. John Smith to Joseph F. Smith, May 31, 1856, Eldred G. Smith Personal Records.

11. John and Hellen Smith to Joseph F. Smith, November 3, 1856, Eldred G. Smith Personal Records.

12. Hellen Smith to Joseph F. Smith, April 4, 1857, Eldred G. Smith Personal Records. Nancy Melissa Lemmon married John Smith on February 18, 1857. They had one son, John Lemmon Smith, born March 16, 1858, who died May 1, 1867. There are few direct references to this second wife, either in John's papers or in church records, but she is mentioned as John's surviving wife in his 1911 obituary.

13. Hellen Smith to John Smith, May [date unclear] 1857, Eldred G. Smith Personal Records. In John's letter to Joseph F. Smith, August 3, 1857, Eldred G. Smith Personal Records, he adds a postscript saying, "It is reported that there is 2500 souldiers acoming out here to hang Brigham Young and all of his assosiates and also those that will not put away Polygamy."

14. Hellen Smith to John Smith, February 20, 1860, Eldred G. Smith Personal Records.

15. John Smith to Joseph F. Smith, April 18, 1860, Eldred G. Smith Personal Records. The Reorganized Church of Jesus Christ of Latter Day Saints was founded April 6, 1860. The group had its beginnings in 1851, and a first conference was held in 1852. Members had been assured that "ere long one of the seed of the Prophet Joseph Smith would be called of God to take charge, as leader, of the scattered sheep." Richard P. Howard, ed., *The Memoirs of President Joseph Smith III, 1832–1914* (Independence, Mo.: Herald Publishing, 1979), 72.

16. Brigham Young, April 16, 1854, cited in Fred C. Collier, ed., *Teachings of President Brigham Young, 1852–1854*, 3 vols. (Salt Lake City: Collier's, 1987), 3:294.

17. *Deseret News*, July 6, 1854.

18. John Smith, Missionary Journal, Eldred G. Smith Personal Records; typescript in authors' possession.

19. Ibid., January 22, 1863.

20. Ibid., February 25, June 16, and July 8, 1863.

21. Ibid., July 2 and 25, 1863.

22. John Smith to Hellen Smith, from Copenhagen, September 23, 1863, Eldred G. Smith Personal Records; photocopy of holograph in authors' possession.

23. John Smith, Missionary Journal, December 4 and 5, 1863, and March 22, 1864.

24. John Smith to Hellen Smith, n.d. [1862 or 1863], Eldred G. Smith Personal Records.

25. Ibid., January 19, 1863.

26. Ibid., October 12, 1863.

27. John Smith to Joseph F. Smith, from Copenhagen, January 2, completed January 7, 1864, Eldred G. Smith Personal Records.

28. Ibid., June 8, 1863.

29. James R. Clark, ed., *Messages of the First Presidency of the Church of Jesus Christ of Latter-day Saints, 1833–1964*, 6 vols. (Salt Lake City: Bookcraft, 1965–75), 2:229–31.

30. Lucy Mack Smith, *History of the Prophet Joseph Smith*, revised by George A. Smith and Elias Smith (Salt Lake City: Improvement Era, 1902). The preface to this edition, reproduced as the "Introduction to First Utah Edition," in Lucy Mack Smith, *History of Joseph Smith by His Mother, Lucy Mack Smith*, with notes and comments by Preston Nibley (Salt Lake City: Bookcraft, 1958), vii–viii, expresses the disappointment of many of the authorities "at the necessity of issuing the [earlier] order to temporarily suppress its further circulation." It was believed that "old and young will be pleased as well as benefitted by the perusal of its pages, and . . . that it may inspire them with renewed zeal. . . ."

31. Jan Shipps, *Mormonism: The Story of a New Religious Tradition* (Urbana: University of Illinois Press, 1985), 101.

32. John Smith to Hellen Smith, March 30, 1864, Eldred G. Smith Personal Records.

33. *Deseret Evening News*, November 7, 1911.

34. John Smith to Emma Smith Bidaman, in Nauvoo, December 2, 1866, Eldred G. Smith Personal Records.

35. Alexander H. Smith, in San Bernardino, to John Smith, San Bernardino, February 8, 1867, Eldred G. Smith Personal Records.

36. Wilford Woodruff, Journal, October 9, 1875, LDS Church Archives.

37. Merle Graffam, ed., *Salt Lake School of the Prophets Minute Book, 1883* (Palm Desert, Calif.: ULC Press, 1981), 48. B. Carmon Hardy drew our attention to this reference. The Word of Wisdom is a health law requiring Mormons to abstain from the use of tea, coffee, alcohol, and tobacco.

38. Ibid., 54.

39. Abraham H. Cannon, Diary, April 6, 1884, LDS Church Archives.

40. Conversations between Ralph Smith and E. Gary Smith.

41. Blessing given by Patriarch John Smith to Nancy Naomi Tracy, Huntsville, Utah, January 30, 1869, Joseph Geisner Family Records, Santa Rosa, Calif.

42. John Taylor to George Q. Cannon, November 7, 1877, John Taylor Papers, Special Collections, Marriott Library, University of Utah, Salt Lake City.

43. Ibid.

44. John Smith to Joseph F. Smith, June 6, 1887, LDS Church Archives.

45. John Smith to Joseph F. Smith, February 25, 1887, LDS Church Archives, replying to an old letter from Joseph F. dated January 26, 1885, which he had mislaid.

46. Wilford Woodruff to John Smith, January 20, 1888, LDS Church Archives. By this time members of the church hierarchy were drawing a subsistence allowance from church funds.

47. D. Michael Quinn, "The Mormon Hierarchy, 1832–1932: An American Elite" (Ph.D. diss., Yale University, 1976), 125–31.

48. John M. Whitaker, "Journal of John M. Whitaker," October 1, 1894, LDS Church Archives, cited in Paul H. Peterson, "An Historical Analysis of the Word of Wisdom," (M.A. thesis, Brigham Young University, 1972), 78. In 1894 the General Authorities were still divided on whether the Word of Wisdom was a commandment or the advice of a loving Father. Also at this time several of the General Authorities were having problems themselves. For details, see *Dialogue: A Journal of Mormon Thought* 14 (Fall 1981). The issue includes essays by Lester E. Bush, Jr., "The Word of Wisdom in Early Nineteenth-Century Perspective," 47–65; Robert J. McCue, "Did the Word of Wisdom Become a Commandment in 1851?" 66–77; and Thomas G. Alexander, "The Word of Wisdom: From Principle to Requirement," 78–88. See also James N. Kimball, "More Words of Wisdom," *Sunstone* 10 (March 1985): 41.

49. Woodruff, Journal, November 7, 1841.

50. Heber J. Grant, General Conference Address, October 6, 1894, Journal History, LDS Church Archives. Historically, there had been resistance to enforcing what was deemed "a principle with a promise." Brigham Young himself, while condemning infractions of the health law and often referring to it as a commandment, displayed a more tolerant attitude than some of the other leaders. On April 7, 1861, he said, "Some of the brethren are very strenuous upon the 'Word of Wisdom' and would like to have me preach upon it, and urge it upon the brethren, and make it a test of fellowship. I do not think I shall do so. I have never done so." *Journal of Discourses by Brigham Young, President of the Church of Jesus Christ of Latter-day Saints, His Two Counsellors, the Twelve Apostles and Others*, 26 vols. (Liverpool: Latter-day Saints Books Depot, 1855–86), 9:35.

51. Conversation between E. Gary Smith and Samuel S. Smith, August 8, 1980.

52. John W. Taylor, *Conference Reports of the Church of Jesus Christ of Latter-day Saints* (Salt Lake City: Church of Jesus Christ of Latter-day Saints, October 6, 1900), 30.

53. Reed C. Durham, Jr., and Steven H. Heath, *Succession in the Church*, (Salt Lake City: Bookcraft, Inc., 1970), 117–18. Durham quotes the October 17, 1901, journal entries of Brigham Young, Jr. and Marriner W. Merrill, respectively, as: "Pres Smith was set apart by all present, his brother Patriarch Jno. S. being mouth by his request," and "Joseph Smith was unanimously sustained as the President and was set apart as such by his brother, Patriarch John Smith."

54. Ibid., 119.

55. John Taylor, "Patriarchal," *Times and Seasons* 6 (June 1, 1845): 922. The question of succession was decided on April 5, 1900, when it was agreed at a council meeting that the Prophet's naming of Hyrum as his successor was "a departure from the general rule . . . the Church had been at sea regarding a

successor to Joseph . . . this was a special revelation from the Lord appointing him; but there had been no departure since the death of Joseph from the rule that now prevails." John Henry Smith, Diary, April 5, 1900, photocopy of holograph in George A. Smith Family Collection, Manuscripts Division, Special Collections, Marriott Library, University of Utah, Salt Lake City.

56. Frank J. Cannon, *Under the Prophet in Utah* (Boston: C. M. Clark, 1911), 248–49. Even as late as January 25, 1973, George F. Richards, Jr., Oral History Interview, No. 11, LDS Church Archives, commented, "Before I went on a mission with father I heard some people complaining that there were too many Smiths in the authority of the Church and it was reputed to have been mentioned to Hyrum M.[Smith] on one occasion, and he answered the observer to the effect that 'The Lord knows what he can do if there are too many of us.'"

57. President Joseph F. Smith, *Conference Reports,* November 10, 1901, 71.

58. Ibid.

59. John Henry Smith, Diary, April 6, 1902.

60. Brigham Young, Jr., Journal, April 6, 1902, New York Public Library, also in LDS Church Archives.

61. John Henry Smith, Diary, June 25, 1902.

62. James B. Allen and Glen Leonard, *The Story of the Latter-day Saints* (Salt Lake City: Deseret Book, 1976), 457.

63. Joseph Smith III to John Smith, December 20, 1909; John Smith to Joseph Smith III, December 29, 1909, Eldred G. Smith Personal Records.

64. Joseph Smith III to John Smith, July 7, 1911, Eldred G. Smith Personal Records.

65. For example, John corresponded with Josephine, the daughter of Don Carlos Smith, the Prophet's youngest brother. Judging by a letter dated July 3, 1908, she seemed quite bitter toward the Utah church but said, "Do not doubt my love for you, good boy and good man that you have always been. I do not forget you nor *anything.*" Eldred G. Smith Personal Records; photocopy in authors' possession.

66. For example, Mary Ann Dowdle, June 25, 1869, in John Clark Dowdle Journal, BYU Archives; Eliza Melissa McGary, March 1, 1875 [unclear], Archives of the Reorganized Church of Jesus Christ of Latter Day Saints, Independence, Mo.; Donnette Smith, April 19, 1882, in Donnette Smith Keeler, "Reminiscences of Donnette Smith Keeler," LDS Church Archives; Lydia Clawson, May 10, 1910, in Rudger Clawson Papers, Special Collections, Marriott Library, University of Utah, Salt Lake City.

67. Blessing of Charlotte Cornwall by Patriarch John Smith, October 27, 1882, cited by Marie Cornwall, "The Gender Question," *Sunstone* 13 (December 1989): 47.

68. *Deseret News,* November 7, 1911.

69. John McDonald to Hyrum F. Smith, November 7, 1911, Eldred G. Smith Personal Records; photocopy in authors' possession.

7

A Question of Primacy

Hyrum G. Smith—Sixth Patriarch, 1912–32

The Presiding Patriarch . . . holds the keys of the Patriarchal blessings upon the heads of all the people. . . . It is his duty, also, to
preside over all the evangelical ministers, or patriarchs, of the
whole church."

—*Improvement Era,* December 1912

President Joseph F. Smith gave little explanation when Hyrum Fisher
Smith, John's oldest son, was not called as Presiding Patriarch following
John's death. Hyrum F. was born in 1856 and was fifty-five years old when
his father died in November 1911. He was primarily a blacksmith and a
farmer, taking responsibility for working the farmlands that came into
his father's possession. He married Hannah (Annie) Marie Gibbs in 1878,
and they had nine children between 1879 and 1902.[1] Hyrum F. was an easy-
going person, known to his grandson as an expert carver of jewel boxes,
rattles, and puzzles. Although Hyrum F. did not have much education,
John Smith would often call on his oldest son to act as scribe when giving blessings, and he demonstrated good penmanship.[2] When he was thir-
ty-nine, he was appointed "Judge & Clerk of Election for Hoytsville Pre-
cinct, Summit County."[3]

Private correspondence reveals several possible reasons why Hyrum F.
was not called to succeed his father. He was separated from his wife when
John died; like his father before him, Hyrum F. had difficulty observing
the Word of Wisdom; and he had demonstrated, at least in recent years,
an inability to keep steady employment or to support his family.[4]

Yet there were those who had faith in Hyrum F. His friend John Mc-
Donald gave him some advice:

Hyrum, we were boys together, we have visited each other through life, we have each other's welfare at heart. therefore what I say may it be taken in the spirit in which it is written Realizing that a word or two in a time like this might make a deep impression. No doubt you are the man to take your Father's place. There is no greater calling. Brother magnify this calling, lay aside the Hoe & Trowel, never mind the cracks in your hands, a little ointment will heal them, remember our Father's work is pressous and thrust in the sycle and reap a blessing like your Father has. You know I know you, and I firmly believe you will surprise many. There are few that know how hard you have studied to prepare yourself and very few know the power of God and what He can do with an unpolished Gem. . . . You may think you are weak but God takes the weak things of the earth to confound the mighty.[5]

Even the family, which had first-hand experience with some of Hyrum F.'s problems, thought that he would not be overlooked by the hierarchy. When John Smith died, Hyrum Gibbs Smith, the oldest son of Hyrum F., was living in Los Angeles, having graduated June 15, 1911, as valedictorian of his dental class at the University of Southern California.[6] He was also serving as president of the Los Angeles branch of the church.[7] Hyrum G. came to Salt Lake City for his grandfather's funeral, and, upon his return to California, he wrote to his father with advice for what he assumed would be the elder Hyrum's call to the patriarchate: "I hope that you are trying to forget the *past* and preparing for the *future*. Get some *chewing gum* and peppermint candies or something of that nature for a while instead of getting that 'Good Luck' or 'Battleax.' I hope you will have no trouble in making your final settlement with one another. I was pleased to see the way Mama acted toward you, and I think if you are careful and make necessary provisions that you can erase the *past* that has been so unpleasant and hurtful to us all."[8]

Succession in the line of direct lineal descent would not be automatic, however. President Joseph F. Smith certainly had a strong interest in keeping the office important and within the Smith family. He faced a dilemma, though: his nephew, Hyrum Fisher Smith, was not a man easy to champion. President Smith apparently chose to abdicate the responsibility for choosing a successor, leaving it to the Quorum of the Twelve, as long as they restricted their choice to the lineal descendants of John Smith.[9] He must have known that the Smiths in the Quorum would adequately protect Smith family rights in this case, while handling the delicate matter of a less-than-acceptable heir apparent.

On March 12, 1912, George F. Richards and George Albert Smith were in Southern California meeting with the California mission president,

John Smith with his sons, John (*center*) and Hyrum Fisher (*right*). Courtesy of E. Gary Smith.

Hyrum Fisher Smith Family. *Left to right:* Hyrum Fisher Smith, John Gibbs Smith (*front*), Hyrum Gibbs Smith (*rear*), Hannah (Annie) Maria Gibbs Smith, and Mary Hellen Smith. Taken about 1885. Courtesy of E. Gary Smith.

Hyrum Fisher Smith, 1856–1923. Eldest son of John Smith. Courtesy of E. Gary Smith.

Hannah (Annie) Maria Gibbs Smith, 1862–1924. Wife of Hyrum Fisher Smith. Courtesy of E. Gary Smith.

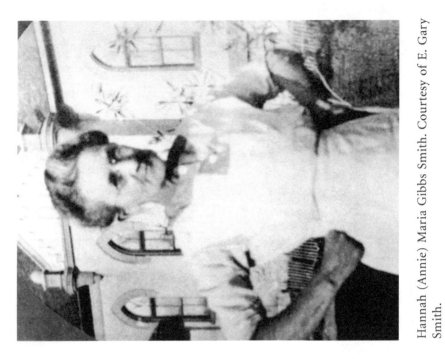

Hannah (Annie) Maria Gibbs Smith. Courtesy of E. Gary Smith.

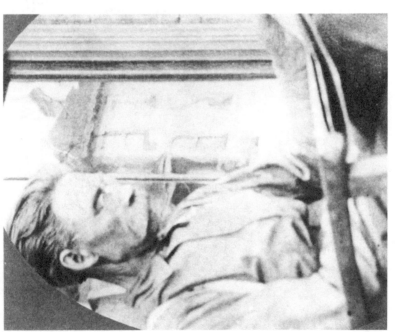

Hyrum Fisher Smith. Courtesy of E. Gary Smith.

Joseph E. Robinson. Robinson took them to the office of the Los Angeles branch president, Hyrum G. Smith, where "they put Hyrum through a lot of questions as to his life and faith etc. all of which he answered satisfactorily."[10] Robinson added his endorsement to Hyrum's character and wrote in his diary, "He is a fine fellow. Of course we all know what this catechism means. He said to George A. when the latter said 'Hyrum I'm glad my ~~good~~ dear brother that you could answer as you did the questions of the brethren.' Hyrum replied, 'I have no concern about them inquirying into my own life but I do wish I knew what they were going to do with my father.' Geo. A. told me this. It means Hyrum for Patriarch I guess and I will have to hunt up another Branch President for the Los Angeles Branch."[11]

Between Hyrum's interview and the announcement of the decision in the April 1912 General Conference, the children of Hyrum F. struggled with what they saw as a humiliating experience for their father. Although John, a younger brother of Hyrum G., had frequently been critical of his father, he was furious when his father was passed over as Patriarch. John wrote to his older brother warning him not to accept the calling—that it would be like taking his father's birthright. He suggested in his letter that it would be better to let "young Joe" (Joseph Fielding Smith, Jr.) have the office, and he predicted trouble at the local stake conference over it. John was angry that "Ol Joe" (President Joseph F. Smith) left the matter to the Twelve rather than defending the rights of Hyrum Fisher Smith.[12]

Predictably, Hyrum Fisher Smith felt bad about being passed over. This was a calling he had expected to be automatic, based on lineal rights of the Smith family. The general feelings were expressed by President Robinson, however: "It is evidently his own fault and none others are to blame." Robinson's diary entry concludes, "Hyrum [G. Smith] is filled with conflicting emotions—poor fellow!—but he sees and will do the right."[13]

On March 21, 1912, Apostle James E. Talmage recorded a meeting of the Twelve where "consideration was given to the functions of the office of the Patriarch to the Church, generally known as the Presiding Patriarch. A detailed report of the proceedings was made to the First Presidency."[14] Although this report is not available, it can be assumed that the nature of the office, as manifested in the incumbency of Hyrum G. Smith, reflected the consensus of the Twelve in that meeting.

At the April 1912 General Conference in Salt Lake City, President Joseph F. Smith said that Hyrum G. Smith, who was "selected to fill the vacancy resulting from the death of the late Patriarch John Smith, is a literal descendant of John Smith, but he is his grandson, and not his own son." The president went on to describe the new patriarch:

[He is] a clean, pure, intelligent boy; he has been faithful and exem-
plary throughout all his life, and has never been addicted to any habits
that he had to abstain from. . . . The question of looking over the children and grandchildren of the Patriarch was submitted to the Twelve
Apostles, as it is the duty of the twelve apostles to look after, and select, and ordain evangelists in the church; and after due consideration,
they have unanimously recommended the grandson of the late Patriarch to fill the place of his grandfather.[15]

Hyrum G. was ordained a high priest and the Presiding Patriarch on
May 9, 1912, by President Joseph F. Smith. The journal entry of Apostle
Talmage for that day, after noting the hereditary nature of the office, comments, "In this instance the son of the late Patriarch, and father of the
new Patriarch, viz., Hyrum Fisher Smith, was not considered worthy of
this high ordination. The newly ordained Patriarch is understood to have
been a man of honorable life and no one who needs reformation to make
him eligible."[16]

Hyrum G. Smith seemed an ideal candidate for the office of Presiding
Patriarch in a church gaining respectability in the larger society. Intelligent and faithful, he was happily married to Martha Gee, great-grand-
daughter of Asael Smith (brother of Joseph Smith, Sr.).[17] They had eight
children between 1905 and 1927.[18] Hyrum G. Smith was not only devoted
to the church but also still in the direct line of eldest-son succession in
an hereditary office.

Included in the ordination blessing by President Smith were the words,
"And we set you apart to be the Presiding Patriarch of the Church of Jesus
Christ of Latter-day Saints in succession to your ancestors."[19] The church
magazine, the *Improvement Era,* announcing the new patriarch, reiterated the description of the office: "The Presiding Patriarch . . . holds the
keys of the Patriarchal blessings upon the heads of all the people, that
whoever he blesses shall be blessed, whatsoever he binds on earth shall
be bound in heaven. . . . It is his duty also, to preside over all the evangelical ministers, or patriarchs, of the whole church."[20]

There was no doubt that he was to be an officer with presiding authority in the church. Perhaps in Hyrum G. Smith, more than in any patriarch before or since, there was the ideal combination of a lineal and
institutional officer. The hierarchy of the church, however, regarded his
ability to function so well in that capacity as a mixed blessing. President
Joseph F. Smith not only approved of Hyrum G.'s assertiveness but also
probably encouraged it; President Heber J. Grant, the second president
under whom Hyrum G. would serve, regarded it as unjustified usurpa-
tion of authority.

Hyrum Gibbs Smith, 1879–1932. Sixth presiding patriarch, 1912–32. Taken when he was a young man. Courtesy of E. Gary Smith.

Hyrum G. Smith upon graduation as valedictorian of his class at the University of Southern California Dental College. It was inscribed, "To Uncle Joseph F.," and sent in 1911 from 1232 South Flower Street, Los Angeles. Courtesy of E. Gary Smith.

Martha Electa Gee Smith, 1883–1968. Wife of Hyrum Gibbs Smith, sixth presiding patriarch. Taken early in their marriage. Courtesy of E. Gary Smith.

The new patriarch commenced his duties immediately. Barely four weeks after his ordination, Hyrum G. called on President Joseph F. Smith and was successful in gaining his approval of a new plan for keeping patriarchal records.[21] During the months that followed, the Patriarch attended many stake conferences, meeting with stake presidents and other leaders, where he would give instructions and counsel to local patriarchs. He presided at many of these meetings, even when members of the Quorum of the Twelve were present. At the General Conference, too, he presided over meetings of patriarchs, answering questions and giving direction.[22]

At one of these gatherings, on April 5, 1913, Hyrum G. was asked to give a ruling on stake patriarchs' charging a fee for blessings. He replied, "We may receive a blessing from those whom we bless. If they wish to give."[23] Sixteen months later, though, the Patriarch cautioned that patriarchs should never permit anyone who has received a blessing to leave feeling that they have paid for that blessing: "Patriarchal blessings cannot be purchased, they are the free gifts of God to his children under the hands of His Patriarchs."[24]

Patriarch Smith also provided moral support for these local patriarchs. On September 8, 1912, several diary entries refer to the patriarchs by name, followed by the reminder "write and encourage" or "instruct and encourage," and there is mention of their visiting him at his home.[25] On many occasions he warned the patriarchs against making extravagant promises and finally included that advice in a circular of instructions sent to all newly ordained patriarchs.[26] He also asked that patriarchs not "unduly advertize ourselves."[27]

In 1922 the Patriarch counseled Joseph A. Quibell, a local patriarch, about "cranks" and others who go about trying to get a blessing from every patriarch they meet: "I think every member of the Church should have at least one blessing . . . and for that purpose the stake patriarchs are placed in the church—as it is an utter impossibility for the Patriarch of the Church to bless all the people. I think all members of the Church may receive blessings in the stakes, and then those who are fortunate enough may receive one from the Presiding Patriarch—then they should be *well blessed* for this *life*."[28]

All of this activity suggests that Hyrum G. took the title of Presiding Patriarch seriously. In his diary during May 1913, he included biographical information about all the previous patriarchs. "Joseph Smith, Sr.," he wrote, "was the first president of the High Priesthood in this dispensation."[29] Although Hyrum G. Smith had no aspirations to be president of the church, he quietly concurred with the statement made in General Conference by his uncle, President Joseph F. Smith, that the Patriarch should be sustained first in the order of General Authorities, as set out

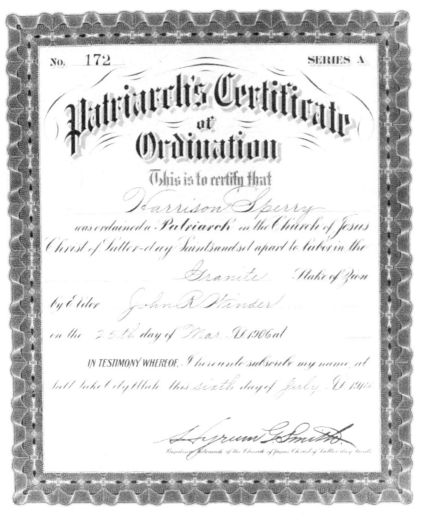

Ordination certificate for the stake patriarch Harrison Sperry issued during the incumbency of Hyrum G. Smith. After President Joseph F. Smith's death in 1918 and before Hyrum G. Smith's death in 1932, in addition to signing all certificates, Hyrum G. Smith ordained 12 out of 276 patriarchs. Courtesy of Gregory P. Christofferson.

RECORD OF PATRIARCHAL BLESSINGS

This record is the property of the Church of Jesus Christ of Latter-day Saints and when the labors of the patriarch are completed, it should be delivered to the Stake Clerk who will forward it to the office of the Church Historian, Salt Lake City, Utah, where it will be filed as a permanent Church Record. Whenever a copy of a Patriarchal record is desired from a record that has been forwarded to the office of the Church Historian, such copy may be obtained upon application to that office.

....Full Name

....Stake of Zion

....Date Ordained

By ....

DUTIES OF PATRIARCH

Bless the worthy members of your stake where you have been called to labor and who desire blessings at your hands.

Record each blessing in your official record and give a copy signed by yourself.

According to the promptings of the Holy Spirit, declare the lineage of those you bless; pronounce blessings and promises; and seal up against the power of the destroyer until the day of redemption.

Avoid extravagant promises and do not make unnecessary repetitions of the name of Diety. Long blessings are not necessary.

A gift or offering may be accepted, but do not permit any person to leave you feeling that he has paid for a blessing. Patriarchal blessings cannot be purchased, they are the gifts of God.

The following is an appropriate heading for Patriarchal blessings and should be made uniform:

Place and date.
A blessing given by (full name,) Patriarch, upon the head of (full name) son or daughter of (father's and mother's full names) born (date at place.)

HYRUM G. SMITH,
Presiding Patriarch.

Example of communications from Presiding Patriarch Hyrum G. Smith to local patriarchs. Courtesy of Gregory P. Christofferson.

in Doctrine and Covenants 124. It may explain the actions of Heber J. Grant in 1918 if we speculate Hyrum G. might have suggested that the Patriarch might be the interim president after a president died and before a new one was chosen and that this was consistent with the primal sustaining position of the Patriarch and with the historical dimensions of the office. This would have acted as a red flag for some apostles. They need not have doubted either Hyrum's motives or his circumspection, however. His own feelings on the subject were expressed in a December 30, 1915, letter responding to a Joseph A. West inquiry about the order of sustaining General Authorities:

> The time is not opportune to publish your ~~letter~~ outline in its present form; that is in quoting revelations which place the office of presiding Patriarch in a different position to that which he is sustained at present. While there is no discount or discredit upon the revelations quoted and referred to yet I feel that this is a matter which concerns the First Presidency of the Church, and adjusted at a more opportune time. Hence, I would defer the teaching of the revelations or passages quoted. . . . [30]

The sustaining order had been a concern of the hierarchy for some time. Some members of the Twelve were probably confused about the sustaining order being tied to presidential succession rights. As recently as 1900 the Twelve had discussed the subject of seniority. They remembered that Brigham Young had ordained two of his sons as apostles, without first submitting their names for approval to the Quorum of the Twelve or to the general church membership. Since the senior member of the Twelve was thought to succeed to the presidency of the church, this was an important question. In that 1900 meeting the Brethren decided that George Q. Cannon, for whose ordination proper procedures had been observed, would be senior to the sons of Brigham Young.[31] In this context, therefore, the idea of the Patriarch as presiding authority, even during a brief interim period, was extremely troubling to the Twelve.

The question became pressing when President Joseph F. Smith was close to death in July 1918. Heber J. Grant, along with two other members of the Twelve, went to Anthon H. Lund and Charles W. Penrose, counselors in the First Presidency, to neutralize what they anticipated might be a claim by Hyrum G. Smith to be the presiding authority in the event of the death of President Smith. They reiterated their understanding that the senior member of the Council of the Twelve should succeed as president. Although they avoided discussing any distinction between temporary presiding authority and selection of a new president, it is likely they feared an interim president would have leverage to claim permanent presidential authority. Even a temporary grant of ultimate authority was totally unacceptable.

Lund and Penrose agreed but decided not to trouble President Smith about the matter.[32] Indeed, neither Grant nor the counselors wished a deathbed statement from President Smith that might support the claims Hyrum G. Smith quietly asserted. The apostles were probably aware that Hyrum G.'s proddings between 1912 and 1918 had been with the approval if not the encouragement of the president.

This incident helps explain why President Grant wanted to do away with the hereditary nature of the office altogether fourteen years later. When Heber J. Grant became president of the church four months after this discussion, in late 1918, the Patriarch continued to be sustained in the customary order, to wit, after the First Presidency and Council of the Twelve. On January 2, 1919, Apostle James E. Talmage recorded in his journal the formalization of the sustaining order:

> At intervals for years past, the Presiding Patriarch of the Church has called the attention of the brethren, mostly in private conversation, to the fact that he finds an inconsistency in the order of the presiding officials of the Church, as these are presented today for the vote of the people, in comparison with Doctrine and Covenants, Section 124, verses 124 & 125. He has repeatedly asked for a consideration of the matter. Today the decision of the First Presidency and Twelve was made a matter of record to the effect that the Presiding Patriarch of the Church ranks in the order of office between the Council of the Twelve and the First Council of Seventy. . . . Revelations to and history combine in making plain the fact that no officer stands between the Council of the Twelve and the First Presidency of the Church.[33]

Talmage goes on to point out, insightfully, that this was not the place that the Presiding Patriarch had claimed. He had asked whether "in view of the Lord's having mentioned his great-grandfather Hyrum Smith first in order of the Priesthood, is not that of the first officer of the church, ahead of the First Presidency." Talmage concluded that "it was the unanimous decision of the Council that the order heretofore observed shall be maintained, unless the Lord reveals another course as the one to be followed."[34] President Grant also adjusted the seating of the Patriarch in the meetings of the General Authorities from between the First Presidency and Council of the Twelve to below the Council of the Twelve.

There is every indication that President Grant and Patriarch Hyrum G. Smith had a warm and respectful personal relationship. Hyrum G. was twenty-four years President Grant's junior, but he possessed many of the personal qualities Grant admired. He was intelligent, well educated, and energetic. They continued to have conflict over the parameters of the patriarchal office, though. During a testimony meeting of the General Authorities, when Hyrum G. expressed a special gratitude for a privilege that none of the others had, that of appointing and ordaining his successor, President Grant corrected him. Ignoring historical precedent, the president said that "no one possessed privileges not held by the President of the Church."[35] While Grant correctly stated the current fact of the matter according to his authority as president of the church, Patriarch Smith was historically correct. The second patriarch, Hyrum Smith, had been appointed and ordained by his own father. When Brigham Young ordained Hyrum's son John, he had said "[We confer] on thee [the office of Patriarch] with the keys as thy grandfather Joseph Smith [Sr.] held them, who conferred them on your father Hyrum Smith, so we confer them instead of thy father, who would have conferred them on thee if he had been alive."[36]

President Grant had not changed Hyrum G.'s views on the subject. When Hyrum G. Smith became seriously ill early in 1932, he was still operating according to his understanding of the earliest family rights to a divine calling. He asked his wife, Martha, to bring his eldest son to him so he could ordain Eldred to the office of Patriarch. Martha reproved Hyrum for imagining he was going to die (he was only fifty-two years old), and the Patriarch accepted her optimistic judgment. He died a few days later without ordaining his son.[37]

Despite health problems, Hyrum G. Smith had been vigorous in fulfilling his duties. He traveled throughout the Northwestern States Mission in 1928, and during that time his letters to Martha reveal the love he had for his family and the sacrifice he had been called upon to make in being away from them.[38] His tour of the mission was apparently not for the purpose of giving blessings, because in one letter to Martha he says, "Everywhere we stop the people are disappointed that I have not come to give them their Patriarchal Blessings but I could not do it and do the other work too. So I just tell them to come to my office when they come to Salt Lake."[39]

Although Patriarch Hyrum G. Smith gave 21,590 recorded blessings during his nineteen years in office, more than any other patriarch gave, he never received a patriarchal blessing himself. At one time he did have an appointment with his grandfather, John Smith, to receive his patriarchal blessing; however, when he met with the Patriarch, John said he did not feel inspired to give one at that time. It was not unusual for John to do this. Hyrum G. did not bother to make any further appointment, saying that his grandfather would approach him when he felt so inclined.[40] John died before a blessing was ever given.

When Hyrum G. Smith died on February 4, 1932, at the age of fifty-two, many members of the Twelve paid tribute to him. Apostle George

Martha Electa Gee Smith, taken late in her marriage to Hyrum G. Smith. Courtesy of E. Gary Smith.

Hyrum G. Smith, taken not too long before before he died at the age of fifty-two. Courtesy of E. Gary Smith.

Hyrum G. Smith with his three sons. *Left to right:* Barden, Hyrum G., Eldred G., and Hyrum. Courtesy of E. Gary Smith.

General Authorities and their families at an outing in the Utah mountains. Patriarch Hyrum G. Smith is holding his hat and standing to the right of the man sitting in the front left. President Heber J. Grant is standing with his hat on right center. Apostle George Albert Smith is standing to the far right. Courtesy of E. Gary Smith.

Albert Smith said of him, "He was a patriarch in his temperament. . . . He was not a man to contend for a thing that he thought was right. He was modest and retiring. But when he believed he was right he was very firm in expressing himself so that his associates knew what his opinion was on such occasions."[41] Joseph Fielding Smith of the Council of the Twelve said of the Patriarch:

> During the nineteen years that he served he gave blessings to twenty-one-thousand five-hundred-ninety individuals, whose blessings are recorded. This is not all the blessings that he gave, but all that were recorded. It is a magnificent work, showing his faithfulness, his integrity, and the confidence on the part of the Latter-day Saints in him and his mission. . . . How greatly he has been honored to hold this mighty position of responsibility and trust and power and Priesthood in the Church, standing not only as a father to the people, but as the one who held the birthright in Israel, the first-born among his brethren by descent, the only one who rightfully, according to the revelations of the Lord, could stand in this place and speak with power and with authority.[42]

Among the letters of condolence was one from President W. R. Sloan, whose Northwestern States Mission Hyrum G. had visited earlier:

> We are all heart stricken in the Northwestern States Mission today over the untimely death of your dear husband, father, and our friend and brother. Few men have ever come into our lives that have so indelibly attached themselves to us as Brother Smith did. We have known and loved him many years, but not until he toured the mission did we really learn his true worth and noble character. . . . You have many things to be thankful for, Sister Smith, your splendid family and your illustrious son on whom I am sure a father's high and holy calling will rest. He will arise through the help of our Father to the honors that shall come.[43]

Despite the respect Hyrum G. Smith had enjoyed, he had, by his very efficiency, aroused some concern. The "Patriarch's Certificate of Ordination" used during his tenure was signed at the bottom by Hyrum G. Smith, "Presiding Patriarch." As such, he had taken on the responsibility for instructing, counseling, and encouraging local patriarchs at stake conferences as well as during general conferences of the church. He compiled and circulated printed "Instructions to Patriarchs," signed by the "Presiding Patriarch." He ordained bishoprics after consulting with the president of the church, instead of referring the matter to the Twelve. He also raised some uncomfortable questions about the primacy of his office.

When the time came to name Hyrum G.'s successor, President Grant's discomfort was evident. In dealing with what he perceived as the problematic nature of the office of Patriarch, Grant would encounter some dissonance in his relationship with the Twelve. The result was an impasse that would last ten years, from 1932 to 1942.

Notes

1. The children of Hyrum Fisher Smith and Hannah (Annie) Marie Gibbs were Hyrum Gibbs, born 1879; Mary Hellen, 1881; John Gibbs, 1883; Gertrude, 1886; Evaline, 1889; Wilford Gibbs, 1891; Ruby, 1895; Ralph Gibbs, 1899; and Annie Ruth, 1902.

2. Recorded interview with Eldred G. Smith by E. Gary Smith on June 18, 1977; typescript in authors' possession.

3. Original certificate dated October 8, 1895, Eldred G. Smith Personal Records, Salt Lake City; photocopy in possession of E. Gary Smith.

4. Hyrum F.'s son, John, mentions his father's employment problems in his letters to Hyrum F. Smith, Provo, January 9 and February 4, 1909, Eldred G. Smith Personal Records; photocopies in authors' possession. There is one possible explanation for Hyrum F.'s inability to achieve a stable financial base. As the eldest son, Hyrum F. was given the task of working on the various properties bequeathed to the Patriarch. When a farm had been developed, his father would sell it, and Hyrum F. would have to move on, which did not allow him to consolidate any enterprise of his own. Interview with Ralph Smith, Hyrum G.'s brother, June 17, 1977.

5. John McDonald to Hyrum F. Smith, November 7, 1911, Eldred G. Smith Personal Records; photocopy in authors' possession.

6. Copy of Hyrum G. Smith's commencement speech is in Eldred G. Smith's Records. Hyrum received the dental school's gold medal for operative techniques in gold.

7. Leo J. Muir, *A Century of Mormon Activities in California*, 2 vols. (Salt Lake City: Deseret News Press, 1951–52), 1:110, 435.

8. Hyrum G. Smith to his father, Hyrum F. Smith, November 17, 1911, Eldred G. Smith Personal Records.

9. *Conference Reports of the Church of Jesus Christ of Latter-day Saints* (Salt Lake City: Church of Jesus Christ of Latter-day Saints, April 6, 1912), 59.

10. Joseph E. Robinson, Diary, March 19, 1912, Archives of the Church of Jesus Christ of Latter-day Saints, Salt Lake City (hereafter LDS Church Archives). D. Michael Quinn brought this to the attention of the authors.

11. Ibid. Crossing out of "good" in the original.

12. Quoted in ibid., April 18, 1912.

13. Ibid., 210.

14. James E. Talmage, Journal, March 21, 1912, Archives and Manuscripts Division, Harold B. Lee Library, Brigham Young University, Provo, Utah. Inserted in the journal, and dated April 1912, is a list of the General Authori-

ties of the church, giving the date of birth, date installed, and date relieved of duties. First he names the president of the church and his counselors, then the Presiding Patriarch, followed by the Twelve.

15. *Conference Reports,* April 6, 1912, 59. The *Deseret News,* April 8, 1912, stated, "The fourth session of the conference held Saturday afternoon was characterized by the appointment of Hyrum G. Smith, a grandson of the late patriarch, to succeed John Smith as the presiding patriarch to the Church."

16. Talmage, Journal, May 9, 1912.

17. Asael Smith was the unofficial Patriarch to the Church between the incumbencies of William Smith and "Uncle" John Smith. Martha's father and mother were first cousins, both grandchildren of Asael Smith.

18. Their children were Cleone, born 1905; Eldred Gee, 1907; Helen, 1909; Miriam, 1913; Barden Gee, 1916; Hyrum Gee, 1919; Verona, 1923; and Donna, 1927.

19. Ordination of Hyrum G. Smith, May 9, 1912, Eldred G. Smith Personal Records.

20. *Improvement Era* 15 (December 1912): 97. This church magazine has been replaced by *The Ensign* and *The Era.*

21. Hyrum G. Smith, Diary, April [date unreadable] 1912, Eldred G. Smith Personal Records.

22. The Patriarch's diary from 1912–15 shows that he continued to preside at meetings for local patriarchs when the General Authorities were in attendance. See also Talmage, Journal, 1912–16.

23. Hyrum G. Smith, Diary, April 5, 1913.

24. Circular letter from Hyrum G. Smith to stake patriarchs, "Instructions to Patriarchs throughout the Church," August 19, 1914, Historical Department of the Church of Jesus Christ of Latter-day Saints, Salt Lake City; copy in authors' possession.

25. Hyrum G. Smith, Diary, September 8, 1912, and October 15, 1912.

26. Hyrum G. Smith, "Instructions to Patriarchs throughout the Church."

27. Minutes of Meeting of Patriarchs, April 8, 1916, LDS Church Archives; copy in Eldred G. Smith Personal Records.

28. Patriarch Hyrum G. Smith to stake patriarch Joseph A. Quibell, October 21, 1922, LDS Church Archives.

29. Hyrum G. Smith, Diary, May [date unreadable] 1913.

30. Hyrum G. Smith to Joseph A. West, December 30, 1915, Eldred G. Smith Personal Records. This question had been raised earlier by President Joseph F. Smith. Apostle John Henry Smith, Diary, April 6, 1902, photocopy of holograph in George A. Smith Family Collection, Manuscripts Division, Special Collections, Marriott Library, University of Utah, Salt Lake City, noted, "During the noon hour the Presidency and Apostles and Patriarch met and talked over the matter of the place the Patriarch of the Church would be sustained in, whether before or after the Apostles. It was decided to leave it over for the present."

31. John Henry Smith, Diary, April 5, 1900.

32. Heber J. Grant, Diary, July 3, 1918, LDS Church Archives.

33. Talmage, Journal, January 2, 1919. At about this time the Quorum of the Twelve began also to be known as the Council of the Twelve.

34. Ibid. The minutes of the meeting of the Twelve Apostles on January 2, 1919 records a very important time in the transition of authority in the office of Patriarch. President Joseph F. Smith, a familial protector of the patriarchate, had just died the prior November. Hyrum Gibbs Smith, who had served as Presiding Patriarch for eight years, voiced his concerns in that meeting as to whether his office was accorded the appropriate dimensions of authority as set forth in D&C 124:91 and 124. Without President Smith to protest, the Quorum responded robustly: No, The Patriarch is not sustained "first," nor is it "first" in any sense of true authority. No, the Presiding Patriarch should no longer be seated with the First Presidency in these meetings, but rather next to the most junior member. No, the Patriarch does not ordain anyone unless specifically authorized by a member of the Quorum. No, the orderly arrangements of portraits in the council room of the Twelve with the Patriarch's portrait next to the First Presidency is by way of "convenience in hanging" and not to indicate authority.

Later Patriarchal Blessings of the Church of Jesus Christ of Latter-day Saints, compiled by H. Michael Marquardt (Salt Lake City: Smith-Pettit Foundation, 2012), pp. xiii–xv, quoting Minutes of the First Presidency and Quorum of the Twelve Apostles, January 2, 1919, transcript in D. Michael Quinn Papers, Special Collections, Beinecke Library, Yale University, New Haven, Connecticut.

35. As told to E. Gary Smith by Eldred G. Smith.

36. Ordination of John Smith by Brigham Young, February 18, 1855, Eldred G. Smith Personal Records.

37. As told by Martha Smith to her son Eldred and related to E. Gary Smith on December 1, 1980, and reiterated February 24, 1990.

38. In one of Martha's letters to her husband she mentions her work on the general board of the church's Mutual Improvement Association. There had been some dissatisfaction with Martha's replacing another woman on some committee, and Martha comments, "I will tell you all about it when you come home, but I have never felt so much like quitting the whole thing as I do to-night." Martha Smith to Hyrum, April 29, 1928, Eldred G. Smith Personal Records.

39. Hyrum G. Smith to Martha, Spokane, Washington, May 4, 1928, Eldred G. Smith Personal Records; photocopy of holograph in authors' possession.

40. Conversation between E. Gary Smith and Patriarch Eldred G. Smith, April 19, 1984.

41. Cited by James H. Wallis, "Death of Hyrum G. Smith," typescript of draft article "Death of Patriarch Hyrum G. Smith," 7, later condensed for publication in the *Millennial Star* 94 (March 17, 1932): 168–69; also in Eldred G. Smith Personal Records.

42. Joseph Fielding Smith eulogy at the funeral of Hyrum G. Smith, quoted in Wallis, draft article "Death of Patriarch Hyrum G. Smith."

43. President and Mrs. W. R. Sloan to Mrs. Hyrum G. Smith and family, February 8, 1932, Eldred G. Smith Personal Records; photocopy in authors' possession.

8

Decade of Uncertainty, 1932–42, and the Compromise

Joseph F. Smith II—Seventh Patriarch, 1942–46

> The office that Hyrum Smith held was more than the office which subsequent patriarchs have held. . . . It is not an administrative office, it is not an executive office, it is a spiritual office.
>
> —Patriarch Joseph F. Smith II, 1944

In the 1930s the United States was desperately attempting to resolve—and survive—fundamental economic and social crises. The Great Depression forced the country's leaders to consider sometimes unprecedented breaks with tradition and procedure. Not untouched by the national situation, President Heber J. Grant was also seeking to guide the church to safer temporal havens, even if it meant breaking with ecclesiastical tradition.

In this generally uncertain period, the death of Patriarch Hyrum G. Smith in 1932 presented both an opportunity and a dilemma. Here was a chance for President Grant to break boldly with tradition and resolve what he saw as the "Patriarch problem" of the past one hundred years, while at the same time strengthening the church's position and reputation in the world. This, however, wrenched time-honored church (and scriptural) precedents such that the Quorum of the Twelve stubbornly opposed President Grant's proposal for change. With different goals for the patriarchal office, the Quorum of the Twelve and the president found themselves at an impasse. President Grant was determined to break with the precedent of lineal succession rights; the Twelve were equally committed to retaining lineal succession rights, although they wanted to eliminate the administrative (line) authority aspects of the office. For ten years, neither would concede to the other.

This decade of uncertainty for the office profoundly affected the attitudes of the church hierarchy toward the office of Patriarch for the following half-century. It also deeply affected the personal life of Eldred G. Smith, heir apparent to the lineal office, who was only twenty-five when Hyrum G. Smith died.

Choosing a successor to the office of Church Patriarch had always been considered only upon the death (or imminent death) of the incumbent. It had been a matter of designating the next one in the nearest lineal order and then determining worthiness. When Hyrum G. Smith died in 1932, not only was the concept of lineal succession questioned for the first time, but also the definition and scope of the office received considerable attention. The reasons for this can be found in the background of President Grant as well as in the development of the patriarchal office itself.

President Grant's tenure as president from 1918 to 1945 saw the transfer of the patriarchal office only once. President Grant, however, brought to the task attitudes developed over a lifetime, toward both the office and the men who occupied it. All the holders of the patriarchal office had been known intimately to either Heber J. Grant or his father, Jedediah M. Grant. Jedediah M. Grant's sister, Caroline Amanda Grant, married William Smith, brother of the Prophet and third patriarch, only a few months after Jedediah's baptism in 1833.[1] Jedediah came to know and revere Joseph Sr., the first patriarch, as well as his successor and eldest son, Hyrum. Jedediah and William Smith traveled together to Philadelphia in 1843 and worked in the Eastern States Missions until 1844, when Jedediah returned to Nauvoo.[2] After Caroline's death in May of 1845 and William's excommunication in October of the same year, Jedediah and William became enemies. Any enemy of the leadership of the church was an enemy of Grant. Jedediah Grant knew and respected Uncle John, the fourth patriarch, who died in 1854. Jedediah was a counselor in the First Presidency when he died, five days after his son Heber was born.

Heber J. Grant was made an apostle in 1882; John Smith had already been serving as the Patriarch for twenty-seven years. For twenty-nine more years, Heber and John served together as general authorities, until John's death in 1911. Grant became president of the church in 1918, and Hyrum G. Smith, who had been the Patriarch for six years at that time, served under Grant for fourteen years.

During these years, Heber J. Grant, along with other leaders, participated in creating a tightrope for incumbents in the office of Patriarch. Michael Quinn has suggested that "whenever a Patriarch to the Church after 1845 tried to magnify his presiding office, the Twelve and Presidency recoiled in apprehension that a vigorous Patriarch to the Church might wield too much authority and dare to challenge the automatic apostolic

Heber J. Grant, 1856–1945. President of the church, 1918–45. President Grant sent this photo to Patriarch Hyrum G. Smith's widow, Martha Electa Gee Smith, three months after Hyrum G. died. It is inscribed, "Sincerely Your Friend and Brother, Heber J. Grant." Courtesy of E. Gary Smith.

succession that has existed since 1844. But when individual Patriarchs to the Church after 1845 seemed to lack administrative vigor, the Quorum and Presidency criticized them for not magnifying their office."[3]

John Smith (1854–1911) fell in the latter of Quinn's two categories. Administrative vigor was not his forte. This, along with John's failure to live by the Word of Wisdom strictly or to embrace polygamy enthusiastically, had been an aggravation to Grant. As John was growing older, Heber J. Grant was a young product of the reformation-attitude his father had helped initiate. Grant valued businesslike aptitude in church leaders, was a confirmed polygamist, and the most strident advocate of strict adherence to the Word of Wisdom that the church has ever known. In short, John was not the kind of Smith young Heber saw as befitting the office of Presiding Patriarch. This undoubtedly influenced Heber J. Grant's conclusion that lineal succession was not appropriate for the office of Patriarch.

There was another reason for Grant's opposition to the office of Patriarch as it had been known. Grant, sixth in seniority in the Council of the Twelve, was present at the emergency meeting held during that noon hour in 1902 following President Joseph F. Smith's announcement that the Patriarch should be sustained first among the General Authorities. He was present when they discussed it again the following June. Although the sustaining order was not changed, the attempt itself was a menacing memory. After Hyrum G. Smith became the Patriarch, the question of order of sustaining persisted. There was also Hyrum G. Smith's possible private assertion that his office would be the presiding authority in the interim between the death of a president and the selection of a new one. The question had again been raised in July of 1918, when President Joseph F. Smith was ill and felt to be close to death. As discussed in the previous chapter, Heber J. Grant and two other members of the Twelve went to Anthon H. Lund and Charles W. Penrose of the First Presidency to neutralize what Heber J. Grant anticipated might be a claim by Hyrum G. Smith to be the presiding authority in the event of President Smith's death.[4]

The occasion followed by many years Heber J. Grant's involvement in analyzing the propriety of strict seniority in apostolic succession. In 1887, when President John Taylor was close to death, Wilford Woodruff was the senior apostle. Heber J. Grant, a junior member of the Quorum, was concerned that George Q. Cannon might want to succeed his uncle, John Taylor, as president, which would have undercut the primary position of the Quorum of the Twelve. In response to Grant's inquiries about the possibilities that the next president could be an apostle other than the senior member of the Quorum, Wilford Woodruff asked for some time to think out his answer. At that time the issue had not been decided firmly as it is today. The Twelve had been debating the subject since 1877, and

Woodruff himself had prophesied that Joseph F. Smith would become the president of the church, a prospect that would have also, at that time, involved a departure from strict Quorum seniority succession. When Woodruff wrote back to Grant on March 28, 1887, however, he emphatically confirmed that the senior member of the Twelve should always succeed as president.[5]

It was a copy of the same 1887 Woodruff letter that President Grant brought to Lund and Penrose in 1918 to shore up what he considered a possible challenge to his own ascendancy, as the senior apostle, to the presidency. At that 1918 meeting, Grant sought confirmation that, as senior member of the Council of the Twelve, he would succeed automatically as president. Lund and Penrose agreed, without discussing the question with President Joseph F. Smith.[6] It should be noted that the 1887 Woodruff letter maintains that the senior member of the Twelve should become president of the church *because* it is the Quorum of the Twelve that becomes the immediate presiding authority upon the death of a president. The senior member of the Quorum is the president of the Quorum; *therefore,* the senior member of the Quorum should be president of the church. With that reasoning, it is apparent why Grant would be concerned if Hyrum G. Smith had suggested that the Patriarch would be even the interim presiding authority. It is not surprising that Grant balked at perpetuating the hereditary nature of the patriarchal office after Hyrum G. Smith's death in 1932.

Even though Hyrum G. had enjoyed the personal respect of President Grant, he was also responsible for some of Grant's misgivings. For the first six years of Hyrum G.'s incumbency, he served under his great-uncle, President Joseph F. Smith, and was well aware of President Smith's preference to return to the original order of sustaining the General Authorities. In private conversations, Hyrum G. brought this up with his colleagues. The Patriarch also asserted openly what he perceived as his privilege of appointing and ordaining his successor, a blessing no other church official had. President Grant strongly disagreed with these positions.

Patriarch Hyrum G. Smith clearly fell into the first of Michael Quinn's categories. He attempted to fill the full limits of what he understood to be the parameters of his calling—a magnification of the office that discomforted those committed to the postmartyrdom, apostolic-oriented hierarchy. When Hyrum G. died, the stage was set for the ensuing decade of uncertainty.

Merlo Pusey, drawing on the personal papers of the George A. Smith family, recounts that following the death of Hyrum G. Smith, Heber J. Grant "asked the Twelve to pray for inspiration in the choice of a successor. George Albert Smith suggested that the office should go to Eldred G. Smith, son of Hyrum G. and a direct descendant of the first patriarch,

Joseph Smith, Sr., in accord with the usual practice. President Grant thought Eldred was too young and inexperienced; so the office was left vacant for a period."[7]

At about this same time, President Grant was in the process of selecting J. Reuben Clark, Jr., as a counselor in the First Presidency, and he wanted a man of similar stature in the office of Church Patriarch. The Quorum of the Twelve demurred. In the April 1932 General Conference of the church, President Grant therefore had no successor to announce. Instead, he said:

> I expect there will be considerable comment when I present the General Authorities seeing that we are not going to fill the vacancy in the First Presidency nor call a man to succeed Brother Hyrum G. Smith as Presiding Patriarch. Some will say: Did you ever hear of such a thing? Yes, way back in 1880, fifty-two years ago, next October, there was a vacancy in the Quorum of the Twelve that lasted for two years; then Brother Orson Pratt died, making two vacancies that lasted a little over a year. When President Brigham Young died there was no First Presidency for three or four years, and when President John Taylor died there was no First Presidency for several years. So this is not so new after all.[8]

The years that followed validated the need to prepare the membership for a substantial hiatus in the patriarchal office. President Grant filled the vacancy in the First Presidency twelve months later with the calling of J. Reuben Clark, Jr., but the Church Patriarch vacancy continued. More than a year later, on October 22, 1933, George F. Richards, Jr., wrote in his diary, "A successor to Presiding Patriarch Hyrum G. Smith some time ago deceased has not yet been appointed. It seems as if the brethren cannot agree on a successor."[9]

President Grant clearly wished to increase the number of eligible candidates for the position, if not eliminate the restrictions of lineal succession altogether. His reasons must have included (1) his personal lack of respect for prior incumbents (particularly William Smith and John Smith); (2) his reaction to what he perceived as past attempts by aggressive descendants of Hyrum Smith to usurp primal sustaining rights, if not presidential succession rights (particularly William, President Joseph F. Smith, and Hyrum G.); and (3) his discomfort with the primal and autonomous nature of an office wherein incumbents had historical precedent for ordaining, if not selecting, their own successor.

Yet, at the same time, Grant maintained that his actual reason was that the Presiding Patriarch he selected should be a man of education, experience, and perhaps prominence—all attributes not found in the twenty-five-year-old Eldred Smith in 1932. Possibly President Grant conclud-

Eldred G. Smith, taken when he was a young man. Courtesy of E. Gary Smith.

ed that if lineal succession were eliminated, then some of the nonthreat-
ening aspects of the previously distinguished office could be salvaged.
President Grant clearly wanted the hierarchy to be made up of men who
would lend prestige to the church. He had selected J. Reuben Clark, Jr.,
to be in the First Presidency during this time, even though Clark's record
of church service paled beside his prominence in government and business affairs.[10]

Grant's premise was that, in order to elevate the office of Presiding
Patriarch through the selection of a prominent, educated, and experienced
man, it was necessary to select from a larger pool of candidates. This does
not make sense, however. Even though Grant was against lineal succession for this purported reason, he did *not* object to the proposal by the
Quorum of the Twelve that the substantive authority of the office be dras-
tically and permanently circumscribed. There would be no need for a man
of such qualifications if the office were to disallow the exercise of any real
authority. It is more likely that the expressed desire for a man of stature
was a public position taken to provide an acceptable reason for oppos-
ing lineal succession at any cost.

Grant found himself caught on the horns of a dilemma. Eldred G.
Smith had completed a mission to Germany, was living the standards of
the church, and was the oldest son following a five-generation tradition.
President Grant was aware of the respect several in the Council of the
Twelve had for that tradition and had no reason to disrespect Eldred as a
person. Grant did not know Eldred personally, other than officiating at
Eldred's wedding, and made no attempt to meet or speak with him until
the stalemate between Grant and the Twelve ended ten years later. Although Eldred was only thirty-five at the end of the decade in question,
it must have been difficult for President Grant to argue Eldred's age as a
deterrent, since Grant had spoken proudly of being a stake president at
twenty-four and an apostle at twenty-six.[11] President Grant frequently
recorded in his journal his supplications to the Lord for guidance. Grant
had no sons, and most of the time he favored calling his son-in-law, Willard Smith, but was counseled against it. One report indicates that, immediately after Hyrum G. Smith's death, President Grant told a stake patriarch by the name of Whitaker that he should prepare himself for the
possibility of being called as Patriarch to the Church. The Quorum immediately objected, so Grant told Whitaker it was not possible after all.[12]

In stark contrast to Grant, the Quorum of the Twelve thought that succession should continue lineally. It wanted to revise the substance of the
office, however, to remove it as a point of friction within the hierarchy.
It wanted to accomplish this by reducing, definitionally, the responsibilities of the office. Both President Grant and the Council of the Twelve

wanted to eliminate threatening or ambiguous aspects of the office, but Grant thought the elimination of lineal succession, *along with* the substantive reductions in historic authority, was necessary.

In March 1933 members of the Twelve undertook researching the history of the patriarchate. The findings were included in a four-page memorandum written to the First Presidency by Apostle Joseph Fielding Smith, Jr., grandson of Hyrum Smith. The memo was a well-researched brief on the succession question. It quoted at length from the ordination blessing of Joseph Smith, Sr., where it speaks of rights, keys, and lineal succession: "Behold the blessings of Joseph by the hand of his progenitor *shall come upon the head of my father and his seed after him, to the uttermost*" (emphasis added by Joseph Fielding Smith, Jr.). The official *History of the Church* was quoted as saying, "Wherever the Church of Christ is established in the earth, there should be a Patriarch for the benefit of the Posterity of the Saints." Also included were verses from section 107 of the Doctrine and Covenants, which state that "the order of this priesthood was confirmed to be handed down from father to son and rightly belongs to the literal descendants of the chosen seed, to whom the promises were made." The apostle quoted from Hyrum Smith's blessing: Hyrum "SHALL STAND in the TRACKS of his father and be numbered among those who hold THE RIGHT OF PATRIARCHAL PRIESTHOOD" (emphasis in the original). The memo then reviewed the history of succession in the office, from incumbent to incumbent, demonstrating the rigid adherence to the lineal tradition.[13]

The memo discussed the calling of literal descendants of Aaron as bishops and then stated:

> I am not here trying to present any argument, but merely a statement of fact. However in discussing this question certain fundamental elements must be considered. Let me ask the following questions: Are these offices, that of Patriarch to the Church, or Presiding Patriarch, and that of Presiding Bishop, subject to the same rule, or order of descent? Are we justified in saying that the law in relation to the Bishopric does not apply to the office of Patriarch?[14] If we make an exception, wherein are we justified by scripture, or word of inspiration coming by authority?

The conclusion of the memo makes the point that the first-born in the patriarchal line has a legal right to the office of Patriarch in the same way a literal descendant and a first-born of Aaron has a legal right to the office of bishop (see figure 1).[15]

On March 22, 1933, four days after the memo was written to the First Presidency, the Twelve sent a letter to President Grant and his counselors asking four questions: What is the most accurate designation of the patriarchal office? What are the functions of the office? What line or lines

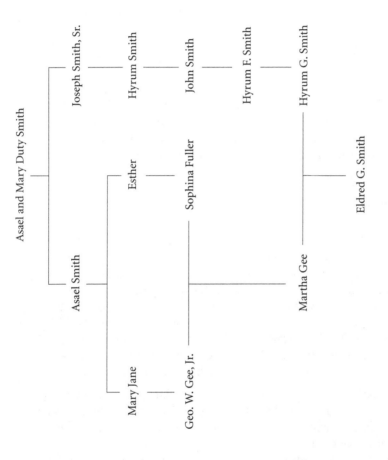

Figure 1: Eldred G. Smith Lineage in Smith Family

Eldred's mother and father were both descended from the original founding Smith family. His mother, Martha Gee, was the daughter of first cousins. The cousins' grandfather, Asael Smith, was a brother of Joseph Smith, Sr. Eldred's father's side descended in eldest son order from Joseph Smith, Sr.

of descent at the present time are eligible to hold the office? Whom shall we recommend to the First Presidency to fill the office?[16]

They then proceeded to answer these questions as follows:

1. Change the name of the office from Presiding Patriarch to Patriarch to the Church. "[The former] carries with it certain uncertainties and implications that in the past have given rise to misunderstandings with reference to the nature of the duties and powers inherent in the office, and may continue so to do."[17]

2. Define the office as being one of blessing and spiritual beneficence rather than an office of executive and administrative functions.[18] (This meant the only aspect of the office left intact was the giving of patriarchal blessings.)

3. Keep lineal succession, with preference to the oldest-son line. "Any male person in the direct lineage of Hyrum Smith, brother to the Prophet, is eligible by way of descent," but, in accordance with scripture and statements by church leaders, as well as the practice of the church both in modern times and during biblical dispensations, it was preferable that the eldest son in the direct line be appointed to the office. The letter pointed out that deviations to the rule of primogeniture have been recognized as exceptions and that when the next in line has been worthy and available, he has inherited the office because "this particular office is and always has been one that descends with the blood, the virtues of which are inherent in the blood itself."[19]

4. In view of these points, the Quorum agreed that Eldred Gee Smith should be appointed Patriarch to the Church, successor to his father, Hyrum G. Smith. It was suggested, however, that he not carry the administrative responsibility of his father. It was also emphasized that if it was decided to go to the line of President Joseph F. Smith, then the eldest son should be the one in line, even though such a procedure "seemed to be fraught with many difficulties."[20]

Despite this letter, for two years President Grant did nothing further to fill the office. In 1935 Rudger Clawson, president of the Twelve, prepared a preliminary draft of another letter to the First Presidency.[21] He pointed out that two former members of the Twelve were not present during the 1933 deliberations and that two new members had been added to the Quorum. Also, additional information was now available. The letter made the following recommendations:

1. The designation of the office should be Patriarch to the Church. It noted that any administrative or executive church duties were given to previous patriarchs by virtue of special callings, not because of the patriarchal office.

2. The rule of primogeniture should be followed in the selection of the

Patriarch to the Church: "It is clear to us, from the revelations, the history and the practice of the church, that the office of 'Patriarch to the Church' belongs to the descendants, in direct lineage, of Joseph Smith, Senior, the first Patriarch to the Church. Indeed, there appears to have been no departure from this view, and certainly not from such practice, during the history of the church. The blessing upon the head of Father Smith points definitely to a continuation of the office in his family."

3. Under this rule Eldred G. Smith, a worthy young man, should be called to be Patriarch to the Church:

> Under the rule of primogeniture, as above stated, we find ourselves unable to depart from the conclusion that, if Hyrum G. Smith's eldest son is worthy in life, and otherwise fitted for this high office, he has a rightful claim upon the office. We have made recent inquiry concerning Eldred Gee Smith, the man in question. He is clean in his life, industrious, of good intelligence, and easily above the average person in natural endowment. At home and on his mission he has conducted himself worthily. We recommend him for the office of Patriarch to the Church. . . .

4. "A departure from the rule of primogeniture or the assignment of another title or executive duties to the Patriarch to the Church should come, as discussed, as a special call from the President of the Church."

President Grant was not easily persuaded, however. This intransigence might seem ironic in view of the advice Grant gave to George Albert Smith when he was ordained as an apostle in 1903. Grant warned the new member of the Twelve not to have set goals when he attended meetings. He related a personal experience that led him to realize he would lose the Spirit if he did. Grant went on, "I can truthfully say that from that day to this, although I have a very tenacious disposition, that I have ever felt ready and willing to surrender my views and that I have not had any such feeling in my heart since to carry a point to this Council."[22]

One of the underlying problems with which church leaders were contending is apparent in the 1935 Clawson letter. They were seeking rational answers to questions that ultimately depended on nonrational sources for their solution. Concerning any possible departure from past practice, Clawson observed that the office of Patriarch was not clearly understood. Why, for instance, should the office descend from Joseph Smith, Sr.? Also, the function of the office had never been clearly revealed. Clawson assured President Grant, "In our deliberations we have been guided by the revelations given, their interpretations by leaders of the Church, and the consistent practice of the Church. We have not felt it proper for us to suggest departures from past practice." In the last sentence of the draft copy, however, Clawson reassured the president that they had kept in mind that continuous revelation was a fundamental principle of the faith and that if he should be inspired to set up a "new course of action, ~~the Council of the Twelve would support to a unit, the procedure proposed.~~"[23] This last sentence was stricken out in the draft stage of the letter—presumably because there were those in the Quorum of the Twelve who were not willing to invite the president to overrule their position on the matter. It should be remembered that George Albert Smith, great-grandson of Patriarch Uncle John Smith, and Joseph Fielding Smith, Jr., grandson of Patriarch Hyrum Smith, were both influential apostles serving in the Quorum of the Twelve at that time. They were strong proponents of lineal succession in the patriarchal calling and had lineal, and probably emotional, ties to those charismatic, family-based beginnings of the church.

While the president and the Twelve parried, Eldred G. Smith went on as best he could under the circumstances. On August 15, 1932, six months after Hyrum G. Smith's death, President Grant performed the temple wedding ceremony for Eldred G. Smith and Jeanne Audrey Ness. George Albert Smith and Joseph Fielding Smith, Jr., were the witnesses. Eldred had previously served a mission to Germany and was trying to earn enough money in the depression years to help support his widowed mother and her family of eight. Although he had studied engineering at the University of Utah and had considerable talent in that area, he did not complete college because his mother and siblings needed him to help support them. He had to quit school and work full-time.

While Eldred was growing up, his mother, teachers, and friends all told him that if he lived worthily, his call to the patriarchate would be automatic. Although he was not treated differently from his siblings, he consciously prepared for what was expected of him. Now the uncertainty following his father's death was troubling him.

In the summer of 1932 Eldred resolved to go directly to President Grant to seek a resolution. In the months since his father's death, Eldred had had no word from any church leader regarding his status. He wanted to know how to plan his life. He was intercepted by Anthony W. Ivins, a counselor in the First Presidency, as he entered the Church Administration Building. Eldred's mother, Martha, had called Ivins and asked him to intercede. Ivins took Eldred aside and told him that President Grant had three objections: (1) he was too young, (2) he had no college degree, and (3) he was not married.[24] Disheartened, Eldred left without talking with the president and made no further attempts to do so.

It was particularly difficult for Eldred during this period because the Brethren gave no public explanation either for his not being called. Most members understood that, unless the oldest son was unworthy, the call was automatic. It is no surprise that assumptions of unworthiness and conjectural gossip played havoc with Eldred's reputation.[25] Ironically, those who disregarded (or did not hear) the rumors created other prob-

Eldred G. Smith and his wife, Jeanne Audrey Ness Smith. Courtesy of E. Gary Smith.

lems for Eldred. His employer explained that Eldred did not get a promotion to store manager because he was a "six-month man." (New general authorities were called at the general conferences, which were held every six months.) Another prospective employer refused to hire him for the same expressed reason.[26] This made the difficult depression years even harder for Eldred, who was struggling to support not just his own family but also his mother and his brothers and sisters.

As the deadlock dragged on between Grant and the Twelve, stake patriarchs, including Nicholas G. Smith of the Salt Lake Stake, were authorized to bless missionaries and members from missions; however, they were never sustained as even acting in the office of Patriarch to the Church. In 1937 seventy-six-year-old George F. Richards, one of the Twelve, was sustained as Acting Patriarch to fill in until the question could be resolved. He continued in that capacity for five years.[27] His son, George F. Richards, Jr., noted the calling in his diary, saying, "This was indeed a great surprise to everybody."[28]

During this time Eldred served as a bishop's councillor, a member of the Ensign Stake High Council, and then as a bishop. He and his wife began their family.[29] Except for the college degree, the objections originally voiced by President Grant had mostly resolved themselves. Throughout, Eldred experienced great frustration as he waited for the decision to be made.

By 1942 George F. Richards wanted to be relieved of his patriarchal duties so that he could give full attention to his calling as president of the Salt Lake Temple. At each general conference during the past ten years the issue had been discussed and then tabled when the impasse appeared. Now Richards suggested a compromise that would effectively remove both primacy and primogeniture and would change the ecclesiastical status and function of the office of Church Patriarch. Richards argued the lineal aspect of the office could be satisfied by opening the call to *any* male descendant of Hyrum Smith without reference to the eldest-son line, while keeping in place the proscriptions on the power and authority of the office suggested by the Twelve. This was not a new suggestion, but apparently President Grant had recently become willing to accept the possibility of a candidate other than Willard Smith, and so the stage was set for the proposal to be renewed.

Richards reminded the Twelve that there was a member of the Joseph F. Smith family of some stature who could serve as the Patriarch: Joseph F. Smith II was the son of Apostle Hyrum M. Smith, a grandson of President Joseph F. Smith, and a professor at the University of Utah.[30] In July 1942 Richards presented his conclusions to the Twelve as to why the office could be occupied by a member of the Joseph F. Smith family instead of continuing in the John Smith family. His reasons are summarized as

George F. Richards, 1861–1945. Acting patriarch to the church, 1937–42. Courtesy of the Utah State Historical Society.

follows:

1. President Heber J. Grant wanted the change made, and the Council of the Twelve was out of harmony with him because it wanted to install the son of Hyrum G. Smith.

2. The Joseph F. Smith line was more faithful, was stronger in character, and had qualified men to fill the measure of the office.

3. Doctrine and Covenants 107:40–41 does not require patriarchal descent from father to eldest son.

4. The Old Testament does not require descent from father to eldest son.[31]

In a letter to John A. Widtsoe, dated August 12, 1942, Richards stated that "all things being equal," descent from father to eldest son might be "the proper and intended order" but that neither he nor President Grant thought that the John Smith line was an appropriate one at that time. Richards quoted Brigham Young as saying, "The right is in the family of Joseph Smith, his brothers, his sons, or some of his relations." This he felt was convincing evidence that any descendant of Joseph Smith, Sr., could occupy the position of Patriarch.[32] Richards did not acknowledge that Brigham Young's statement was made during the succession crisis of 1844, when the oldest son of Hyrum was too young to be called, and that Young was attempting to determine the next nearest relative during the boy's minority.

Richards's belief that the Joseph F. Smith family was "stronger and more qualified for the office" than the family of John Smith echoed the view of President Grant, who felt that Eldred G. Smith lacked the necessary stature for the office. Their concerns, however, apparently went much deeper. Richards objected to the idea that the Patriarch should be designated "a prophet, seer, and revelator." As for Hyrum Smith's being so described in Doctrine and Covenants 124:94, Richards suggested that "the office of prophet, seer, and revelator, does not go with the office of patriarch except in the case of Hyrum Smith. Otherwise would not all the [stake] patriarchs of the Church be prophets, seers, and revelators? This I do not regard to be the case." In fact, John Smith and Hyrum G. Smith had both been sustained as prophets, seers, and revelators, and there were other distinctions between the Patriarch to the Church and local patriarchs. Richards explained these disparities by concluding, "I know of no other patriarch having been called by revelation to be a prophet, seer, and revelator to the Church."[33] Richards apparently did not feel Hyrum's designation as prophet, seer, and revelator was connected to the patriarchal office.

One month after Richards's letter to Grant, Richards repeated his suggestions to the Twelve. On September 13, 1942, Grant called on Richards at his home and "talked freely over patriarchal matters." Grant affirmed his objections to the recommendations of the Twelve, and he revealed his choice for the office of Church Patriarch.[34] It was at this time, apparently, that Grant finally abandoned his hope that his son-in-law, Willard Smith, would become the Patriarch.

How consensus was achieved after the ten-year standoff cannot be explained definitively. However it was managed, Heber J. Grant, instead of continuing to debate the issue with the Twelve as a group, contacted each of the apostles individually. Two of those most opposed to any departure from primogeniture were George Albert Smith, great-grandson of Patriarch Uncle John Smith, and Joseph Fielding Smith, Jr., grandson of the second church patriarch, Hyrum Smith. Joseph Fielding Smith, Jr., related the circumstances of his own response many years later to Eldred G. Smith. He said that President Grant telephoned him and said that all the other members of the Quorum had agreed to the compromise appointment of Joseph F. Smith II as the Patriarch. Not wishing to be the only holdout, the apostle reluctantly agreed. Joseph Fielding Smith, Jr., learned later that George Albert Smith had not been contacted until after Grant's call to him.[35] Indeed, the diary of Apostle George Albert Smith recounts a conversation he had with President Grant on Thursday, October 1, 1942, two days before the General Conference announcement of the decision and most probably after all the other apostles had been polled:

> President Grant came to see me and we had a conversation about the appointment of a Patriarch to the Church. He feels that he will not be happy in appointing Eldred but thinks that Joseph F. Smith, son of Hyrum M. Smith [descendant of Hyrum's youngest son, Joseph F. Smith, and cousin of the Joseph Fielding Smith, Jr., in the Quorum of the Twelve], would be the right man at this time. I am very disappointed that Eldred will not be sustained. I am sure that Martha and Eldred will feel bad about it. The President has the right to make the nomination in all these matters but I have felt that Eldred was in line for the appointment and have so expressed myself several times in the years that have elapsed since the death of his father. But the President is assuming the responsibility and I will sustain his appointment.[36]

Certainly it could have been the case that everyone was tired of the issue and wanted it resolved. In any case, agreement was reached; Joseph F. Smith II would be put forward as Patriarch to the Church at the October 1942 General Conference.

During the evening of Friday, October 2, 1942, Eldred G. Smith, now bishop of the North Twentieth Ward, was attending a stake leadership meeting. He was handed a note from President Grant asking him to go immediately to the president's office at 47 East South Temple Street. Eldred went directly to President Grant's office for the first and only meeting between the two men on the subject of the patriarchal office.

President Grant advised Eldred that he was calling Joseph F. Smith II to the office of Patriarch the next day. Eldred wanted to know why he had been asked to come speak with the president if another was to be called. Grant said it was to assure Eldred that the decision had nothing to do with his worthiness. Grant explained that he could not feel right about calling a descendant of John Smith, a man who, even though the eldest son of Hyrum Smith, could not live the Word of Wisdom. Eldred pointed out that he was only five years old when his great-grandfather died and that he hardly knew him. He asked if that was not penalizing him because of something his great-grandfather did. President Grant replied, "You can put it that way if you want to." Eldred said that he had tried to live worthy of the office of Patriarch all his life and that he felt there was no reason to depart from the normal method of succession. Grant replied, "Oh, yes. I get good reports of your activity in the ward. It's not because of your unworthiness personally." But the decision was final. Eldred concluded, "Well, you're the President of the Church. That's up to you. You're responsible for that."[37]

Once more, no public explanation was given for failing to call Eldred to the office. He would again become the object of speculation. Joseph F. Smith II became Patriarch to the Church the next day.[38]

The Sunday priesthood session of General Conference followed one day after the announcement of the call of Joseph F. Smith II as the new patriarch. Bishop Eldred G. Smith attended and sat with the other bishops in the tabernacle. He was among those chosen to pass the sacrament, and when he passed the sacrament to Apostle Joseph Fielding Smith, Jr., sitting on the stand, Eldred asked if he could be among those chosen to bear testimony that day. When the members of the Council of the Twelve took microphones to members of the congregation, Eldred received one. He said that he had no ill feelings toward the church and that he sustained Joseph F. Smith in his new calling. He said that his birthright had passed him by but that they could not take away his testimony of the truthfulness of the gospel. Eldred commented years later that "maybe that was not a good expression because they criticized me for saying that after, because they said I had no birthright."[39]

There were those among the General Authorities who were pleased with his remarks, however. George Albert Smith noted in his diary, "Sunday, October 4, 1942. Tabernacle meeting began 10:00A.M. and lasted until 4:40 P.M. Testimonies were borne afterward. House full. Eldred Smith bore testimony and *pleased many people*. Broke my fast at 5:00 P.M. and went to bed exhausted. It has been a very satisfactory conference. Eldred Smith's testimony has pleased many people."[40] Not long afterward Eldred moved with his family to Oak Ridge, Tennessee, where he began work as an engineer on the federal Manhattan Project. He founded and became president of the Oak Ridge branch of the church.

With the call of Joseph F. Smith II, it had been decided that instead of having to stay with the eldest son of an incumbent, the president could call any descendant of Hyrum Smith. At the same time, the authority and function of the office were diminished. This represented an important turning point in the history of the office of Patriarch to the Church.[41] Discretion regarding future appointees and removal of any primal characteristics allowed the office to be more easily assimilated within the structure of the institution.

When the announcement of the appointment of Joseph F. Smith II was made, David O. McKay, the second counselor in the First Presidency, said, "I will repeat Elder [Joseph F.] Smith . . . is the grandson of the late President Joseph F. Smith and a great-grandson of Hyrum Smith, the Patriarch. Elder Smith's right to this office, therefore, is not only by lineage, but by direct inspiration to the President who holds the keys of this high Priesthood."[42]

When the new patriarch was ordained on October 8, 1942, the former acting patriarch, George F. Richards, Sr., noted in his journal, "At this meeting President Grant said he was sure that it was inspiration from the Lord that Joseph F. Smith had been chosen and set apart. He thanked me before the Council for initiating the move and for the information I had given them concerning the call of ancient Patriarchs etc. This I regarded as a very great compliment, as he acknowledged the inspiration in it."[43]

When the new patriarch was called to assume the office, he was head of the Speech Department at the University of Utah, and, although without a Ph.D., he had personal prestige and a demonstrated competence in public relations. He was also president of the National Speech Association. The announcement of his church appointment in the *Deseret News* twice noted that he was "a prominent member of the University of Utah faculty."[44] He was, at the time of his call, a member of the Mutual Improvement Association (MIA) General Board of the church. In his new calling the Patriarch displayed humility both in his acceptance speech in the tabernacle and in his response to the responsibilities given to him. According to his secretary, Patriarch Smith was robust, masculine, neat-appearing, well-dressed, and organized. At times he could be intimidating and was quite a contrast to her previous boss, George F. Richards, whom she described as quiet, humble, and very retiring.[45]

Without any public acknowledgment of changes in function, the title of the office became "Patriarch to the Church" instead of "Presiding Patriarch," and the incumbent was no longer allowed to ordain or supervise stake patriarchs, although he could counsel them if necessary. The Patriarch still maintained a close association with the local patriarchs, however. He was concerned for their well-being and diligent in his calling. He kept files on each stake patriarch, sent each of them birthday cards, and gave encouragement when needed. He also kept records of blessings they gave and advised the Brethren when new patriarchs were needed. He traveled to stake conferences, but always with another general authority. On these occasions he always met with the local patriarchs. He continued to be sustained in General Conference after the Twelve. He was close friends with President Grant, Harold B. Lee, Richard L. Evans, and others of the General Authorities.[46]

The parameters of the patriarchal office received some formal definition in a May 25, 1943, circular, issued by the First Presidency and entitled "Suggestions for Stake Patriarchs." The circular stated that all future stake patriarchs would be selected and ordained by the Twelve and would be supervised by the stake presidents. The circular also reaffirmed that the office was one of blessing, not of administration.[47]

One year later, in a priesthood session of General Conference on October 7, 1944, Patriarch Joseph F. Smith II attempted to reconcile the historical dimensions of the office with the current official definition. Referring to Patriarch Hyrum Smith's nineteenth-century calling as associate president during the years before the martyrdom, he stated:

> That calling [the one held by Oliver Cowdery and which was given to Hyrum at the time he was called to be Patriarch] was over and beyond his office of patriarch. He was a special witness to his brother and was shown the keys of the presidency. Now this situation has been unique in the history of the Church. Since that time that has not been necessary. There are thousands of persons who now are witnesses of the divinity of the Prophet Joseph Smith, so the office that Hyrum Smith held was more than the office which subsequent patriarchs have held. . . . It is not an administrative office, it is not an executive office, it is a spiritual office.[48]

This interpretation assisted in distancing the current office of Church Patriarch from any administrative function. While inconsistent with the actual historical authority of the calling as held by Hyrum Smith (discussed in chapter 3), it illustrates an interesting parallel between Joseph F. Smith II and Uncle John Smith with respect to their nonconfrontational incumbencies.

Joseph F. Smith II's tenure as Patriarch lasted barely four years. Disquieting allegations of some involvement in homosexual activity had earlier reached the office of the First Presidency, but, because they were re-

Joseph F. Smith II, 1899–1964. Seventh patriarch to the church, 1942–46. Courtesy of the University of Hawaii.

layed by a police captain who was also the uncle of Eldred G. Smith, the information was disregarded.[49] Joseph was a man of spiritual sensitivity and upright moral character, and the charges seemed incredible. One day in April or May 1946, Joseph did not come into the office as was usual. Later that day, one of the General Authorities came in and told his secretary that Joseph F. Smith II was not to give any more blessings. She was flabbergasted. His secretary never saw Joseph F. Smith II again. She continued to work as a secretary and arranged for several local patriarchs to come in and give blessings during the period the office was vacant.[50]

In the journals of the General Authorities, references are sympathetic, ambiguous, and discreet. On July 10, 1946, George Albert Smith, who had become president, recorded in his diary, "Met in office with Council of Presidency & Twelve. . . . Jos Patriarch case considered. Bad situation. Am heartsick."[51] The next day President Smith records, "Met in Church Council room with Presidency and Twelve. . . . Discussed condition of Patriarch Jos F."[52] The First Presidency then met with Patriarch Smith the next day, July 12. President Smith went to see the Patriarch on September 6 and noted in his diary, "a pitiable case."[53]

On September 16, George Albert wrote, "Restless night. At office 8:15. Met with Presidency and Joseph F. Patriarch Ruth Browning and son present. A. E. Bowen also listened. Regret that the evidence is not satisfactory."[54] Two days later George Albert noted, "Hyrum Smith and Harold Beecher came to consider Joseph Patriarch position."[55] On October 3 President George Albert Smith wrote that it had been decided "Joseph F. Smith Patriarch unable to carry on," and the Patriarch to the Church was released, "a sad happening."[56]

At General Conference on October 3, 1946, President McKay read to the assembled Saints a letter written by Joseph F. Smith II. Among other things, the Patriarch said:

> As you know I have been very ill for many months. While I am slowly gaining strength and hope soon again to be able to do some work, I do not know when, if at all, I shall be able to stand the full drain upon my energy incident to the office of Patriarch to the Church. As you know, the duties of the Patriarch entail heavy exhaustion. Since but one man holds that office, if he is immeasurably incapacitated, its work must in that degree suffer. I know, of course, that one neither resigns nor asks to be released from such a calling. . . . Bearing these things in mind, I am writing to say that if you desire me to carry on I shall do my best. If, however, in the circumstances, you should feel that the interests of the Church would be best served by releasing me at this time, I want you to feel at liberty to do so.[57]

President George Albert Smith's diary entry for the day states, "Tabernacle & Assembly hall filled . . . Jos F. Smith released. A sad happening."[58]

Soon after, the family left for the University of Hawaii, where Joseph F. resumed his career as a teacher of English and drama. No church trial was ever held, and no formal action was taken against him; however, the church authorities in Hawaii were instructed that Joseph F. was not to assume any responsibilities or callings. Ten years later his stake president and bishop appealed to President David O. McKay to lift the restrictions, and after it was determined that Joseph F. had confessed to his wife and had written a full confession to the First Presidency, all restrictions were lifted.[59] At the time of his death on August 29, 1964, he was serving as a stake high councillor.

By September 1946 Eldred G. Smith had returned to Salt Lake City from Tennessee, and George Albert Smith had become the president of the church. In April 1947 Joseph Fielding Smith, Jr., called to tell Eldred that the president wished to speak with him at the president's home. After questioning Eldred about his worthiness, President Smith asked Eldred to accept the calling that his father had held. On April 10, 1947, Eldred Gee Smith was ordained as Patriarch to the Church. What Heber J. Grant, now deceased, had labored so long to accomplish in terms of succession to the office, was seemingly reversed by President George Albert Smith, great-grandson of Patriarch Uncle John Smith.

Notes

1. Gene A. Sessions, *Mormon Thunder: A Documentary History of Jedediah Morgan Grant* (Urbana: University of Illinois Press, 1982), 7.

2. Ibid., 33, 34; Erastus Snow, Journal, May 11, 1843, Huntington Library, San Marino, Calif.

3. D. Michael Quinn, "From Sacred Grove to Sacral Power Structure," *Dialogue: A Journal of Mormon Thought* 17 (Summer 1984): 17.

4. Heber J. Grant, Diary, July 3, 1918, Archives of the Church of Jesus Christ of Latter-day Saints, Salt Lake City (hereafter LDS Church Archives).

5. Reed C. Durham, Jr., and Steven H. Heath, *Succession in the Church* (Salt Lake City: Bookcraft, 1970), 97.

6. Grant, Diary, July 3, 1918.

7. Merlo J. Pusey, *Builders of the Kingdom: George A. Smith, John Henry Smith, George Albert Smith* (Provo, Utah: Brigham Young University Press, 1981), 290–91.

8. *Conference Reports of the Church of Jesus Christ of Latter-day Saints* (Salt Lake City: Church of Jesus Christ of Latter-day Saints, October 3, 1942), 17. What President Grant did not acknowledge were the peculiar circumstances in 1880. At that time the anti-bigamy statute of 1862 had been affirmed as constitutional in the Reynolds test case regarding polygamy in the church.

In 1882 the Edmunds Act was approved, calling for punitive action against polygamists. The Edmunds-Tucker Act of 1887 gave teeth to the earlier law. Most of the leaders of the church had plural wives, and John Taylor was in hiding when he died in 1887. The Church Manifesto officially ending polygamy was announced in 1890.

9. George F. Richards, Jr., Diary, October 22, 1933, LDS Church Archives.

10. See D. Michael Quinn, *J. Reuben Clark, Jr.: The Church Years* (Provo, Utah: Brigham Young University Press, 1983), 16, 17, 28–43, 197, 205, 288, n.80. Thomas G. Alexander, *Things in Heaven and Earth: The Life and Times of Wilford Woodruff, a Mormon Prophet* (Salt Lake City: Signature Books, 1991), 268, points out that "those among the church leadership like Heber J. Grant who believed in the basic virtue of political, economic, and social cooperation with non-Mormons would prevail . . . the church abandoned attitudes which may have served well while a persecuted sect concentrated in the remote vastness of the West but which became potentially ruinous if not altogether irrelevant to a nationally and internationally prominent church."

11. Heber J. Grant quoted in "Taught the Youth and Lived as Example," *Church News*, May 3, 1980, 13.

12. Reported by Martha Smith to her son Eldred Smith and by Eldred to E. Gary Smith on February 24, 1990, and on other earlier occasions.

13. Joseph Fielding Smith, Memo, n.d., LDS Archives Archives; also appears as first item in Patriarchal Reference Book 18, March 18, 1933. He was quoting Joseph Smith, *History of the Church of Jesus Christ of Latter-day Saints*, 2d rev. ed., ed. B. H. Roberts, 7 vols. (Salt Lake City: Deseret Book, 1978), 3:381.

14. *Doctrine and Covenants of the Church of Jesus Christ of Latter-day Saints* (Salt Lake City: Deseret Book, 1955), 68:16–18, maintains that literal descendants of Aaron have a legal right to the office of bishop. Historically, however, bishops in the church have been chosen without any reference to their ancestry.

15. Joseph Fielding Smith, Memo; Joseph Fielding Smith also mentioned the lineal *rights* to the patriarchal office when he spoke at the funeral of Hyrum G. Smith.

16. Draft of letter written by the Council of the Twelve to President Heber J. Grant, March 22, 1933, in Council of the Twelve Correspondence, LDS Church Archives.

17. Ibid.

18. There was no mention of the directive found in John A. Widtsoe, *Priesthood and Church Government in the Church of Jesus Christ of Latter-day Saints*, compiled under the direction of the Council of the Twelve (Salt Lake City: Deseret Book, 1939). This states that the local patriarchs appointed in the branches of the church are all "subject to counsel and instruction from the Patriarch to the Church, as he is directed by the First Presidency or the Council of the Twelve" (127). This book is regarded as a permanent guide and reference regarding priesthood and its functions. Nor is John Taylor's "Patriarchal," *Times and Seasons* 6 (June 1, 1845): 921, mentioned, which states that Patriarch William Smith, by right of office, would preside over local patriarchs.

19. Council of the Twelve to Grant, March 22, 1933.

20. Ibid. When they referred to "difficulties," they probably had in mind that President Joseph F. Smith was the son of Hyrum Smith and his second wife, Mary Fielding, and that Eldred G. Smith was descended from Hyrum's first wife, Jerusha Barden.

21. Rudger Clawson to President Heber J. Grant and Counselors, April 4, 1935, in Council of the Twelve Correspondence, LDS Church Archives, cited in E. Gary Smith, "Heber J. Grant and the Office of Presiding Patriarch: A Decade of Uncertainty, 1932–1942" (Paper presented at the Mormon History Association annual meeting, Laie, Oahu, Hawaii, June 14, 1990).

22. "Instructions Given to Elder George A. Smith at the Council Meeting of the First Presidency and Apostles of October, 1903, Being the First of Their Meetings Held and Attended by Brother George A. after He Had Been Chosen and Sustained as One of the Quorum of Twelve Apostles," 9, George A. Smith Family Collection, Manuscripts Division, Special Collections, Marriott Library, University of Utah, Salt Lake City. Grant's perspective had undoubtedly changed with his advancement to the position of Prophet and President of the Church.

23. Clawson to Grant, April 4, 1935.

24. Conversations between Eldred G. Smith and E. Gary Smith on February 24, 1990, and on other earlier occasions.

25. When reminiscing with E. Gary Smith in January 1991, Eldred asked, "What are they saying now about why I am emeritus?"

26. Telephone conversation between Eldred G. Smith and E. Gary Smith, January 21, 1991. Wallace Bennett was the employer, and Adam S. Bennion was the prospective employer.

27. During the 1932–42 hiatus, other local patriarchs also assisted, such as Frank Woodbury, George F. Richards, Sr., and James H. Wallis. It is interesting that in Widtsoe, *Priesthood and Church Government* (1939), 243, the office of Patriarch to the Church is stated to be an inherited office, "but a person must be appointed and ordained by the First Presidency and sustained by a vote of the Church in order to hold the office. The office carries with it recognition as a Prophet, Seer and Revelator, and comes as a special call of the First Presidency."

28. George F. Richards, Jr., Diary, May 2, 1937. George F. Richards, Sr., had served as a local patriarch prior to his call as an apostle. During 1883 there are several entries in his diary stating that he had acted as scribe for Church Patriarch John Smith at $2.50 per day. George F. Richards, Sr., Diary, February 5, 6, and 7, 1883, LDS Church Archives.

29. Eldred G. Smith and Jeanne Audrey Ness Smith had five children: Miriam, born 1935; twins, Eldred Gary and Audrey Gay, born 1938; Gordon Raynor, born 1941; and Sylvia Dawn, born 1948.

30. This Joseph F. Smith was often referred to with "II" after his name to distinguish him from other notable Smiths with the same name.

31. George F. Richards, Sr., to the Twelve, July 1942, as paraphrased in Dale C. Mouritsen, "A Symbol of New Directions: George Franklin Richards and

the Mormon Church, 1861–1950" (Ph.D. diss., Brigham Young University, 1982), 238–40. Doctrine and Covenants 107:40–41 states, "The order of this priesthood was confirmed to be handed down from father to son, and rightly belongs to the literal descendants of the chosen seed, to whom the promises were made. This order was instituted in the days of Adam, and came down by lineage in the following manner." The verses that follow include a recital of the patriarchs from Adam to Noah.

32. George F. Richards to John A. Widtsoe, August 12, 1942, cited in Mouritsen, "A Symbol of New Directions," 237–40. Brigham Young's speech of August 8, 1844, is in Joseph Smith, *History of the Church,* 7:241.

33. Richards to Widtsoe, August 12, 1942, cited in Mouritsen, "A Symbol of New Directions," 239–40.

34. George F. Richards, Diary, September 13, 1942, cited in Mouritsen, "A Symbol of New Directions," 240–41.

35. As told to E. Gary Smith by Eldred G. Smith on several occasions, including April 12, 1983, and February 24, 1990.

36. [President] George Albert Smith [1870–1951], Diary, October 1, 1942, LDS Church Archives. See also George A. Smith Family Collection, Manuscript Division, Special Collections, Marriott Library, University of Utah, Salt Lake City.

37. Conversations between E. Gary Smith and Eldred G. Smith, including February 4, 1990, and other earlier occasions. The journals of Heber J. Grant at the LDS Church Archives were not available at the time of first publication of this book, but now, through the Quinn Papers at Yale Library as quoted by Marquardt in *Later Patriarchal Blessings of the Church of Jesus Christ of Latter-day Saints,* p. xxv, the following quote from Grant's journal for October 2, 1942 is now available:

At 6 o'clock Eldred Smith, son of Hyrum G. Smith, who had expected always to be named as Patriarch to the Church, called at my request and I told him that the unanimous vote of all the brethern of the Presidency and Apostles was for Joseph F. Smith, commonly konwn as Joseph F. Smith, III, that he had been decided upon to be sustained as Patriarch to the Church. He wanted to know what he had done that he could not succeed his father. I told him there were no charges of any kind against him, but the inspiration for the brethren was that the line should be changed from John Smith, his great grandfather, to Joseph F. Smith's grandson. He said he could not understand it, he had tried to live a perfect life, etc. It was anything but a pleasant task to tell him. He said that he would of course sustain whomever the Presidency and the Apostles decided to choose. He manifested a good spirit, but of course was greatly disappointed and I could not blame him. He felt it would be a great disappointment to his mother, she had felt that he was sure to be sustained as the Patriarch. It was one of the most unpleasant tasks I have ever had. . . . I took a warm bath and tried to get to sleep tonight, but had a miserable night.

38. *Conference Reports,* October 3, 1942, 17.

39. Recorded interview with Eldred G. Smith by E. Gary Smith, June 18,

1977. Also conversation between E. Gary Smith and Selvoy J. Boyer in the winter of 1958.

40. [President] George Albert Smith, Diary, October 4, 1942.

41. In 1958 there was an interesting parallel development in the Reorganized Church of Jesus Christ of Latter Day Saints. When W. Wallace Smith, a descendant of Joseph Smith, Jr., was ordained prophet, he broke the tradition of lineal descent in the office of Patriarch. Instead of calling Lynn Smith, the son of the outgoing patriarch, to the position, he called Roy Cheville to the office. Later, after a 1984 revelation allowing women to hold the priesthood, many schisms developed. To date there are 221 independent local groups, and some of these fundamentalists believe that "passing over Lynn Smith for Presiding Patriarch was the first sign that W. Wallace Smith was in apostasy." William Dean Russell, "Defenders of the Faith: Varieties of RLDS Dissent," *Sunstone* 14 (June 1990): 14–19.

42. *Conference Reports,* October 3, 1942, 17.

43. George F. Richards, Sr., Diary, October 8, 1942. The possibility that Joseph F. Smith II might be appointed was not new; it was in accord with Heber J. Grant's own suggestion as early as 1933. Mouritsen, "A Symbol of New Directions," 239.

44. *Deseret News,* October 3, 1942.

45. Interview with Joseph F. Smith II's secretary, October 5, 1991.

46. Interview with Ruth Smith, wife of Joseph F. Smith II, April 4, 1981.

47. Suggestions to Patriarchs, May 25, 1943, Eldred G. Smith Personal Records, Salt Lake City.

48. *Conference Reports,* October 7, 1944, 110.

49. Interview with Ralph Smith, uncle of Eldred G. Smith, June 17, 1977. In 1944 Ralph went with his brother John, a police inspector, to tell President Grant about Joseph F. Smith II's alleged homosexual activity. Eldred G. Smith Personal Records.

50. Interview with Joseph F. Smith II's secretary, October 5, 1991. Some of the local patriarchs who helped out were Frank Woodbury, Charles Jones, and Nicholas B. Smith.

51. [President] George Albert Smith, Diary, July 10, 1946.

52. Ibid., July 11, 1946.

53. Ibid., September 6, 1946.

54. Ibid., September 16, 1946. Michael Quinn has suggested that a comma was perhaps omitted from the September 16 entry and that it should read "Met with Presidency and Joseph F. Patriarch [and] Ruth[,] Browning and son present."

55. Ibid., September 18, 1946.

56. Ibid., October 3, 1946.

57. *Conference Reports,* October 3, 1946, 157.

58. [President] George Albert Smith, Diary, October 3, 1946.

59. David O. McKay, Diary, April 10, 1957, July 10, 1957, December 9, 1957, LDS Church Archives.

9

The End of the Line
Eldred G. Smith—Eighth Patriarch, 1947–79

> Administrative capacity would then not come to be regarded as
> a determining factor in the selection of the Patriarch . . . as it may
> have been in times gone by.
>
> —Council of the Twelve to George Albert Smith, June 1949

Eldred Gee Smith was proposed for sustaining vote as the new patriarch in the April 1947 General Conference. No public reason had ever been given for the lapse of fifteen years during which the hereditary office was not held by the eldest son of the former patriarch. In later years he recalled that between 1932 and 1947 some people in the church assumed he had not been called to the office because there was something wrong with him—something of which he had need yet to repent.[1]

When the new patriarch was called without warning out of the audience to make his acceptance speech in General Conference on April 10, it was an opportunity to explain to the membership that he had not had anything of which to repent and that he was entitled to, as well as worthy for, the office. Eldred said:

> Brethren and sisters, I think you are all aware of the fact of the hereditary nature of the office to which I have been called. For that reason I was prepared to give a speech for this occasion fifteen years ago, but not today. Maybe it's because I don't want to get burned in the same fire twice. . . . Many people said, after that occasion, I was not called because I was not worthy, and I would like to say something regarding that now. I don't think that I have had to do any reforming or change my habits in order to make myself worthy of this calling. When President Grant called Joseph F. Smith to this position a few years ago, the

Friday evening preceding, he called me into his office and told me what
he was going to do. I don't know why it was any business of mine. . . . I
asked him the question, "President Grant, are you doing this because I
am not worthy." "Oh, no, no, on the contrary. In fact you have made
quite a reputation for yourself in your Church activities."[2]

Eldred went on to declare his faith and testimony. That evening the
Brethren assembled to ordain and set apart Eldred as the Patriarch. President George Albert Smith spoke first in what seems to have been an attempt at least to leave open the lineal succession aspects of the office,
while at the same time reluctantly confirming the decreased administrative role upon which the apostles were insisting. He said that Eldred represented a long line of men who have held the priesthood: "You belong
to a race that have been greatly honored by our Heavenly Father in being represented in the Church in high positions." He remarked that people expect patriarchs to be older men and that "the people looked for an
older man, but I think you are old enough and have had experience
enough, that there is no duty that you cannot adjust yourself to. . . ." President Smith stressed that the office was one of love, commenting that
"your ordination . . . places you on a pinnacle, as it were, among the people of the Church . . . [there is] just one Patriarch to the Church. . . ."[3]

Before beginning the ordination, President Smith instructed the new
patriarch that he was to be sensitive in the giving of blessings and that
this would be his primary responsibility since his work would be con-
fined to his office and the local vicinity. Eldred was advised to put his
office in order and was told that Apostle Joseph Fielding Smith, Jr., would
act as his supervisor. He was not to meet with the First Presidency and
the Twelve, as his father had done, unless invited. Then the president told
Eldred that he would not travel in his job as would the other Brethren
and that he would not be presiding over stake patriarchs as his father had
done. Finally, Eldred was told that he would be sustained as "Patriarch
to the Church" instead of "Presiding Patriarch, as in your father's
day . . . [because] the brethren concluded that that was not the proper
title."[4]

George Albert Smith was attempting to walk a tightrope. Although he
must have preferred that more responsibility be associated with the calling of the Church Patriarch, he had apparently concluded that he could
not avoid the reduction in authority desired by most apostles and probably by at least one of his counselors. But he wanted to minimize the in-
roads being made on the principle of succession and at the same time
wanted to initiate the reduction in responsibilities in a kind and gentle
way.

What happened following the ordination blessing by the president of the church was one of the dramatic hierarchical confrontations between an apostle and a president in the history of the church. George F. Richards not only was offended by Eldred's acceptance talk that day but also remembered well the comments Eldred had made in the general priesthood testimony meeting five years earlier.[5] In 1942 Richards had sided with President Grant, maintaining that the descendants of the President Joseph F. Smith line were more faithful and stronger in character than were the descendants of John Smith.[6] He was anxious now, in 1947, to end the concept of lineal succession that purportedly gave rights to the descendants of John Smith. Although President Smith had referred to Eldred's position in the "long line of men who have held the priesthood" and to the "race" to which Eldred was so greatly honored to belong, George Albert had stopped short of outright affirmation of the traditional succession rights. The very tentativeness of the president's remarks and his natural desire to avoid conflict with the Brethren probably suggested to Apostle Richards that he could succeed in reversing any imminent resurgence of inherent rights. He said, "I would like to say a few words to Brother Eldred, and if I should exceed my authority or my views are not in harmony with the views of you brethren, I would like to be corrected." He then pointed out that the Twelve had considered descent from father to son some years ago in a meeting and decided that *any* worthy descendant of Hyrum was eligible for the office—subject to the approval of the president of the church. Richards continued:

The remark that you made, Brother Eldred, in Conference at the time that Joseph F. Smith was sustained as Patriarch—I think that you made the statement that you had been deprived of your birthright. I want you to know how I feel about that, that you had no birthright nor does anybody else have a birthright to the office of Patriarch to this Church except that he is a descendant of the Patriarch Hyrum Smith. One of Joseph F. Smith's sons might have said with just as much propriety that he was deprived of the birthright as you. You are your father's oldest son. The Lord did say that this order of Priesthood should descend from father to son, but he did not say from the father to the oldest son.[7]

After referring to biblical exceptions to the tradition of the oldest son's inheriting the birthright, Richards continued:

The apostles, when they made that decision that this office might rightly be given to any one of the male descendants of Hyrum Smith, indicated that everything else being equal, it would be proper to descend from father to son; and if you entertain those views now, Brother Eldred, it is contrary to our understanding and you ought to know it. You ought not to repeat such things as you said in Conference. There have been very adverse reports made on what you had to say in Conference. . . . Now you are to be the Patriarch to the Church because you have been chosen by the President of the Church . . . and sustained by this Council . . . not because of any rights that you have, or any other man who is a descendant of Hyrum Smith. Now that is my understanding, President Smith. Having said that much, if I have said too much or am in error, I would like to be corrected. We ought to understand alike.[8]

The gauntlet was thrown. President Smith, apparently not feeling that direct confrontation was appropriate at the time, sidestepped to a certain extent by suggesting that, from what Eldred said in his talk that morning, it appeared that Eldred also felt anyone in or out of the hereditary line of the oldest son, if ordained a patriarch by proper authority, would be a patriarch. President Smith "concluded that he thought Eldred believed as President Richards had indicated, and upon being asked by President Smith if he were right, the Patriarch said, 'That is right.'"[9]

That night George F. Richards wrote in his journal, "I gave a talk on Patriarchal order and set right the Patriarch, showing his attitude had been wrong in thinking that the office was his birthright. . . . My talk was characterized by a member of the Presidency as a masterful stroke. Most all members of the Twelve told me after the meeting how much they appreciated my presentation. The Patriarch wept and thanked me."[10] Later, Patriarch Smith did not recall thanking Elder Richards, nor did he recall weeping in gratitude for his remarks.

In subsequent years President George Albert Smith attempted to expand the authority of the patriarchal office by small increments and through private lobbying, but he did not meet with much success. Eldred was ordained as Patriarch to the Church by institutional appointment, to an office now with its heritage of succession to the oldest son in doubt, and with its office authority limited more than at any other time in its history. The significance of what had happened, however, was not apparent to Eldred at first.

Shortly after his ordination, someone in the historical department of the church gave Eldred a revised version of John Smith's 1855 ordination as Presiding Patriarch. Apparently someone did not wish Eldred to learn of the authority that his great-grandfather had had as the Patriarch, because certain phrases had been removed, such as "and we confirm thee to be the first in the Church of Jesus Christ among the Patriarchs, to set apart, ordain, and confirm other Patriarchs." Also omitted were the words "and we bless thee with all the keys belonging unto you from your Father."[11]

Eldred Gee Smith, 1907– . Eighth patriarch to the church. Ordained in 1947 and placed on emeritus status in 1979. Courtesy of E. Gary Smith.

The Brethren continued to suggest that Eldred owed an apology for his maiden talk at General Conference. Eldred went to President George Albert Smith for advice. Together they went over the transcript of the talk, and President Smith indicated he saw nothing for which to apologize. Eldred said, "Well, if there's something I'm to apologize for, I want to do it, but I want to know what I'm talking about." President Smith replied, "That's all right. Forget it," and passed it off.[12]

Despite the assurances of the president, it was apparent with the passage of time that some of the apostles continued to feel more was required of the new patriarch to compensate for his remarks about hereditary rights and about his meeting with President Grant six years earlier. In the October 1947 General Conference, the new counselor in the First Presidency made statements that could have been seen as a reaction to Eldred's comments at the previous April General Conference. J. Reuben Clark, Jr., said, "We may claim no honor, no reward, no respect, nor special position or recognition, no credit because of what our fathers were or what they wrought. We stand upon our own feet in our own shoes. There is no aristocracy in this Church." He went on to speak against the incessant adulation of prominent pioneer leaders of Mormonism.[13]

Eldred had been taught from an early age that he was foreordained to be the Patriarch and that he had a responsibility to live up to what was expected of him in that regard. On his eleventh birthday he was given a patriarchal blessing by his father, Hyrum G. Smith. In it he was told, "Thou art an heir through faithfulness to blessings of the Holy Priesthood, which have been promised would be handed down from father to son."[14] Eldred was not claiming aristocratic privilege. He was trying to live up to what he believed both his family and the Lord expected of him. He was caught in the middle.

Until President George Albert Smith's death in 1951, the president did what he could to try and restore some of the privileges of the patriarchate. Soon after Eldred's ordination, President Smith encouraged members of the Twelve to take Eldred with them on conference assignments so they could get to know him. During his tenure Eldred, by assignment, accompanied members of the Twelve to hundreds of conferences, many of which were to reorganize or create stake presidencies. These were faith-promoting experiences for Eldred as well as the members who heard him and worked with him. His humble spirit served the church and the members as he completed these assignments. There were numerous times when he set apart and ordained stake leaders when asked to do so by the apostle with whom he traveled. This continued until the creation of church regions and the calling of regional representatives, at which time his assignments gradually diminished and then disappeared for a while. Throughout, Eldred regularly gave talks in the semiannual general conferences. When questions came to him, he forwarded them for answer to the apostle currently assigned to supervise him.

In 1949 President George Albert Smith requested that the Twelve consider inviting the Patriarch to meet with the First Presidency and the Twelve in their weekly temple meetings, consistent with earlier practice.[15] On June 22, 1949, the president received the written response from the Council of the Twelve stating that they had made this a matter of much discussion and that in their judgment "it would not be wise to reinaugurate a practice which, in our opinion, does not seem to fully carry out the revealed order in church government." The letter from the Twelve went on to point out that the First Presidency was the chief directing authority and that the Twelve, acting under the direction of the First Presidency, were invested with the authority to "build up the Church and regulate all the affairs of the same in all nations" and "also to ordain and set in order all the other officers of the Church." The Twelve concluded that they could not see the place of the Patriarch in such an administrative council and suggested that "he would not seem to be vested with the right to vote in the proceedings . . . [since] it is generally agreed his office is one of blessing and is not executive in nature. His inclusion in the administrative meetings would seem to us to be somewhat confusing to the order of the Church."[16]

The same letter addressed the question of sustaining the Patriarch as "Prophet, Seer, and Revelator." The writers confessed an inability to understand fully the meaning of these terms as applied to anyone other than the president of the church and concluded that perhaps each man "may be deemed to be a Prophet, Seer and Revelator within the sphere of his particular calling or that these designated powers are conferred to be held in abeyance until such time as the person . . . so designated shall be called to act in the chief administrative office." It was agreed that the office of Patriarch came by right to one of the "blood" who must, if worthy, be chosen. As far as the functions of the office were concerned, however, "administrative capacity would not come to be regarded as a determining factor in the selection of the Patriarch as . . . it may have been in times gone by."[17]

Eldred G. Smith's ordination blessing did not mention the sealing powers that had figured so prominently in previous ordinations.[18] Eldred was given the privilege of sealing in the temple, however, shortly after his ordination. He asked President George Albert Smith for permission in November 1947, and the president deferred to Eldred's memory of what his father did in the office. Based on that verification, it was approved.[19] Thereafter, Eldred performed temple weddings at his discretion. In 1950

President Smith succeeded in extending to Eldred and his wife, Jeanne, the privilege of receiving the private second anointing ordinance in the temple, an ordinance reserved for only a relatively few in the church.[20]

By 1951, however, the careful observer was aware that the authority and visibility of the office of Patriarch had been circumscribed. Official church handbooks, messages to stake presidents, and remarks in stake conferences gradually phased out references to the function of the Patriarch to the Church. Responsibility for selecting, ordaining, and instructing stake patriarchs was placed in the hands of the Twelve and later the stake presidents; and meetings of patriarchs in conjunction with general conferences were presided over by one of the Twelve.[21] The Patriarch to the Church only gave patriarchal blessings. It was stated repeatedly that he did not preside over stake patriarchs.[22]

When President George Albert Smith died in 1951, the new president, David O. McKay, was sustained in a solemn assembly in the tabernacle, where the priesthood voted in quorums. In interesting contrast to the stated policy at the time, however, the stake patriarchs, along with the Patriarch to the Church, voted together as a quorum of patriarchs in accordance with the historical pattern to sustain the new president—a vestige of the time when such a quorum was acknowledged.

The Brethren did ask Eldred to assist the Twelve in their responsibilities. He was assigned to set apart missionaries when needed, and in 1966 the First Presidency assigned Eldred to tour the missions in Australia for the purpose of giving patriarchal blessings. There followed several assignments to travel to missions in countries around the world. Most such countries had never before had a patriarch. Hundreds of blessings were given, and he was well received wherever he went. These assignments suggested President George Albert Smith's statement that Eldred would be restricted in his travels was no longer applicable. By extension it also put into question the relevance of the other restrictions stated back in 1947.

In 1967 Eduardo Balderas, a stake patriarch working as a staff assistant in the translation department of the church, accompanied Spencer W. Kimball on a trip to South America, during which Balderas gave 250 blessings to the members in the mission field.[23] This seems to have been an incursion into an area of Eldred's authority that the Brethren had not disputed, that is, only the Patriarch to the Church was to give patriarchal blessings to members not living within established stake boundaries. Although the Church Patriarch had authority to give blessings to any members of the church throughout the world, whether or not they lived in established stakes, it is true that Eldred G. Smith followed the tradition set by Church Patriarchs in the twentieth century of giving patriarchal blessings primarily to individuals who came to him from areas where there were no local patriarchs.[24]

The Brethren occasionally questioned the Patriarch about how he was performing his job. In a temple meeting in 1968 the Twelve had asked President Joseph Fielding Smith to speak with the Patriarch about several of their concerns. The questions were sent to him in a note.[25] Eldred had been taking his summer vacation when the temple was closed, a time when fewer members traveled to Salt Lake City from the "mission field" and thus a time of decreased demands for blessings. The Brethren questioned the timing of the vacation. They apparently were not aware of the impact of the temple closure and had perhaps forgotten, until Eldred pointed it out, that his predecessor, Joseph F. Smith II, had gone to Canada for three entire months during his summers.

Another concern of the apostles in 1968 was that people had been seen waiting in the hall prior to their blessings. The Patriarch explained that there was no waiting room and that he could not move people in and out quickly as could be done when setting apart missionaries. Patriarchal blessings were profound moments in the lives of the recipients, and a rapport and spiritual atmosphere needed to be established for these occasions. This took time, and sometimes some members were required to wait for a while.

The third concern was Patriarch Smith's refusal to allow his office and equipment to be used by "substitute" patriarchs when he was absent. Patriarch Smith maintained that there was no such thing as a "substitute patriarch" for the Patriarch to the Church, since stake patriarchs were not authorized to give blessings to persons living outside their own stake boundaries. He cited the *General Handbook*.[26] Later, President David O. McKay personally confirmed this limitation on stake patriarchs.[27]

Although he diligently fulfilled his calling and performed his duties, Eldred continued, from time to time, to ask the Brethren in private about inconsistencies between the historical prerogatives of the patriarchate and the limited authority and responsibility attached to the office as he held it.

In 1969 Eldred was again sent to tour a foreign mission, and he gave patriarchal blessings in London. The Brethren, however, were reluctant to give undue public attention to the patriarchal office. The editor of a church magazine wrote to Eldred G. Smith in 1968, advising him that permission to use an interview with Eldred was denied. He explained that the Quorum of the Twelve was apparently in charge of patriarchal blessings.[28]

In 1971 Eldred received an assignment to go to a stake conference with one of the assistants to the Twelve. Eldred knew he was the junior when he went with an apostle, but he asked Apostle Ezra Taft Benson whether he or the assistant to the Twelve would be senior when assigned together. He was told the assistant to the Twelve was to be senior in this instance. When the assistant was shortly thereafter made an apostle, Eldred felt the distinction might have been more in deference to the man's inchoate authority as an apostle-to-be than a ruling on the inherent seniority between the Patriarch and assistants to the Twelve.

Shortly thereafter Patriarch Smith became aware of the upcoming dedication of the Independence Visitors Center. He mentioned to Apostle Spencer W. Kimball that he had a great interest in church history and would love to be part of the dedication services in some way. This prompted Kimball to reflect on the scope of activities that would be appropriate for the Patriarch. A few days later Kimball asked Eldred to prepare a list of his predecessors' responsibilities, to be discussed at the next meeting of the Twelve. Kimball suggested that many of the apostles did not know much about the history of the office and that perhaps it was time to take another look at and possibly increase Eldred's activities. Eldred had not meant to stir the waters to that extent; although hopeful about a reevaluation, he also feared the other members of the Quorum would perceive it as a complaint on his part.

Eldred submitted a short written list of responsibilities he thought should be associated with his office, but Kimball told him he wanted a little more "chapter and verse." "You mean like a lawyer arguing a case?" asked Eldred. "Yes, something like that," Kimball replied.[29] In the meantime, the Twelve prepared its own brief. Its research was limited to obtaining a copy of the minutes for the meeting in 1947 when Eldred was ordained, including the remarks of George F. Richards. These were produced by Joseph Anderson at a meeting of the Twelve on April 15, 1971.

After reading the earlier minutes, the Twelve recommended that Elder Howard W. Hunter prepare a statement outlining Patriarch Eldred G. Smith's comments along with a summary of the interview with him prior to his ordination. He was to review this with Patriarch Smith. The Twelve also recommended that Eldred be given other responsibilities, such as visiting the missions and stakes of the Church to give blessings. They also recommended that he be given the opportunity to be a sealer in the temple.[30]

The Twelve met again on April 22. The apostles read the 1947 minutes in their entirety, and some suggested that Eldred's mother might have influenced him unduly in the years that he was not called to serve as the Patriarch. Spencer W. Kimball asked for suggestions on things to occupy Eldred's time. Gordon B. Hinckley suggested that he travel throughout the church to give blessings. Richard L. Evans suggested that the Patriarch could, on such trips, ordain bishops and members of the Quorum of the Seventy, but this was not approved. A senior apostle objected to the fact that while some of the apostles sat on the second row in General Conference, Eldred sat at the end of the first row near the First Presidency.[31] These and other concerns with respect to the patriarchal office were eventually resolved, and it was unanimous that the Patriarch be required to accept, in writing, the recommendations made to him.[32]

In the meantime, Patriarch Smith had submitted the "brief" requested of him. The document is dated May 28, 1971; however, he remembers distinctly that he submitted this document before the meeting between him and the committee from the Twelve, which records show as having occurred on May 21, 1971. There is no reference to this document in the minutes of the meetings of the Twelve, and it is presumed that it was received after its last meeting of April 22 and before the meeting with Eldred on May 21.

Eldred's brief made the following points concerning predecessors in the office:

> (1) [They] met with the Quorum of the Twelve & the First Presidency in their regular weekly temple meeting. An old moving picture . . . shows all the prescy & the 12 & the patriarch coming out of their meetings in the temple. This change was made when I came into office. We sustain the patriarch with the counselors to the first presidency and the quorum of the twelve apostles, *all* as prophets, seers & revelators. . . . This needs no proof. The records verify it. The general membership of the Church all know it.
>
> (2) [The Patriarch] assisted the quorum of twelve in Stake Conferences and in the missions. . . . I have father's notebooks showing his assignments and activities to stake 1/4 Conferences. This covers most weekends over a period from 1912 to 1932. (Some trips took weeks). . . . Why couldn't I too be delegated to assist the 12 in this work?
>
> (3) [The Patriarch] ordained and set apart *all other* officers, including bishops and patriarchs. . . . There has been no question in the past (as far as my knowledge is concerned) that previous patriarchs have ordained & set apart other officers.
>
> (4) [The Patriarch] has presided as president of the quorum of patriarchs.[33]

In support of the last of these items, Eldred quoted from the June 1, 1945, John Taylor article in the *Times and Seasons;* he quoted from the November 7, 1877, letter from John Taylor to George Q. Cannon, which contains the suggestion that the Patriarch preside over a quorum of patriarchs; and he referred to the wording of the ordinations of John Smith and Hyrum G. Smith. He also pointed out that he had copies of thirteen certificates of ordination substantiating the claim that his father had ordained local patriarchs.[34]

On Friday, May 21, 1971, Eldred met with a committee of three apostles: Spencer W. Kimball, acting president of the Quorum; Howard W.
Hunter, the church historian; and LeGrand Richards, the son of George
F. Richards. The apostles reviewed with Eldred the comments made by
George F. Richards in 1947, and they told him that he was not to teach
his son that he had any right to the office. This surprised Eldred, because
he thought the meeting was about the administrative functions of the
office. The question of succession had not been a part of any of their discussions. Eldred replied that he did not need to teach his son, that his
son would know by simply reading the scriptures. When they asked for
the scripture to which he was referring, Eldred read from Doctrine and
Covenants 124:91: "And again, verily I say unto you . . . that my servant
Hyrum may take the office of Priesthood and Patriarch, which was appointed unto him by his father, by blessing and also by right." Richards
responded by maintaining that no one had any right to any office in the
church. Eldred replied that all he wanted "was what the Lord wants, and
if the Lord wants my son to succeed me, He'll take care of it." He pointed out that those present would probably not be the ones who would
make the decision when the succession question next came up, so a discussion at that time was really moot. It should be remembered that Eldred was considerably younger than most of the members of the Council of the Twelve and presumably would outlive most of the incumbents
sitting in 1971, leaving the question of succession to be decided by others
upon Eldred's death. This comment displeased the committee, despite the
fact that Eldred concluded by assuring them that he would do whatever
he was asked to do.[35]

Before the meeting adjourned, the committee read to Eldred the list
of approved activities. A paraphrased version of the list is as follows:

1. Possibly be sent to foreign missions to give blessings;

2. By invitation, set apart missionaries, fifteen to twenty every week;

3. Administer to the sick who come to the building, thus relieving the
Brethren;[36]

4. Become a sealer in the temple under the direction of the temple president, if desired;

5. Accept the fact that there was no Quorum of patriarchs;

6. Receive other assignments that would be given by the Twelve;

7. At General Conference, sit between the Twelve and the assistants to
the Twelve (instead of on the top row);

8. Keep regular hours "like everyone else, whether there are people to
give blessings to or not.[37]

Eldred's response to this in his personal notes was, "I couldn't understand what there was to accept. There was no new program."[38] He was

never told what the Brethren wished him to do in his office at the Church
Administration Building when there were no appointments for blessings.
He had no administrative or other "office" duties.

A week later Spencer W. Kimball sent a letter to Eldred stating,
"Though you made the statement that you would do whatever you were
asked to do, our Committee members felt that your spirit was such that
it was not a satisfactory adjustment and it could not be concluded on that
note." Eldred was asked to accept the program "with a good spirit, a kindly
attitude and an evident appreciation for the great privileges made available to you."[39]

The tension between Apostle Kimball and Patriarch Smith at this time
was so acute that at the last minute Kimball withdrew the assignment he
had earlier made, but never communicated to Eldred, for Eldred to give
the benediction at the dedication of the Independence Visitors Center—
the event that had initiated the entire reexamination of the office parameters.[40] Eldred saw his name on the program, after the fact, and asked
Kimball about it. The apostle explained what had happened and apolo-
gized.

In less than a month Kimball sent a conciliatory letter, reassuring the
Patriarch that the Quorum felt "very kindly" toward him and saying that
"you are the one man in the world who has this great privilege of repre-
senting the Lord as the patriarch to His Church." He asked if they could
hear from Eldred soon regarding the "activities suggested."[41] Eldred was
unclear about what additional reply was wanted. He felt he had already
communicated that he would comply with whatever their instructions
were. Apostles Marion G. Romney and Ezra Taft Benson both consulted
with Eldred at different times in an effort to assist in putting the matter
to rest. Benson suggested that the Patriarch write a letter restating his
willingness to accept the new "program," and Benson suggested some appropriate wording for a note to that effect.[42] Eldred wrote a note dated
June 25 that simply said he was reaffirming his willingness to accept any
assignments given to him by the Twelve or the First Presidency. He closed
by saying, "I have no personal ill feelings toward any one and hope and
pray my services in the future will be acceptable by the Lord and my
brethren of the twelve and the first presidency."[43]

Consistent with the outline provided by the Twelve, in late 1971 the First
Presidency called Eldred to tour the Scandinavian missions to give patriarchal blessings. In early 1972 he toured missions in Europe, and in 1973
he returned to Europe and also went to the Far East. Above and beyond
the activities outlined by the apostles were his several assignments to accompany apostles to stake conferences in the months that followed.

In the following years, however, Patriarch Smith received communications from the Council of the Twelve that questioned absences from his office, undue amounts of time spent with recipients of blessings, and comments made during interviews that were deemed beyond the limits of his authority. Eldred replied to all of these complaints with a puzzled courtesy.[44] Yet his personal notes reveal his discomfort. "Why do the brethren always keep me on the defensive?" he wrote. "How can I have the spirit of blessing etc. when the brethren keep me constantly in a turmoil? . . . Why, when I offer to help them with their tremendous load, do they continue to cut me lower and deeper, just because I wanted to help?"[45] In the official church publications, references to the Church Patriarch were minimal, and he was treated as a guest at meetings of stake patriarchs.

Then the unexpected occurred. In May of 1975 Spencer W. Kimball, who had been president of the church for seventeen months, called Eldred into his office and advised him that he was to assume the full responsibilities of a prophet, seer, and revelator. He was to go to stake conferences with each of the members of the Council of the Twelve, after which he would be given his own assignments. All prior restrictions were to be removed.[46] This was confusing to Eldred but was received with relief and anticipation. The turnabout was particularly surprising given the lack of any descendants of the founding Smith family in the hierarchy to encourage the change. Joseph Fielding Smith, Jr., had died in 1972, and he was the last of the Smiths.[47] The announcement also demonstrated President Kimball's personal openness on the question, evidenced during the 1971 exchange of views, and his willingness to depart from a long-accepted course if he felt inspired to make a change.[48]

Although Eldred thereafter did accompany two of the Twelve to stake conferences, his involvement in such activities apparently did not meet with the approval of some of the apostles, who once again began to examine what they felt were the proper dimensions of the office. In February 1976 Apostle Boyd K. Packer requested the staff of the church research department to gather information on any possible historical precedents for allowing stake patriarchs or fathers to take over some of the duties that up to that time had been the responsibility of the Church Patriarch.[49] The next month the Patriarch was asked for information about his sons.[50] Eldred found this a surprising request, but coupled with the expansion of responsibilities indicated by President Kimball for the office, he interpreted the inquiry as a positive development. His reply to the Brethren included the information that his eldest son was a member of the high council in the Los Angeles Stake and was a partner in a law firm there.

Without notice, however, Eldred's stake conference assignments mysteriously stopped in 1976. When he asked President Kimball about this, the president simply said he had been required to make some changes in

Eldred G. Smith near the time he was placed on emeritus status. Courtesy of E. Gary Smith.

Jeanne Ness Smith, 1907–77. Wife of Eldred G. Smith. Courtesy of E. Gary Smith.

his plans in that regard. Things returned to the way they were before President Kimball's announcement in May 1975 that the patriarchal office was going to be expanded.

In June 1977 Eldred's wife, Jeanne, died. President Kimball called Eldred into his office and gave him his warm condolences. He told Eldred that his travel assignments would increase, not decrease; however, Eldred never received another assignment. In May 1978 Eldred married Hortense Child, then a counselor in the general presidency of the church's Young Women's organization of the Mutual Improvement Association. She had served in responsible positions in the church for many years and became a great source of comfort and assistance to Eldred in his work.

It was a complete surprise to Eldred when President Kimball called him into his office in 1979 and said Eldred would be designated an emeritus general authority. This was inconsistent with President Kimball's earlier attempts to find a way to give the office meaning and responsibility. It is not known what dynamics might have combined to cause Spencer Kimball to retire the office of Church Patriarch. Perhaps it was the desire to end more than a century of tension over the proper parameters of authority for the office and to finally put to rest the question of lineal rights of succession. In keeping with Kimball's sensitive approach to the problem was his assurance to Eldred that he would be allowed to continue giving patriarchal blessings to those who came with proper recommends.

The announcement was made at the October General Conference by President Nathan E. Tanner, counselor in the First Presidency, that "because of the large increase in the number of stake patriarchs and the availability of patriarchal service throughout the world, we now designate Elder Eldred G. Smith as a Patriarch Emeritus, which means that he is honorably relieved—not released [laughter][51]—of all duties and responsibilities pertaining to the office of Patriarch to the Church."[52] The announcement was sustained by the congregation.

Although the announcement suggests that Patriarch Smith was being retired (his status was being changed to that of "emeritus"), in fact it was the office that was actually being retired. The latter was accomplished through the former. No replacement Church Patriarch was ever called. With respect to Eldred's activities the action was redundant and unnecessary. Any previous involvement of the Patriarch in administrative matters so troublesome to the hierarchy had been gradually phased out. Eldred continued to have the privilege of giving patriarchal blessings—the only official church activity in which he had been engaged for some time prior to his emeritus designation. Patriarch Eldred G. Smith had given 17,517 blessings in his thirty-two years in office. Following his emeritus status, he continued to give patriarchal blessings, although fewer in number, at his office in the Church Office Building.

Eldred G. Smith was the last of the church patriarchs who have had to confront the impossible task of operating within the parameters of an office that was created and defined when the church was led by Smiths and had "lineal authority" but existed in a modern church fueled by office and hierarchical authority. Perhaps an anachronism, perhaps a perceived threat of some kind to institutional order, the office and its history can only hint at the emotional roller coaster and the chronic uncertainty in which Eldred and his family lived their lives, subject to various political and personal winds blowing through the Twelve from time to time. That is the deeply personal, certainly painful, and almost tragic aspect of the story of the last church patriarch.

Notes

1. Speculation about why Eldred had not been called as Patriarch has been painful to him. One friend had staunchly defended him in a Sunday School class in Provo when the teacher had stated authoritatively that only unworthiness could have precluded Eldred's appointment. The bitter debate that followed caused estrangement between the participants that lasted for many years. Martha Smith related this story to her son Eldred G. Smith.

2. Conference talk as given. Eldred was asked to edit the talk before publication. He submitted a revision, but a different version yet was actually published in "A Testimony of the Truth," in *Conference Reports of the Church of Jesus Christ of Latter-day Saints* (Salt Lake City: Church of Jesus Christ of Latter-day Saints, April 1947), 6.

3. Minutes of the Council of the Twelve, April 10, 1947, Archives of the Church of Jesus Christ of Latter-day Saints, Salt Lake City (hereafter LDS Church Archives).

4. Ibid.

5. See the previous chapter for Eldred's remarks after Patriarch Joseph F. Smith II was sustained in Conference.

6. George F. Richards, Sr., to the Twelve, July 1942, as paraphrased in Dale C. Mouritsen, "A Symbol of New Directions: George Franklin Richards and the Mormon Church, 1861–1950" (Ph.D. diss., Brigham Young University, 1982), 239–40.

7. Minutes of the Council of the Twelve, April 10, 1947, as quoted in Minutes of the Council of the Twelve, Salt Lake Temple, April 15, 1971, at 8:00 A.M. and April 22, 1971, at 8:00 A.M., LDS Church Archives.

8. Ibid.

9. Ibid.

10. George F. Richards, Sr., Diary, April 10, 1947, LDS Church Archives.

11. Eldred G. Smith Personal Records, Salt Lake City; copies of both versions of John Smith's ordination in the authors' possession.

12. Recorded interview between Eldred G. Smith and E. Gary Smith, June

18, 1977. After the death of Hyrum G. Smith, George Albert Smith, then an apostle, had been "more or less a second father" to the family.

13. Quoted in D. Michael Quinn, *J. Reuben Clark, Jr.: The Church Years* (Provo, Utah: Brigham Young University Press, 1983), 103.

14. Patriarchal blessing given by Hyrum G. Smith, to his eldest son, Eldred Gee Smith, January 9, 1918, Eldred G. Smith Personal Records.

15. This would be contrary to the instructions the president had given Eldred just prior to his ordination. John Henry Smith, Diary, 1875–1911, photocopy of holograph in George A. Smith Family Collection, Manuscripts Division, Special Collections, Marriott Library, University of Utah, Salt Lake City, notes that Patriarch John Smith attended these meetings in the Salt Lake Temple during his incumbency. Patriarchs Hyrum G. Smith and Joseph F. Smith II also attended the weekly meeting with the First Presidency and the Twelve.

16. Council of the Twelve to President George Albert Smith, June 22, 1949, LDS Church Archives.

17. Ibid.

18. Eldred G. Smith Personal Records; copy of ordination blessing in authors' possession.

19. Transcript of telephone conversations between George Albert Smith and Eldred G. Smith, November 24, 1947, Eldred G. Smith Personal Records; copy in authors' possession. On January 8, 1948, Brother Haycock confirmed to Eldred that he had authority to seal in the future.

20. The second anointings were received January 6, 1950. The practice of giving second anointings was reinstituted toward the middle of the twentieth century through the efforts of Apostle George F. Richards.

21. See, for example, minutes of the meeting of patriarchs of the church with the General Authorities held in Barratt Hall, Salt Lake City, on October 11, 1958, at 8:00 A.M., LDS Church Archives; copy in authors' possession.

22. See for example, a First Presidency letter to all stake presidents, June 28, 1957, along with many other official publications of the church, LDS Church Archives.

23. *Church News,* December 23, 1967, 6. Walter Krause was ordained a patriarch by President Spencer W. Kimball in 1973 and given the extraterritorial assignment to give blessings to worthy Saints behind the iron curtain. Percy K. Fetzer, a regional representative and an ordained patriarch, made similar trips for several years before that. *Church News,* July 11, 1992, 4.

24. Eldred G. Smith, General Conference talk entitled "Your Patriarchal Blessing," *Conference Reports,* April 6, 1960, 65.

25. Eldred G. Smith Personal Records. Joseph Fielding Smith's note to Eldred G. Smith was handwritten on a reminder sent to Joseph Fielding Smith by D. Arthur Haycook, August 22, 1968.

26. Ibid.; Eldred G. Smith to President Joseph Fielding Smith, September 4, 1968, Eldred G. Smith Personal Records.

27. Conversation between Eldred G. Smith and his son E. Gary Smith, April 20, 1993.

28. Jay Todd to Eldred G. Smith, n.d. [1968], Eldred G. Smith Personal Records.

29. Notes by Eldred G. Smith recounting discussions with Spencer W. Kimball, May 21, 1971, Eldred G. Smith Personal Records.

30. Minutes of the regular meeting of the Council of the Twelve, Salt Lake Temple, April 15, 1971, at 8:00 A.M.

31. After this Patriarch Smith's seat was changed both in General Conference and in the monthly meeting of the General Authorities. In both instances he was moved from between the Presidency and the Twelve to below the Twelve.

32. Minutes of the Council of the Twelve, Salt Lake Temple, April 22, 1971, LDS Church Archives.

33. Eldred G. Smith to Elder Spencer W. Kimball, May 28, 1971, Eldred G. Smith Personal Records.

34. Copies of the original certificates are in the possession of E. Gary Smith. On another occasion Eldred told the Brethren that his father had presided at meetings of patriarchs even when members of the Twelve were present. His father had called on apostles to speak, and they acknowledged that Hyrum G. Smith presided in his capacity as Church Patriarch.

35. Eldred G. Smith notes on his meeting with apostles Spencer W. Kimball, Howard W. Hunter, and LeGrand Richards, May 21, 1971, Eldred G. Smith Personal Records.

36. Ibid. There was never a time when anyone was referred to the Patriarch for this purpose, either before or after this discussion.

37. Ibid.

38. Eldred G. Smith, Personal Notes, n.d., Eldred G. Smith Personal Records. This was a personal note rather than a diary as stated in Irene Bates, "Transformation of Charisma in the Mormon Church: A History of the Office of Presiding Patriarch, 1833–1979" (Ph.D. diss., University of California, Los Angeles, 1991), 342, n.58.

39. Spencer W. Kimball to Eldred G. Smith, May 28, 1971, Eldred G. Smith Personal Records; copy in authors' possession.

40. The Visitors Center was dedicated May 31, 1971. Bates, "Transformation of Charisma," 342, n.60.

41. Council of the Twelve to Eldred G. Smith, June 16, 1971, Eldred G. Smith Personal Records.

42. Apostle Benson was in a good position to give advice on dealing with disputes with the Brethren since he had himself been in that position many times. See D. Michael Quinn, "Ezra Taft Benson and Mormon Political Conflicts," *Dialogue: A Journal of Mormon Thought* 26 (Summer 1993), 1–87.

43. Eldred G. Smith to Council of the Twelve, June 25, 1971, Eldred G. Smith Personal Records; copy in authors' possession.

44. First Presidency letters to Eldred G. Smith, September 9 and October 9, 1975; Eldred G. Smith letters to the First Presidency, in reply, September 25 and October 30, 1975, Eldred G. Smith Personal Records. See also Bates, "Transformation of Charisma," 343–44, n.64. Many of the criticisms had their

genesis with Eldred's secretary, who, Eldred felt, was officious and meddling. Repeated attempts to replace her met with resistance from the Brethren.

45. Eldred G. Smith, Personal Notes, n.d., Eldred G. Smith Personal Records. This appears in a personal note rather than in a "diary" as stated in Bates, "Transformation of Charisma," 344, n.65.

46. The previous January President Kimball had called Eldred to be a sealer in the Salt Lake Temple. Spencer W. Kimball to Elder Eldred G. Smith, January 21, 1975, Eldred G. Smith Personal Records; copy in authors' possession.

47. Much later Russell Ballard, a descendant of Hyrum Smith, would become an apostle.

48. President Kimball is known for his 1978 revelation removing the restrictions that had prevented black members of the church from holding the priesthood.

49. Boyd Packer Research Request, February 1976, Historical Department of the Church of Jesus Christ of Latter-day Saints, Salt Lake City. The request asked for precedents for stake patriarchs' giving blessings outside their stake boundaries; information on declaring lineage in patriarchal blessings; and information on whether fathers have the right to declare lineage in patriarchal blessings on their children.

50. The oral inquiry by the Brethren was made March 17, 1976. Eldred G. Smith, Personal Notes, Eldred G. Smith Personal Records.

51. The aside with respect to being "relieved" as opposed to being "released" was not in the published account.

52. "Sustaining of Church Officers," *Conference Reports*, October 6, 1979, 25.

10

———⟫●⟪———

Unique Emeritus

Eldred G. Smith—Patriarch/General Authority Emeritus, 1979–2013

When the first edition of *Lost Legacy* was published in 1996, Eldred G. Smith was eighty-nine years old and still going strong. He continued to lead a vigorous life for another seventeen years, until his death in 2013 at age 106. This chapter discusses the thirty-four years of his unique emeritus status, from 1979 to 2013. If his emeritus years are counted as "General Authority" years, he was a General Authority for sixty-six years—longer than anyone in the history of the LDS Church. Because Eldred was never released, he continued to serve in a limited way as Church Patriarch. The office lived on in a kind of twilight existence until his death. Thus the sun did not fully set on that office until April 2013.

To understand the uniqueness of Eldred's emeritus status, it is necessary to review the emeritus status as it has come to be for other General Authorities. Before 1978 the term "General Authority" was used to designate full-time, lifetime, ecclesiastical leaders of the LDS Church with world-wide (Church-wide) authority. The First Quorum of Seventy was created in October 1976.[1] Following that addition, General Authorities included the three-member First Presidency, the Council of the Twelve Apostles, the Patriarch to the Church, members of the First Quorum of Seventy (including the Seven Presidents of the Seventy), and the three-member Presiding Bishopric.

In 1978 the Church announced its first limit on lifetime callings for General Authorities. Except for the Patriarch to the Church, all those placed on "emeritus" status since 1978 have come only from the First

Quorum of Seventy. N. Eldon Tanner of the First Presidency provided this explanation at the October 1978 General Conference:

> The very rapid growth of the Church across the world, with the attendant increase in travel and responsibility, has made it necessary to consider a change in the status for some of the Brethren of the General Authorities. Some of our associates have served for many years with complete and unselfish dedication, and they deserve every honor and recognition for such devoted service. It is felt advisable at this time to reduce somewhat the load of responsibility that they carry. After a long period of prayerful consideration and counsel, extending, indeed, over several years, we announce a new and specific status to be given from time to time to Brethren of our associates in the General Authorities. We announce that some Brethren have been designated as emeritus members of the First Quorum of the Seventy. These Brethren are not being released but will be excused from active service. It is out of consideration for the personal well-being of the individuals, and with deep appreciation for their devoted service, that this designation will be given from time to time to designated members of the General Authorities.[2]

Nothing in this initial announcement indicated any particular age to which the emeritus status applied. The first three Seventies to be given emeritus status in September 1978 were aged seventy-two, seventy-four, and seventy-nine.[3] Four more were emeritized later that year; they were aged seventy-five, eighty-nine, sixty-eight, and seventy-four.[4] The only one to receive emeritus status the next year, in 1979, was Patriarch to the Church Eldred G. Smith, who was seventy-two years old. The General Authority chart published in the *Ensign* magazine in May 1979 shows Eldred to the right of the Council of the Twelve and above all the other General Authorities, his one-of-a-kind office graphically apparent by appearing on the side of the page. The seven emeritus General Authorities were then pictured at the bottom of the chart. Six months later, after Eldred's emeritization, he is pictured at the bottom of a revised chart with the emeritus Seventies, first of the eight pictured.

Until May 1989, General Authorities placed on emeritus status continued to be shown in the same chart as active General Authorities. By November 1990 the emeritus General Authorities were no longer shown.

Eventually, emeritus status was routinized so that since November 1991 members of the First Quorum of the Seventy serve until age seventy, at which time they are automatically given emeritus status.[5] Those on emeritus status continue to receive a modest retirement payment and have the title of "Emeritus General Authority." They are otherwise de facto released

General Authorities
of The Church of Jesus Christ
of Latter-day Saints

The First Presidency

President N. Eldon Tanner, First Counselor — President Spencer W. Kimball — President Marion G. Romney, Second Counselor

The Council of the Twelve

Ezra Taft Benson — Mark E. Petersen — LeGrand Richards — Howard W. Hunter — Gordon B. Hinckley — Thomas S. Monson

Boyd K. Packer — Marvin J. Ashton — Bruce R. McConkie — L. Tom Perry — David B. Haight — James E. Faust

Patriarch to the Church

Eldred G. Smith

The Presidency of the First Quorum of the Seventy

Franklin D. Richards — J. Thomas Fyans — A. Theodore Tuttle — Neal A. Maxwell — Marion D. Hanks — Paul H. Dunn — W. Grant Bangerter

Additional Members of the First Quorum of the Seventy

Theodore M. Burton — Bernard P. Brockbank — Robert L. Simpson — O. Leslie Stone — Robert D. Hales — Adney Y. Komatsu — Joseph B. Wirthlin — Hartman Rector, Jr. — Loren C. Dunn — Rex D. Pinegar — Gene R. Cook

Charles A. Didier — William R. Bradford — George P. Lee — Carlos E. Asay — M. Russell Ballard — John H. Groberg — Jacob de Jager — Vaughn J. Featherstone — Dean L. Larsen — Royden G. Derrick — Robert E. Wells

G. Homer Durham — James M. Paramore — Richard G. Scott — Hugh W. Pinnock — F. Enzio Busche — Yoshihiko Kikuchi — Ronald E. Poelman — Derek A. Cuthbert — Robert L. Backman — Rex C. Reeve, Sr. — F. Burton Howard

Teddy E. Brewerton — Jack H. Goaslind, Jr.

The Presiding Bishopric

H. Burke Peterson, First Counselor — Victor L. Brown, Presiding Bishop — J. Richard Clarke, Second Counselor

Emeritus Members of the First Quorum of the Seventy

Joseph Anderson — William H. Bennett — James A. Cullimore — Sterling W. Sill

Henry D. Taylor — John H. Vandenberg — S. Dilworth Young

General Authority Chart for May 1979. (Source: *Ensign*, May 1979)

General Authorities
of The Church of Jesus Christ
of Latter-day Saints

The First Presidency

President N. Eldon Tanner
First Counselor

President Spencer W. Kimball

President Marion G. Romney
Second Counselor

The Council of the Twelve

Ezra Taft Benson | Mark E. Petersen | LeGrand Richards | Howard W. Hunter | Gordon B. Hinckley | Thomas S. Monson

Boyd K. Packer | Marvin J. Ashton | Bruce R. McConkie | L. Tom Perry | David B. Haight | James E. Faust

The Presidency of the First Quorum of the Seventy

Franklin D. Richards | J. Thomas Fyans | A. Theodore Tuttle | Neal A. Maxwell | Marion D. Hanks | Paul H. Dunn | W. Grant Bangerter

Additional Members of the First Quorum of the Seventy

Theodore M. Burton | Bernard P. Brockbank | Robert L. Simpson | O. Leslie Stone | Robert D. Hales | Adney Y. Komatsu | Joseph B. Wirthlin | Hartman Rector, Jr. | Loren C. Dunn | Rex D. Pinegar | Gene R. Cook

Charles Didier | William R. Bradford | George P. Lee | Carlos E. Asay | M. Russell Ballard | John H. Groberg | Jacob de Jager | Vaughn J. Featherstone | Dean L. Larsen | Royden G. Derrick | Robert E. Wells

G. Homer Durham | James M. Paramore | Richard G. Scott | Hugh W. Pinnock | F. Enzio Busche | Yoshihiko Kikuchi | Ronald E. Poelman | Derek A. Cuthbert | Robert L. Backman | Rex C. Reeve, Sr. | F. Burton Howard

General Authorities Emeritus
Members of the First Quorum of the Seventy Emeritus

Patriarch Emeritus

Teddy E. Brewerton | Jack H. Goaslind, Jr.

Eldred G. Smith | Joseph Anderson | William H. Bennett | James A. Cullimore

The Presiding Bishopric

H. Burke Peterson
First Counselor | Victor L. Brown
Presiding Bishop | J. Richard Clarke
Second Counselor

Sterling W. Sill | Henry D. Taylor | John H. Vandenberg | S. Dilworth Young

General Authority Chart for November 1979. (Source: *Ensign*, May 1979)

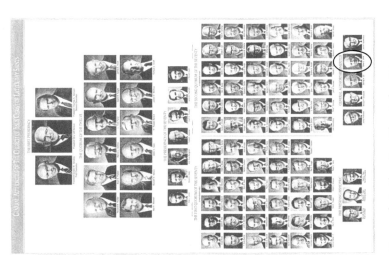

General Authority Chart for November 1990. (Source: *Ensign*, Nov. 1990)

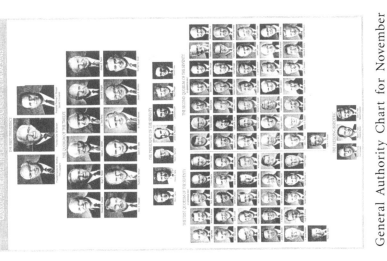

General Authority Chart for May 1989. (Source: *Ensign*, May 1989)

from all General Authority responsibilities and privileges. Many emeriti have been called as temple presidents or to other Church callings. Some have returned to their earlier profession or occupation. For some it was a challenging adjustment. One emeritus Seventy quipped, "In a sense we've become defrocked."[6]

The emeritus status of Patriarch Eldred G. Smith was unique from that of the emeritus General Authority Seventies in three ways: First, and most important, he was the first and only "prophet, seer, & revelator"[7] to be named emeritus. As a result, he continued with many of the accoutrements of an active General Authority. Second, he spent his emeritus years giving "fireside" presentations to thousands of people about the precious Smith family artifacts he had inherited. Third, his emeritus tenure—and by extension, the office—continued for thirty-four years, creating a continuing anachronism for Patriarch Smith as well as for the hierarchy.

The fact that Eldred, as Patriarch to the Church, was sustained as a prophet, seer, and revelator probably had more to do with the uniqueness of his emeritus status than with his designation as Patriarch to the Church. Today, only the First Presidency and Council of the Twelve Apostles carry the designation of prophet, seer, and revelator. That designation incorporates the concept that any man so designated has the potential, or the inchoate authority, to become the President/Prophet of the Church.[8] In established procedure, the Apostle with the most senior ordination date as an Apostle (whether a member of the First Presidency or the Council of the Twelve) becomes the new President/Prophet upon the passing of the incumbent.[9]

As early as 1949 the Council of the Twelve Apostles expressed in a letter to the First Presidency their concern over sustaining Patriarch Eldred G. Smith as "prophet, seer, and revelator." In a lengthy letter to the First Presidency on June 22, 1949, they explained their concern as follows:

> The fact that the Patriarch is sustained in General Conference as "Prophet, Seer, and Revelator," together with members of the First Presidency and Council of the Twelve, has received our attention. While we confess our inability to understand fully the meaning of these traditional terms as applied to anyone other than the President of the Church it does seem reasonably clear to us that the application of the terms does not operate to place on all the men to whom they are applied an equality of authority and privilege. Were it not so every man would be on a par with the President. The construction that seems most tenable to us is that each man shall be deemed to be a "Prophet, Seer, and Revelator" within the sphere of his particular calling or that these designated powers are conferred to be held in abeyance until such time as the person or

persons so designated shall be called to act in the chief administrative office. The President of the Church is the "Prophet, Seer, and Revelator" to the whole Church in all matters. There are undoubtedly some limitations in this respect on the Twelve and very likely further limitations on the Patriarch to the Church. We do not know that the limitations have ever been defined, but we feel sure they must exist.[10]

When President Spencer W. Kimball placed Eldred on emeritus status in 1979, he must have been, again, wrestling with the application of the "prophet, seer, and revelator" designation as it applied to the Patriarch to the Church. It was particularly problematic when seen against the backdrop of the question raised by Patriarch Hyrum G. Smith, Eldred's father, in 1919. Hyrum G. Smith postulated that the Patriarch should be sustained in General Conference even before the President of the Church.[11] His rationale was based on the 124th section of the Doctrine and Covenants. Verse 123 of that section reads: "Verily I say unto you, I now give unto you the officers belonging to my priesthood, that ye may hold the keys thereof, even the Priesthood which is after the order of Melchizedek, which is after the order of mine Only Begotten Son." Verse 124 lays out the order of those priesthood leaders: "*First*, I give unto you Hyrum Smith to be a patriarch unto you, . . ." (italics added). Verse 125 then names Joseph as the presiding elder, to be a "translator, a revelator, a seer, and a prophet." The following verses name, in order, Joseph's counselors in the First Presidency, then Brigham Young as President of the Quorum of the Twelve, and then the members of the Quorum of the Twelve. Earlier, verse 94 in section 124 appointed Hyrum, the newly called Church Patriarch, a "prophet, and a seer, and as a revelator unto my church, as well as my servant Joseph."

The ambiguity of Hyrum being named ahead of Joseph and also being named a prophet, seer, and a revelator in this scripture created tensions between the sitting Presiding Patriarch and the other Brethren for generations.[12] With that history, the continuing sustaining of Eldred as a prophet, seer, and revelator throughout his incumbency was likely a consideration at the time of Eldred's designation as an emeritus General Authority. It is clear that the Patriarch to the Church could not now, in the modern Church, ever be in line for the Presidency, but the question still remained: What problems might be created by placing a "prophet, seer, and revelator" on emeritus status? Would it create an unwelcome precedent, opening the door to further application to other Church officers holding that designation? These considerations, along with a sensitivity to the historical significance of the longstanding hierarchical office of Church Patriarch, likely contributed to the unique context of Patriarch Eldred G. Smith's emeritus status.

Patriarch Eldred G. Smith at 105 years old in his office.

Eldred's emeritus status was different from that of the emeritus Seventies in other ways as well. Except for his invisibility (for example, no longer
on the General Authority chart, no longer visiting at stake conferences,
no longer speaking at General Conference), his emeritus status left his
duties virtually the same as when he was an active General Authority.
Even before the announcement of his emeritus status, his duties had been
limited to giving patriarchal blessings to any member in the world who
came to his office with appropriate recommends from his bishop and stake
president. That authority continued after he was an Emeritus General
Authority. All prior administrative dimensions of the office had already
been curtailed, including presiding over the other patriarchs and visiting
at stake conferences. As was the case with the Seventies before becoming
emeritus, Eldred also had an office, a secretary, and a reserved parking
space. He also attended the monthly General Authority meetings in the
Salt Lake temple on the third Thursday of each month and he received
his temple recommend directly from the President of the Church rather
than from his stake president. These things ceased for the Seventies once
they were placed on emeritus status, but not for Eldred. Like the Seventies,
Patriarch Smith was told he was being "relieved, not released." However,
this was not really the case with Seventy emereti, who were de facto released. With Patriarch Smith, it was true: he was not released. Although

he was not required to continue to serve, he was told that at his option he could continue as before, and everything was provided that was needed for him to continue as an active General Authority—except for visibility. He understood that the office of Patriarch was intended to be retired, but he, personally, was not being retired. He continued to be provided with an office, a secretary, a parking space; he attended the monthly General Authority meetings and received his special temple recommend from the President of the Church. He attempted to walk the tightrope of "invisible General Authority" for the next thirty-five years.

Eldred's assigned office was located at the rear of the second floor of the Joseph Smith Memorial Building. A sign was posted near the elevators: "Church Patriarch."

For the first few years, some members continued to come to Eldred from throughout the world to receive their patriarchal blessings; however, the number diminished over time as people became less aware of his availability until, for the last few years, virtually no one came. In later years the Church telephone operators apparently were no longer aware of his availability and began to tell those who inquired that the Church Patriarch was no longer giving blessings. His part-time secretary faithfully checked on Eldred and transcribed blessings as needed. While in his office, when there were no other matters to occupy him, he would read the Church magazines, go through his mail, and sometimes visit with people who, out of curiosity, would come by.

Most probably the Brethren assumed Eldred would voluntarily relinquish the connections to his active office status at some point. However, throughout the rest of his life Eldred continued to go to his office—even when his attendance dwindled down to just Tuesdays. His calling as Church Patriarch was his lifelong purpose. He had an immovable faith in the divine origin of the Church, and he felt an obligation to live up to the expectations of generations of Smith patriarchs who had gone before him. So he continued to participate in everything that was possible in connection with his calling. He regularly attended the General Authority monthly meetings in the Salt Lake Temple, the last one being the day before his death in April 2013. President Monson would occasionally ask Eldred to bear his testimony at these meetings and was always kind and gracious toward him. While Eldred no longer spoke at General Conferences, or sat on the stand, he did have reserved seats near the front, and went with other General Authorities through the tunnel, from his reserved parking space next to the Church offices to the Conference Center. President Monson would sometimes acknowledge him as he went in and out of General Conference sessions. Eldred also worked as a sealer at the Salt Lake Temple one day a week up until shortly before his death.

CHURCH
PATRIARCH

LDS FOUNDATION

CHURCH HOSTING

VISITORS'
ACTIVITIES

Sign after 1979 indicating location of the office of the Church Patriarch—on
second floor of Joseph Smith Memorial Building in Salt Lake City.

For many years, Eldred kept, in a cabinet next to his office, the hard copies of the patriarchal blessings he had given.[13] At least two General Authorities requested, from time to time, that he release them to be digitized and kept in the Church Archives, but Eldred resisted those requests. To him they represented his life's work, and he felt proprietarily responsible. Eventually, however, he allowed them to be taken away. Toward the end of his life he visited the Church Archives and was reassured that they had not only been digitized, but also that the original hardcopies were still being kept. He was pleased.

The uniqueness of Patriarch Smith's emeritus status, while giving him some continued status, ironically served to exacerbate the frustration he felt about the office not being given the full historical dimensions he thought it deserved. Perhaps it would have been better for all parties to have given him the traditional emeritus status where he would have been more insulated from any perception of continuing recognition as a General Authority. As it was, he occasionally vented his frustration too freely.

A second unique dimension to Eldred's emeritus years was his response to hundreds of requests that he increase the availability of his "firesides,"[14] where he displayed historical artifacts[15] and told restoration stories about the relics. Before emeritus status his firesides were scattered and few. After, he presented up to fifty such firesides per year. With his wife, Hortense Child Smith,[16] he took the artifacts in the car or on the plane, and unpacked them for groups of from fifty to five hundred. These artifacts are described in three categories:

1. The most historically significant of the artifacts was the clothing that Hyrum Smith was wearing when he was murdered in 1844. This consisted of pants, shirt, and vest in amazingly good condition, with blood stains on the shirt and bullet holes in all three garments. Hyrum's widow, Mary Fielding Smith, carried all the artifacts with her after the martyrdom from Nauvoo, Illinois, to Winter Quarters, and then, in 1848, on to the Salt Lake Valley. When she died in 1852 they went to Hyrum's eldest son, John, and then down through the eldest-son line to Eldred. Eldred would explain how Hyrum was killed by a mob, along with his brother, the Prophet Joseph Smith, in Carthage Jail, Illinois, when a bullet came through the door, striking him in the head just to the left of his nose. After Hyrum fell to the floor, Joseph jumped out the window and the mob upstairs turned around and went back down the stairs to participate in the murder of the Prophet. Then the mob returned upstairs, turned over the lifeless body of Hyrum, and shot him in the back; a bullet passed through his body, stopping up against Hyrum's watch, which was in

Brother Alvin's tool box said to contain the golden plates translated by the Prophet Joseph Smith.

Clothes worn by Hyrum Smith when murdered, with blood stains and bullet holes.

Alvin's tool box, owned by Hyrum Smith, and borrowed by Joseph Smith. Mock up of golden plates inside.

The footstool owned by Lucy Mack Smith, mother of Joseph and Hyrum Smith.

his front vest pocket. The very watch, damaged from the bullet, was then also displayed.

2. Another artifact Eldred displayed was a box owned and possibly made by Alvin Smith, older brother to Hyrum and Joseph. Alvin carved his name in the edge of the box, and it is still visible. The family account is that after the box went to Hyrum upon Alvin's death, Joseph borrowed it from Hyrum to lock up the gold plates after first receiving them from the Angel Moroni. Lucy Mack Smith's autobiography recounts how Joseph asked his younger brother, Don Carlos, to go to Hyrum's cabin to ask Hyrum to bring the box up to the frame home so the plates could be locked inside. Hyrum dumped the contents of the box on the floor and ran with Don Carlos back up to the frame home. Lucy said, "When the chest came, Joseph locked up the record."[17]

3. Other artifacts Eldred showed and discussed in his firesides included Hyrum's Nauvoo Legion dress sword, his hunting rifle, the Smith family dinner bell, Hyrum's sunglasses, and a stool owned by Lucy Mack Smith, mother of Hyrum and Joseph.

As he grew older, Eldred became one of the relics, and many thousands of people attended his presentations throughout the United States, and even overseas. It is interesting to note that these firesides were public demonstrations of the importance of the Smith family in early Church history—back when familial charisma had primary authority. It is perhaps fitting that as Patriarch Smith was playing out the final years of his life, and the final years of the life of the familial office he held, these firesides served as a dramatic reminder of the family heritage that was once so visible and important for the Church. He did not want the members to forget the important role the early Smith family played in the Restoration of the Gospel.

In another undertaking that also involved keeping the memory of Hyrum Smith alive, Eldred, as president of the Hyrum Smith Family Foundation,[19] spearheaded the raising of sufficient money to purchase the home in which Hyrum and Jerusha lived in Kirtland, Ohio, in the 1830s. The house was then gifted to the Church as a historical site. Eldred was also active in the Joseph Smith Sr. and Lucy Mack Smith family organization and did much to promote good relations between the posterity of Hyrum and Joseph.[20]

The third unique element about Eldred's emeritus years was simply its duration. It lasted thirty-four years, two years longer than his active incumbency. He was 106 when he passed away in April 2013, having served as a General Authority for sixty-six years. His family was somewhat prepared for his passing when he reached one hundred years old. However, he then announced, humorously, that he was the Fourth Nephite.[21] By the time he reached 106 his family was, again humorously, taking him at his word, and no longer expecting him to die.

In about 2012, in one of the monthly General Authority meetings in the temple, President Boyd K. Packer, then age eighty-eight, alluded to how difficult it was to grow older. Eldred, at 105, sitting toward the rear of the group, said rather too loudly, "Tell me about it!"

At his age it was difficult for him to dress for the temple meeting that followed the monthly Thursday meeting, so two of the Seventy were assigned to help him dress each time. He appreciated the kindly service but was also somewhat embarrassed by its necessity, once commenting that he felt like a rag doll as he was being dressed. He referred jokingly to his emeritus status as "emer-*itis*"—a disease with no cause, no treatment, no cure.

He enjoyed driving a car throughout his life. However, after he turned 104 his family leaned on him to give up driving. He was adamant that he was a good driver and would not stop. At first his family hid the keys to the car. He found other keys. Then in February of 2012, when Eldred was 105, the First Presidency sent him a letter instructing him not to drive. At that point his family hid the cars. Eldred was not happy but finally allowed others to do the driving. He did remain a back-seat driver and enjoyed going to the grocery store, where he could drive the electric cart around the store.

Eldred's first wife died after forty-five years of marriage, at age sixty-nine. When he married Hortense Child less than two years later, everyone expected her to outlive Eldred, given that she was twelve years younger. However, Hortense passed away in May 2012. He had been married to Hortense for thirty-four years and had been married a total of seventy-nine years. Shortly after Hortense died, Eldred, age 105, confided with a twinkle that he had decided not to look for another wife.[22]

Two of the things Eldred enjoyed doing during his very old age were watching Perry Mason reruns on television and attending the BYU football games. He and Hortense were graciously welcomed into the BYU president's box at home games. He stayed mentally alert and followed the games with appropriate critique. For Eldred's last couple of birthdays, President Thomas S. Monson kindly came to his home to visit him. They enjoyed a special friendship over many years. President Monson was age forty-two when Eldred was placed on emeritus status and had been a member of the Council of the Twelve for six years at that time. They had traveled together to Australia on Church business, as well as other places.

The day before Eldred died he attended the monthly General Authority meeting, and then attended a closing on some real estate he was buying. He was alert and mentally sharp to the last day. What was the secret to his longevity? He would say, "Keep breathing." It may have been the shredded wheat he ate every morning, or the hamburgers, Dr. Pepper, ice cream, or chocolate he loved so much. It certainly was not "exercise," since he believed exercise that did not produce some tangible result was a waste of time. Possibly it was his determination to stretch out as long as possible the last vestige of his historic hierarchical office.

Patriarch Eldred G. Smith faced serious challenges throughout his service in the office of Patriarch. He grew up being taught by his parents that the office was his birthright and lifetime calling. When his father died at the early age of fifty-two, Eldred, age twenty-five, faced the challenge of hanging on for ten years and not knowing whether he would be called. In the ensuing five years he faced the challenge of adjusting to the idea the office would never be his. Then he had the challenge of being called unexpectedly to the office by President George Albert Smith. Eldred was not exactly gracious in his acceptance speech, and this, along with other less-than-politic comments he had made over the years, brought him into the office facing some overt hostility from a few of the Brethren.[23] For thirty-two years he tried to live up to what he saw as his calling, under the weight of scrutiny and criticism of some of the Brethren. He was not always sensitive or politically astute in the way he met that challenge. Then came the challenge of emeritus status. The unique nature of the role was probably a result of the Brethren trying to avoid unwanted precedents but also as genuine kindness toward Patriarch Smith. For the next thirty-four years, he faced the challenge of dealing with his own perceived failure and the struggle to be fully active in his calling to the extent it was possible. The unique emeritus status to which he was assigned left him some vestige of dignity but also left him virtually invisible and irrelevant to the Church membership.

This additional chapter dealing with Eldred's years as Emeritus Church Patriarch is a necessary conclusion to the history of this once-important Church office. The simple fact is that the office did not end as long as Eldred was alive. Indeed, it was impossible to separate the office from the man as long as the man continued to operate within the framework of the office. In confirmation of Weberian theory, as explained in this book's opening chapter, the death of Eldred G. Smith represented the final and complete transition from familial authority in the Church to that of office authority. It is logical that the process of changing authority within an institution results in profound effects on the individuals caught in that process. Eldred was, by natural endowment, an engineer. He was intelligent, but he was not an academic.[24] He was not a natural writer or speaker. He sometimes naively charged windmills with his perception of how the office ought to be, rather than working carefully within the realistic parameters available to him. He was a good man, out of his natural environment. His passing tolled not only his own life, but also the death of the last vestige of "familial authority" as reflected by the office of Church Patriarch.

Notes

1. Conference Report, October 1975, 3; or Ensign, November 1975, 4.

2. N. Eldon Tanner, "Revelation on Priesthood Accepted, Church Officers Sustained," Ensign, November 1978, 16. As of October 6, 2012, there had been eighty-one general authorities placed on emeritus status.

3. James A. Cullimore, Henry D. Taylor, and S. Dilworth Young, respectively.

4. Sterling W. Sill, Joseph Anderson, William H. Bennett, and John H. Vandenberg, respectively. "News of the Church," Ensign, November 1978.

5. Lds.org, The Quorums of the Seventy, Elder Earl C. Tingey of the Presidency of the Seventy, August 2005. There were other restrictions on lifetime appointments that applied to the newly created Second Quorum of the Seventy.

6. Richard Alger, personal online journal, "Marlin K. Jensen Conversations," June 29, 2013.

7. Hyrum was given the title of prophet, seer, and revelator at the time he was called to be the Presiding Patriarch. Doctrine and Covenants 124:91-94.

8. Council of the Twelve to President George Albert Smith, June 22, 1949. LDS Church Archives.

9. Conference Report, April 1983, 4; or Ensign, May 1983, 6: ". . . each member of the Quorum of the Twelve 'holds the keys of this dispensation in latent reserve. Inherent in that divine residual is the assured ongoing leadership of the Church.'"

10. Council of the Twelve to President George Albert Smith, June 22, 1949. LDS Church Archives.

11. Thomas G. Alexander, Mormonism in Transition: A History of the Latter-Day Saints, 1890-1930 (Urbana: University of Illinois Press, 1986), 116.

12. These tensions have been discussed throughout other chapters in this book.

13. He gave approximately eighteen thousand blessings.

14. "Firesides" are known among the LDS membership as informal presentations on church subjects outside the regular church meeting agendas.

15. The artifacts are now in possession of the LDS Church and are currently being displayed in the Church History Museum in Salt Lake City.

16. Hortense Child Smith had served as a counselor to Ruth Funk in the General Presidency of the Young Women's Program of the Church.

17. Historical accounts referring to the plates actually being kept and locked in Alvin's box include Joseph's mother, Lucy, as well as Joseph's fourteen-year-old sister, Katherine. Lucy Mack Smith, Biographical Sketches of Joseph Smith the Prophet and His Progenitors for Many Generations (Liverpool, Eng.: Richards, 1853; New York: Arno/New York Times, 1969), 109. Katherine said,

"[When Joseph came back from the woods,] we got a chest and locked the records up in the house." Katherine Smith Salisbuy's 1895 RLDS Conference Talks, reconstructed from April 11, 1895, *Kansas City Times* and *Kansas City Journal, Saints Herald, Zion's Ensign, Independent Patriot,* and *RLDS Conference Minutes* from the Official William Smith Home Page; Andrew H. Hedges, "'Take Heed Continually': Protecting the Gold Plates," *Ensign,* January 2001. Messenger [Berkeley, California], October 1954, p. 1 at p. 6. Mary Salisbury Hancock, "The Three Sisters of the Prophet Joseph Smith," *Saints' Herald* 101 (January 25, 1954): 10-11, 24.

18. A few years before Eldred G. Smith died he asked his son, E. Gary Smith, and his wife, Elizabeth Shaw Smith, to take over the presentation of his traditional fireside utilizing the Smith family artifacts. In 2013 the BYU religion department loaned a mockup of the gold plates to Gary and Elizabeth to put inside Alvin's box, to photograph, and then to use the photograph in their PowerPoint presentation, which was part of the fireside. The "plates" fit inside the box with the lid closed.

19. This was a 501(c)(3) organization.

20. Joseph's children did not go west with Brigham Young and were involved in the establishment of the Reorganized Church of Jesus Christ of Latter-day Saints, a competing branch of the original Church. During the days of polygamy in Utah, these two organizations, and the respective families, had a sometimes-tense relationship.

21. The Book of Mormon tells of three Nephite Disciples who, after Christ's appearance in the Western Hemisphere following his crucifixion, were told they could remain on earth until Christ's second coming—much like what is thought to have been the case with John the Beloved of Jesus's original apostles.

22. Conversation between Eldred G. Smith and E. Gary Smith, May 2012.

23. See chap. 9, p. 203.

24. Eldred worked as an engineer in the Manhattan Project during World War II in Oak Ridge, Tennessee. He was awarded a certificate that read: "United States of America, War Department, Army Service Forces—Corps of Engineers, Manhattan District: This is to certify that Eldred G. Smith, Tennessee Eastman Corporation, has participated in work essential to the production of the Atomic Bomb, thereby contributing to the successful conclusion of World War II. This certificate is awarded in appreciation of effective service. 6 August 1945, Washington D.C. [signed] Secretary of War." He obtained patents in his name, one of which had to do with a valve that was incorporated into the atomic bomb.

Conclusion

In me thou see'st the glowing of such fire,
That on the ashes of his youth doth lie,
As the death-bed whereon it must expire,
Consum'd with that which it was nourished by.

—William Shakespeare, Sonnet 73

It is not surprising that the office of Church Patriarch was retired. In fact, its elimination was probably inevitable. The office and those who filled it served the membership of the Mormon church well, but significant substantive changes within the church after its origin put the office of Patriarch on a collision course with the expanding church organization. Such changes are to be expected in a religious movement embracing the concept of continuing revelation.

Weberian theory holds that "familial charisma" and "office charisma" are inherently incompatible in the long-term life of an institution. Although both are forms of "traditional authority" that are each capable of long-term institutional stability, only one can exist with any real power at any one time. This Weberian precept is classically borne out in the study of the office of the Mormon Church Patriarch.

The office of Patriarch was instituted in the unique context of the early innovative and charismatic movement, which was only partly institutional and still very much "Smith family." In the beginning the patriarchate was endowed with both hereditary rights and primal authority. As time passed, the historical place of the patriarchal office within those early beginnings, which had given it such special meaning then, became the very cause of a dilemma within the fully institutionalized church hierarchy. It can be said the seeds, or impulses, that gave such vigorous life to the office of Church Patriarch contained, from the beginning, the cause of its death.

The familial nature of the patriarchal office explains why it was so vulnerable to its own history, while other offices, like that of apostle, were not. As noted in chapter 2, the historian Jan Shipps has pointed out the powerful effect of Joseph Smith's family on the genesis of the church and the tendency to sometimes see Joseph Smith, Jr., in a vacuum, apart from his family: "a proper prologue to a study of Mormonism does not open with the visions of the Mormon prophet, the coming forth of the Book of Mormon, and the organization of the church, but with the story of the life and hard times of Joseph Smith's family. . . . accounts of Mormon beginnings are incomplete when so much emphasis is placed on Joseph Smith, Jr., that his family recedes into the background."[1]

The pre-1844 church had a Smith family dimension often overlooked by those who see history through the lens of the modern institution. The office of Church Patriarch was a calling within the Smith family. The calling of apostle was not. Theoretically, either familial charisma or office charisma *could* have led the church, but the historical fact is that the direct hierarchical role of the Smiths, as a family, ceased suddenly and permanently with the martyrdom of Joseph Smith and Hyrum Smith in 1844. The office of Church Patriarch lingered as an anachronism within the hierarchy from 1845 to the time of its de jure retirement in 1979, and its de facto retirement in 2013, tolerated for the most part for 135 years but never considered authoritative. Consistent with Weberian theory, the office of Church Patriarch was a "familial office" without authority within an institution governed by leaders having "office charisma" authority.

The tensions that existed between the Twelve and the church patriarchs from 1844 to 1979 were basically rooted in the inherent dilemma between the two forms of authority; however, the conflicts were never articulated in that context. The tensions simply were. To live with the tensions, the Twelve ignored or changed the pre-1844 nature of the patriarchal office,[2] and the incumbent patriarchs from time to time attempted, unsuccessfully, to revive the pre-1844 patriarchal authority by referring to that early history. It is with some irony that the formal demise of the office might have been rationalized, at least in part, by reference to pre-1844 patriarchal functions. The research request made in 1976 by an influential apostle[3] and the increased emphasis given in recent years to the role of fathers in giving blessings to their own children[4] suggest that the Brethren, inadvertently perhaps, obtained a clearer view of one of the original purposes of the patriarchal office, that is, to be a father for the fatherless. Not only did John Taylor point this out in his 1845 *Times and Seasons* article,[5] but also some of the actual blessings of early recipients stated that the Patriarch was only standing in for those first generation Mormons who did not yet have a worthy priesthood father to give them a patriarchal blessing. There were, however, many members who did have worthy fathers who still sought blessings from the Patriarch.

It is ironic that by discovering an early aspect of the patriarchal office instead of continuing to ignore its history, the apostles could have concluded that the office of Church Patriarch had a special relevance that was unique to that first generation of the institution. They did not give this as their reason for retiring the office, however. Moreover, while this rationalization might have a historical base, it does not, of course, constitute an explanation for the elimination of the office. Taken to its necessary conclusion, such a rationalization would also make stake patriarchs redundant, yet they have not been eliminated. The actual reason behind the rationalization that the Twelve might have used comes back to the inherent incompatibility between office authority and the tribal, Old Testament, familial authority personified in the patriarchate.

Notwithstanding the reasoning it was based on, coming to grips with the incongruity of the charismatic patriarchal office in the modern institutional framework was overdue. Generations of church patriarchs, as well as apostles, had struggled with the symptoms of the problem without looking for the cause, far less the cure. This book's purpose has been to analyze and explain both the problems and the causes, with a view to understanding the cure better. There are five chief symptoms of the problem, or tension.

The first concerns succession, always a problem for any charismatic movement, when authority is invested in a specific individual. During the lifetime of the Prophet Joseph Smith there was no opposition to the idea that the worthy eldest son of the incumbent would succeed to the office of Patriarch by lineal right. Of course, there had been only one example of succession during Joseph's life—when Hyrum succeeded his father in 1840—but the idea was securely in place by that time. When Joseph Smith, Sr., was ordained as Patriarch in 1833, the Prophet also said that Hyrum would "stand in the tracts [tracks] of his father and be numbered among those who hold the right of patriarchal priesthood."[6]

Brigham Young thus called William Smith, albeit reluctantly, to be Church Patriarch in 1845 to satisfy the one-generation-old tradition. At that time the tension between the Patriarch and the hierarchy resulted from disagreement over the nature and authority of the office, not from any question about eldest-son succession. William was not Hyrum's oldest son, but, as the oldest living Smith brother, he was understood to be acting in lieu of young John Smith, as was Uncle John Smith, who followed William. Young John was only twelve when his father, Hyrum, was killed. Indeed, Hyrum's oldest son became the Church Patriarch as soon as he was old enough.

After John's death in 1912, the succession tradition was maintained even though the immediate candidate—John's eldest son—did not seem qualified and perhaps was not considered worthy. While skipping a generation, the office stayed strictly within the oldest-son line by going to the grandson of the deceased incumbent.

Official church pronouncements and publications in the twentieth century confirmed that this calling was to be handed down from father to eldest son. In 1933, after the death of Hyrum G. Smith, the idea of succession was severely challenged. The president of the church, Heber J. Grant, wished either to abandon succession entirely or to broaden it to include any descendant of Hyrum Smith. Apostle Joseph Fielding Smith, Jr., with the acquiescence of the Council of the Twelve, still asserted that "this particular office is and always has been one that descends with the blood, the virtues of which are inherent in the blood itself."[7] Even when a departure from the precedent of strict primogeniture was officially sanctioned in 1942 with the appointment of Joseph F. Smith II, homage was paid to the tradition when it was pointed out that he was still of the Hyrum Smith lineage.[8] When Joseph F. Smith II resigned four years later, President George Albert Smith, a protector of the Smith traditions to the extent he was able, called Eldred G. Smith to be the Patriarch and thereby returned the office to the eldest-son line.

But other apostles, while generally deferring to George Albert Smith during his presidency, continued to share President Grant's belief that the office should not have any succession rights, at least not to the extent of conferring a right on the eldest son, even if personally worthy. This was never again tested since the office was retired during the lifetime of Eldred G. Smith. The fact that this decision was on the horizon, to be faced eventually, probably contributed to the reexamination of the office, which in turn led to its elimination.

Although not discussed in this study, it should be acknowledged that world institutional systems in general were also becoming disenchanted with lineal forms of authority. Not only has hereditary monarchy lost its political power in Britain and other parts of the world, but even as a decorative form it is declining in popularity. Certainly the leaders of the LDS Church were not immune to those forces of science and enlightenment that cast doubt on the idea of inherent virtues' being passed by the blood. Indeed, we see a clear trend beginning with Joseph Smith, when family and blood were completely accepted as an authoritative source; to Brigham Young, who kept to the tradition with some reluctance; to George F. Richards, who saw some blood lines as more "worthy" than others; to Spencer W. Kimball, who finally concluded that "blood," whether in blacks or Smiths, really made no inherent difference at all.

A second source of tension, symptomatic of the inherent inconsistency between familial and office authority, was the question of the Patriarch's authority vis-à-vis the Prophet. The primal authority of the Patriarch was essentially historical—disappearing after William's death—but some apostles continued to fear its reemergence. Ambiguities in the relevant Doctrine and Covenant scriptures did not help. In 1841 the patriarchal office had primal honorary authority as well as a share in primal administrative authority. When Hyrum Smith was installed as the second church patriarch, he was taken out of the First Presidency to assume the office of Patriarch. This was considered a promotion. By revelation, the Prophet Joseph declared that Hyrum was henceforth to be "a prophet, and a seer, and a revelator unto my church as well as my servant Joseph, that he may act in concert also with my servant Joseph, and that he shall receive counsel from my servant Joseph."[9] In the same revelation, Hyrum, as Patriarch, was placed first, ahead of even the Prophet Joseph Smith, in the order for sustaining officers in the church.[10]

Although Hyrum shared in administrative authority, it appears the primal dimension was mostly honorary—or spiritual. The fatherly, or patriarchal, position can be compared with that which Lehi had with Nephi, in the Book of Mormon, and Jacob had with Joseph of Egypt, in the Bible. Perhaps authority to bless and authority to preside were considered separate but equal in the beginning. Douglas James Davies has suggested it "would be easier to see [the office of Patriarch] in relation to the priesthoods as the balanced relation of mystical to jural power."[11]

The hierarchy after 1844 did not see concurrent roles for the two types of authority. When succeeding church patriarchs referred to the premartyrdom period as precedent for the scope or meaning of the patriarchal calling, others in the hierarchy became concerned. Some apostles maintained that Hyrum received two separate callings in Doctrine and Covenants 124—as the Patriarch and associate president—and that all references to primal authority in the revelation refer to the office of associate president only. Although, as discussed in chapter 3, this is probably not an accurate view of that historical period, the argument nevertheless goes on to conclude that, since the office of associate president died with Hyrum, the Church Patriarch cannot claim authority from those passages in the Doctrine and Covenants.

Whatever the meaning of those words in the revelation, and whatever might have been the nature of the office of Church Patriarch during Hyrum Smith's time, presiding patriarchs since Hyrum have not been acknowledged by the hierarchy (the Twelve) to have the authority Hyrum had. Reminders by subsequent patriarchs of the revelations referring to Hyrum have only served to increase the tensions.

A third source of tension was uncertainty about the relationship between the Patriarchs and the Twelve. Prior to 1844 the Church Patriarch was regarded as "above" the Twelve in the church hierarchy. After 1845 he became subordinate to the Twelve. This was true even though some vestiges of the earlier ranking remained in some of the formalities. For example, for several years he was sustained in General Conference immediately after the First Presidency and before the Twelve, and in the monthly meetings of the General Authorities he was for many years seated between the First Presidency and the Quorum of the Twelve.[12]

As discussed in chapter 5, the positioning of the office of Church Patriarch necessarily altered when the apostles, who were previously beneath the Patriarch in ranking, *became* the Presidency of the church in 1844. Either the Patriarch became the president himself (as argued by William Smith) or the Patriarch became, for the first time, subject to the Twelve. The latter occurred de facto but was never articulated or made de jure by the Twelve until much later. The tensions over this issue occurred primarily from continuing reminders by incumbent church patriarchs of a time when the Patriarch stood with the president, and none stood between them. These reminders constituted an implicit criticism of the change from that early time.

One of the fascinating scenarios in this history is the time when Joseph F. Smith and John Smith, brothers and sons of Patriarch Hyrum Smith, came together as president and Patriarch, mirroring the premartyrdom relationship in form, but not, of course, in substance. Even though the Patriarch ordained his brother as president of the church, the attempts at déjà vu only succeeded in engendering concern among the apostles about the potentially troublesome nature of the otherwise benign patriarchal office. These concerns manifested themselves years later and also contributed to the elimination of the office.

The fourth source of tension: In addition to the issue of whether the office had primal administrative authority, there was also tension after 1844 over whether the office had any administrative authority at all and, if so, its parameters. There were two areas of potential nonprimal authority: presiding over a quorum of patriarchs and performing special administrative assignments from the General Authorities.

During the years following the martyrdom, the office continued to be defined as potentially one of presidency over local patriarchs. The concept of a council, or "quorum," of patriarchs was confirmed in 1845 when John Taylor was defining the office of Church Patriarch.[13] There is evidence that a quorum was again organized later in the nineteenth century and that it operated at least from time to time well into the twentieth century. That such a quorum was acknowledged can be seen in the voting procedures in solemn assemblies (held when a new president is sustained), where patriarchs voted as a quorum along with other priesthood quorums.[14]

Certainly Hyrum G. Smith, the sixth patriarch, took his presiding role seriously. Under the initial tutelage of his great-uncle, President Joseph

F. Smith, he functioned more completely and successfully in that capacity than did any other church patriarch since Hyrum Smith. After his death in 1932, incumbents were denied the role of presiding over local patriarchs. Later church manuals indicated that "the Patriarch to the Church does not preside over stake patriarchs," and, after 1943, the official *General Church Handbook* assigned the stake president the task of supervising the work of stake patriarchs.[15] In 1973 Elder Delbert L. Stapley, a member of the Council of the Twelve, was delegated the supervision of stake patriarchs. In addressing a meeting of more than a hundred local patriarchs, he said, "I mentioned that you work directly under the Quorum of the Twelve. There is no quorum of patriarchs. In earlier days it was different than it is now but the revelations place the responsibility of patriarchs directly under the Twelve." He conceded that many of those present "learned ere this that the patriarchs of the Church dangle in a sense because they are unattached; but I hope your stake presidents will give you some attention."[16]

After 1933 the only authority the Church Patriarch exercised was that which was specifically granted by the First Presidency or Quorum of the Twelve on an ad hoc basis, and it was never the type that allowed real administrative decisions. It included occasional stake conference assignments (but always with and subject to another general authority), setting apart missionaries, speaking at general conferences, speaking occasionally at other meetings, and offering prayers.

The different names the office went by is an indication of the variations in administrative authority extended and, to some degree, the varying degrees of dissonance. The title fluctuated between "Patriarch over the whole Church," "Patriarch of the Church," "Presiding Patriarch," and "Patriarch to the Church." During the 1932–42 hiatus, it was determined that the name should henceforth be "Patriarch to the Church."

The vacillating and ambiguous administrative role of the Church Patriarch created tensions within the hierarchy. On the one hand, John Smith was censured because he was perceived to be ineffective in presiding over the local patriarchs. On the other hand, Eldred G. Smith was criticized for believing a quorum of patriarchs ought to exist. Eldred's desire for his office to have some administrative authority came in conflict with the Brethren's lack of willingness to grant authority to the office. Yet the Brethren criticized the Patriarch for not being busy with the duties of his office, even at times when there were few candidates asking for patriarchal blessings. It is important to see these dynamics not as petty squabblings but as symptoms of the inevitable incompatibility of a familial office within an office institution.

A fifth tension was the question of whether the Patriarch could ordain his successor, which involved the family aspect of the calling. Father Smith ordained Hyrum, much as Abraham passed the torch to Isaac, and Hyrum was expected to pass the office to his son, just as Isaac, in turn, passed the birthright to Jacob. But Hyrum was killed before he could gather his family and bestow the office on young John. It is an interesting study in transition to see Brigham Young, the first of the primary officeholders, making reference to and reverencing that purely family aspect of the hierarchy when he ordained young John to be Patriarch: "[We] ordain thee to the High Priesthood of Almighty God, conferring on thee all the powers and blessing and authority of the Priesthood, with the keys as thy Grandfather Joseph Smith held them, who conferred them on your father Hyrum Smith, so we confer them instead of thy father who would have conferred them on thee if he had been alive."[17]

The office changed hands three times after that pronouncement by Brigham Young. It is not known if John was tempted to ordain his somewhat wayward son, Hyrum Fisher Smith, in advance of his own death. The only other known time the practice was considered was when Hyrum G. Smith asked for his son to be brought to him for that purpose, even though he knew the current president of the church did not accept such a concept and practice. Hyrum put off the ordination not because the Brethren did not approve but because he believed he would have years to accomplish it. However, he died shortly thereafter and thus never did ordain Eldred. Reference to this as even a possible practice became a source of tension between the patriarchy and the rest of the hierarchy. Not so at the time Brigham Young ordained young John, obviously, but comments about such a privilege by both Hyrum Gibbs Smith and Eldred G. Smith served to increase the distance between the patriarchy and the Brethren.

Apart from these five problems, there have been other dynamics operating in the relationship between the hierarchy and the patriarchy. Primary among these were the personalities of the protagonists. Space does not allow for the exposition the subject deserves. Suffice it to say that the men and women who played a part were, at different times and in different situations, heroic, flawed, humble, proud, sincere, disingenuous, and at all times fascinatingly human. They all shared a real and fervent commitment to the gospel of Jesus Christ as taught by the church and generally acted in a way that each saw as serving the mission of the church. B. H. Roberts said it well:

The position is not assumed that the men of the New Dispensation— its prophets, apostles, presidencies, and other leaders—are without faults or infallible, rather they are treated as men of like passions with their fellow men. Bearing indeed a heavenly treasure, no less a thing than delegated authority from God to teach the gospel and administer its ordinances of salvation to the children of men. . . . But while the officers and members of the church possess this spiritual "treasure," they carried it in earthen vessels.[18]

There were aggressive leaders, such as Brigham Young and Heber J. Grant. There were faithful followers, such as Uncle John Smith. There were peripheral players who had an interest and impact, such as John Taylor, President Joseph F. Smith, George F. Richards, Joseph Fielding Smith, Jr., and President George Albert Smith. There were those thrust into the drama who found the experience ultimately a negative one, such as William Smith, Hyrum Fisher Smith, and perhaps Joseph Fielding Smith II. The interaction of these personalities contributed to some extent to the ebb and flow of the tensions created between "family" and "institution," but the personalities were probably incidental to the basic cause of incompatibility and of the retirement of the office.

The retirement of the office of Patriarch to the Church did not basically change the way in which members of the church were able to obtain their patriarchal blessings. Patriarch Emeritus Eldred G. Smith was specifically authorized by President Spencer W. Kimball to continue giving blessings to members of the church in the same way he did in the past, and he continued to give blessings in his office in the Church Office Building to those who properly apply. In 1976, three years before the retirement of the office of Church Patriarch, preliminary steps were taken with a view to expanding the ability of local patriarchs to give blessings outside their own stakes.[19]

While the Church Patriarch traditionally gave blessings primarily to those who did not live in established stakes of the church, there were examples of local patriarchs acting beyond the geographical boundaries of their own stake even before the retirement of the office of Church Patriarch. When there were few local patriarchs in the mid-nineteenth century, stake boundaries probably did not constitute a rigid proscription requiring patriarchs to give blessings only within their stake. In the early 1930s the local patriarch James H. Wallis was authorized to give blessings throughout Europe and later in mission areas of the United States.[20] Since 1979 various stake patriarchs have received assignments to give blessings to members in mission areas of the church throughout the world. This is a practice that could have been implemented to exclude the Church Patriarch at any time after the first local patriarchs came into existence in 1837 and does not constitute an explanation for either the timing or cause of the retirement of the office in 1979.

Once the full history of the office of Patriarch is examined, it becomes less surprising that it was removed from the institutional structure. Change is inevitable in a growing church, even without the inherent incompatibility that existed because of the familial nature of the patriarchal office. The church has experienced the birth and demise of the office of assistants to the Quorum of the Twelve; the Quorum of Seventy has gone through significant changes, moving from a quorum of the hierarchy, to only Seven Presidents of Seventy, and now to both the First Quorum of Seventy and the Second Quorum of Seventy. The scope and authority of other hierarchical offices have changed also, such as that of the Presiding Bishopric. The number of counselors to the president has fluctuated significantly over time. There will no doubt be further adjustments in the hierarchical structure as the church continues to grow in size and in the diversity of its members.

A comparative study of the history of other charismatic movements would, no doubt, reveal parallel organizational challenges and shifts. Within such movements, according to Max Weber, the death of the founder (together with the passage of time and the growth of the organization) will bring problems dealing with such things as the nature and source of authority, patterns of succession, the distribution of power in the light of expansion, and the need to respond to cultural change in the society at large. Chapter 1 of this study refers to the way in which Methodism, for example, adapted following the death of its founder, John Wesley. Max Weber terms these necessary adjustments the transformation or routinization of charisma, the pure type of which, he states, is inherently unstable. Weber explains that "all modifications have basically one and the same cause: The desire to transform charisma and charismatic blessings from a unique, transitory gift of grace of extraordinary times and persons into a permanent possession of everyday life."[21]

This study of one aspect of Mormonism's solution is a classical example of Weber's theory. Weber states that "the most frequent case of a depersonalization of charisma is the belief in its transferability through blood ties . . . that household or lineage groups are considered magically blessed, so that they alone can provide the bearers of charisma."[22] As this power recedes, another charismatic power is needed, and "normally," according to Weber, "this can only be a hierocracy."[23]

Mormonism, in accomplishing its own transformation of charisma, has been able to incorporate a unique element in its evolution from a familial charismatic movement to a worldwide corporate institution. Its leaders and members strongly affirm a belief in continuous revelation. This belief, that God is directing the daily affairs of the church, serves the religion well in explaining and allowing acceptance of changes within the authority structure of the organization. It contributes to the ongoing vitality and flexibility needed for an organization in a fast-changing culture. It has been able to embrace paradox.

Mormonism, however, in combining biblical literalism with modern revelation in the office of Church Patriarch, illustrates the difficulties of trying to accommodate, structurally as well as ideologically, within a modern corporate institution, a "restitution of all things" from ancient cultures, including a charismatic patriarch. The concept of continuous revelation allows for the resolution of such conflicts, though. The heritage of Mormonism, still full of the excitement of paradox, becomes a rich tapestry for those willing to accept its complex interweavings. The history of the office of Church Patriarch is just one thread in that tapestry.

Notes

1. Jan Shipps, *Mormonism: The Story of a New Religious Tradition* (Urbana: University of Illinois Press, 1985), 4, 9.

2. The reaction of the apostolate was not limited to the office of Patriarch but applied to the historical involvement of the Smith family in general. The first joint declaration by the First Presidency and Quorum of the Twelve Apostles on August 23, 1865, was the recommendation that Mormons destroy Mother Lucy Mack Smith's *Biographical Sketches of Joseph Smith*, printed in 1853, a work that attributed much of the early movement to the family. See D. Michael Quinn, "150 Years of Truth and Consequences about Mormon History," *Sunstone* 16 (February 1992): 12, 13.

3. Boyd K. Packer research request, 1976, and response by researcher, David M. Mayfield, February 1976, Historical Department of the Church of Jesus Christ of Latter-day Saints, Salt Lake City.

4. Church manuals.

5. John Taylor, "Patriarchal," *Times and Seasons* 6 (June 1, 1845): 920–22. (See chapters 4 and 9 for a discussion of this issue.)

6. Joseph Smith, Jr., blessing of Hyrum Smith, December 18, 1833, quoted in Joseph Fielding Smith, comp., *Teachings of the Prophet Joseph Smith* (1938; Salt Lake City: Deseret Book, 1969), 40.

7. Council of the Twelve to Heber J. Grant, March 22, 1933, Council of the Twelve Correspondence, Archives of the Church of Jesus Christ of Latter-day Saints, Salt Lake City (hereafter LDS Church Archives), cited in E. Gary Smith, "Heber J. Grant and the Office of Presiding Patriarch: A Decade of Uncertainty, 1932–1942" (Paper presented at the Mormon History Association annual meeting, Laie, Oahu, Hawaii, June 14, 1990).

8. Previous chapters explain departures from primogeniture: they include the appointments of William Smith and "Uncle" John Smith because the heir-apparent was a minor and the by-passing of Hyrum F. Smith, son of John Smith, in 1912, because he was regarded as unsuitable to hold the office.

9. *Doctrine and Covenants of the Church of Jesus Christ of Latter-day Saints* (Salt Lake City: Deseret Book, 1955), 124:91–95.

10. *Doctrine and Covenants* 124:123–24ff.

11. Douglas James Davies, *Mormon Spirituality: Latter Day Saints in Wales and Zion* (Nottingham, England: Department of Theology, University of Nottingham, 1987), 118.

12. Even the official *Priesthood and Church Government* continued to state that the Patriarch to the Church is under the direction of the First Presidency, not the Twelve. John A. Widtsoe, *Priesthood and Church Government in the Church of Jesus Christ of Latter-day Saints,* compiled under the direction of the Council of the Twelve (Salt Lake City: Deseret Book, 1939), 187.

13. Taylor, "Patriarchal," 920–22. Earlier chapters discuss the subject of a quorum of patriarchs.

14. Solemn assemblies are called on special occasions, for example, when a new temple is dedicated or when a new Prophet/President is installed. They are held in the temple and are modeled on the solemn assemblies of ancient Israel. When President David O. McKay assumed the presidency in 1951, the third priesthood quorum to vote was that of the patriarchs. Roy W. Doxey, *The Latter-day Prophets and the Doctrine and Covenants,* 4 vols. (Salt Lake City: Deseret Book, 1963–65), 4:316–17.

15. See, for example, the *General Church Handbook,* no. 18 (Salt Lake City: Church of Jesus Christ of Latter-day Saints, 1960), 8–9.

16. Delbert L. Stapley address at the meeting of stake patriarchs, Salt Lake City, April 6, 1973. The *General Handbook of Instructions 1968* (Salt Lake City: Church of Jesus Christ of Latter-day Saints, 1968), 9, includes among the duties of the stake president that he supervise the work of patriarchs in his stake.

17. Ordination of John Smith by Brigham Young, February 18, 1855, Eldred G. Smith Personal Records, Salt Lake City.

18. B. H. Roberts, *A Comprehensive History of the Church of Jesus Christ of Latter-day Saints: Century I,* 6 vols. (Salt Lake City: Deseret News Press, 1930), 1:viii.

19. Boyd K. Packer research request, 1976. The request asked for information regarding historical precedents for stake patriarchs' acting outside the boundaries of their stakes.

20. James H. Wallis, Diaries, 1931–40, LDS Church Archives. Wallis received a special calling as a traveling patriarch to Great Britain in June 1931. He later served the same function in Canada. See Gloria Rytting, *James H. Wallis: Poet, Printer and Patriarch* (Salt Lake City: R. & R. Enterprises, 1989).

21. Max Weber, *Economy and Society: An Outline of Interpretive Sociology,* 3 vols., ed. Guenther Roth and Claus Wittich; trans. Ephraim Fischoff et al. (Berkeley: University of California Press, 1978), 3:1121.

22. Ibid., 3:1136.

23. Ibid., 3:1147.

Appendix A

Presiding Patriarchs and Presidents
of the Mormon Church

Patriarchs	Dates of Office	Presidents	Dates of Office
Joseph Smith, Sr.	Dec. 1833–Sept. 1840	Joseph Smith, Jr.	1830–44
Hyrum Smith	Jan. 1841–June 1844	Joseph Smith, Jr.	
William Smith	May 1845–Oct. 1845	Quorum of Twelve (Brigham Young President of the Twelve)	1844–47
Uncle John Smith	Dec. 1847–May 1854 (Sustained in 1847)	Brigham Young	1847–77
John Smith	Feb. 1855–Nov. 1911	Brigham Young	
		John Taylor	1880–87
		Wilford Woodruff	1889–98
		Lorenzo Snow	1898–1901
		Joseph F. Smith	1901–18
Hyrum Gibbs Smith	May 1912–Feb. 1932	Joseph F. Smith	
		Heber J. Grant	1918–45
George F. Richards (Acting Patriarch)	Oct. 1937–Oct. 1942	Heber J. Grant	
Joseph F. Smith II	Oct. 1942–Oct. 1946 (Released)	Heber J. Grant	
		George Albert Smith	1945–51
Eldred G. Smith	Apr. 1947–Oct. 1979 (Emeritus)	George Albert Smith	
		David O. McKay	1951–70
		Jos. Fielding Smith	1970–72
		Harold B. Lee	1972–73
		Spencer W. Kimball	1973–85

Appendix B

Mormon Presiding Patriarchs
(with blood relationships)

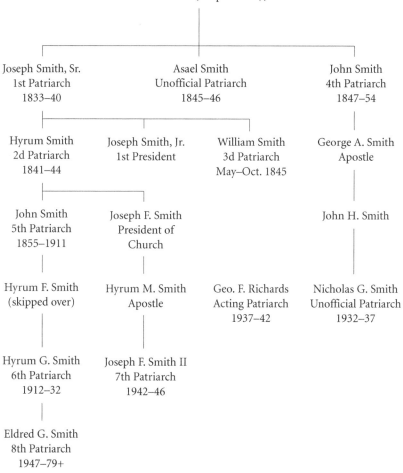

Asael Smith
Grandfather of Joseph Smith, Jr.

Joseph Smith, Sr.
1st Patriarch
1833–40

Asael Smith
Unofficial Patriarch
1845–46

John Smith
4th Patriarch
1847–54

Hyrum Smith
2d Patriarch
1841–44

Joseph Smith, Jr.
1st President

William Smith
3d Patriarch
May–Oct. 1845

George A. Smith
Apostle

John Smith
5th Patriarch
1855–1911

Joseph F. Smith
President of
Church

John H. Smith

Hyrum F. Smith
(skipped over)

Hyrum M. Smith
Apostle

Geo. F. Richards
Acting Patriarch
1937–42

Nicholas G. Smith
Unofficial Patriarch
1932–37

Hyrum G. Smith
6th Patriarch
1912–32

Joseph F. Smith II
7th Patriarch
1942–46

Eldred G. Smith
8th Patriarch
1947–79+

Bibliography

Abbreviations

BYU Archives: Archives and Manuscripts Division, Harold B. Lee Library, Brigham Young University, Provo, Utah

BYU Studies: Brigham Young University Studies

HDC: Historical Department of the Church of Jesus Christ of Latter-day Saints, Salt Lake City, Utah

LDS Church Archives: Archives of the Church of Jesus Christ of Latter-day Saints, Salt Lake City, Utah

RLDS Church Archives: Archives of the Reorganized Church of Jesus Christ of Latter Day Saints, Independence, Mo.

Manuscript Sources

In citing sources, the authors give priority to public availability. For manuscripts in restricted archives, typed transcriptions and photocopies are also sources.

Alger, Richard. Personal on-line journal. "Marlin K. Jensen Conversations," June 29, 2013.

Anderson, J. Max. "Succession in the Patriarchal Priesthood," n.d. (typescript). LDS Church Archives.

Bigler, Henry W. Diary, Book A, 1846–50 (holograph). Huntington Library, San Marino, Calif.

British Mission Manuscript History, March 8, 1839–January 15, 1843. LDS Church Archives.

Cahoon, Reynolds. Journal, 1831–32. LDS Church Archives.

Cannon, Abraham H. Journal, 1879–95. LDS Church Archives.

Clawson, Rudger. Papers. Special Collections, Marriott Library, University of Utah, Salt Lake City.

Clayton, William. Diaries, 1840–53. LDS Church Archives.

Council [Quorum] of the Twelve. Correspondence, March 22, 1933; April 4, 1935; June 22, 1949. LDS Church Archives.

———. Information and Suggestions for Patriarchs, 1943–80. LDS Church Archives.

Crosby, Caroline Barnes. Journal and Memoirs, 1807–82. Utah State Historical Society, Salt Lake City.

Dowdle, John Clark. Journal, 1836–1908. BYU Archives.

Fielding, Joseph. Diary, 1832–59. LDS Church Archives.

First Presidency. Correspondence, June 28, 1857. LDS Church Archives.

Geisner, Joseph. Family Records. Santa Rosa, Calif.
Grant, Heber J. Diaries, 1880–1933. LDS Church Archives.
———. General Conference Address, October 6, 1894. Journal History, LDS
    Church Archives.
Grant, Jedediah. Sunday Tabernacle Discourse, March 23, 1856. Journal His-
    tory, LDS Church Archives.
Hyde, Orson. Diary, 1832. LDS Church Archives. Also in Special Collections,
    Marriott Library, University of Utah, Salt Lake City, which includes "Or-
    son Hyde Biography," by his son Joseph Hyde.
Ivins, Stanley S. Notebooks. Utah State Historical Society, Salt Lake City; copy
    in New York Public Library.
Johnson, Benjamin F. Letter to George Gibbs, 1903 (typescript). Huntington
    Library, San Marino, Calif.
Journal History. LDS Church Archives.
Kane, Thomas L. Reply to President James Fillmore, July 11, 1851. Journal His-
    tory, LDS Church Archives.
Keeler, Donnette Smith. "Reminiscences of Donnette Smith Keeler." LDS
    Church Archives.
Kirtland Elders Quorum Minutes, April 29, 1836; May 21, 1836. RLDS Church
    Archives.
Kirtland High Council Minute Book. LDS Church Archives.
Knecht Family Records. In possession of William L. Knecht, Moraga, Calif.
Lyon, John. "Sacred to the Memory of John Smith Patriarch," July 20, 1854
    (holograph poem). LDS Church Archives.
McKay, David O. Diary, 1932–61. LDS Church Archives.
Manuscript History of the Church. LDS Church Archives.
Minutes of General Conference, Quincy, May 4–5, 1839. LDS Church Archives.
Minutes of a Grand Council at Kirtland, Ohio, May 2, 1835. Manuscript in-
    cluded in Patriarchal Blessing Book 2, LDS Church Archives.
Minutes of Meetings of Patriarchs, April 8, 1916; October 11, 1958; April 6, 1973.
    LDS Church Archives.
Minutes of the Quorum [Council] of the Twelve, May 27, 1843; April 10, 1947;
    April 15, 1971; April 22, 1971. LDS Church Archives.
Moffit, John Clifton. "Isaac Morley on the American Frontier," n.d. HDC.
Monroe, James. Diary, 1845. Holograph in Coe Collection, Yale University
    Library, New Haven, Conn.; copy in Huntington Library, San Marino,
    Calif.
Nauvoo Temple Record. Special Collections, Genealogical Library, Salt Lake
    City.
Packer, Boyd K. Research request, 1976, and response by David M. Mayfield,
    February 1976. HDC.
Patten, David. Journal, 1832–34. LDS Church Archives.
Richards, George F., Jr. Diaries, 1895–1953. 19 vols. LDS Church Archives.
———. Oral History Interview, No. 11, January 25, 1973. LDS Church Archives.
Richards, George F., Sr. Diaries, 1880–1950. 24 vols. LDS Church Archives.
Richards, Willard. Diaries, 1836–52. 19 vols. LDS Church Archives.

———. Letter to Brigham Young, June 30, 1844. Manuscript History of the Church, LDS Church Archives.

Robinson, Joseph E. Diaries, 1910–12. LDS Church Archives.

Sessions, Patty Bartlett. "History of Patty Bartlett Sessions: Mother of Mormon Midwifery, 1795–1893" (typescript). Huntington Library, San Marino, Calif.

Sessions, Perregrine. Diary, 1814–86. Holograph in LDS Church Archives; typescript in Huntington Library, San Marino, Calif.

Smith, Bathsheba Bigler. Record Book, 1822–1906. BYU Archives.

Smith, Caroline. Letter to Jedediah M. Grant, May 5, 1844. LDS Church Archives.

Smith, Eldred G. Personal Records. Salt Lake City. In July 1993 some of these records were donated to Brigham Young University and are currently being catalogued at the Harold B. Lee Library for a new special collection to be named for the Joseph Smith, Sr., family.

Smith, George A. [1817–75]. Comments at meeting to ordain Eldred G. Smith as Patriarch to the Church, April 10, 1947. Minutes of ordination meeting, LDS Church Archives.

———. Family Collection, 1731–1969. Manuscripts Division, Special Collections, Marriott Library, University of Utah, Salt Lake City.

Smith, George Albert [1870–1951]. Diary, 1890–1951. LDS Church Archives; copy in George A. Smith Family Collection, Manuscripts Division, Special Collections, Marriott Library, University of Utah, Salt Lake City.

Smith, Hyrum. Patriarchal blessing given to Phebe S. Merrill, January 2, 1841. RLDS Archives.

———. Patriarchal blessing given to Susanna White, September 8, 1841. RLDS Archives.

Smith, Hyrum G. Diary. Eldred G. Smith Personal Records, Salt Lake City.

———. "Instructions to Patriarchs throughout the Church," August 19, 1914. HDC.

———. Letter to Joseph A. Quibell, October 21, 1922. LDS Church Archives.

Smith, John [1781–1854]. Journal. LDS Church Archives; copy in Manuscript Division, Special Collections, Marriott Library, University of Utah, Salt Lake City.

———. Letter to George A. Smith, January 1, 1838. LDS Church Archives.

———. Letter to George A. Smith, January 15, 1838; January 7, 1841. Journal History, LDS Church Archives.

———. Papers. LDS Church Archives.

———. Patriarchal blessing given to Catherine Campbell Steele, January 26, 1846. LDS Church Archives.

Smith, John [1832–1911]. Letter to Joseph F. Smith, February 25, 1887. LDS Church Archives.

———. Letter to Joseph F. Smith, June 6, 1887. LDS Church Archives.

———. Missionary Journal, 1862–64. Original in Joseph Smith, Sr., Family Collection, BYU Archives; copy of typescript prepared by E. Gary Smith in possession of authors; copy of holograph and typescript in LDS Church Archives.

———. Patriarchal blessing given to Eliza Melissa McGary, March 1, 1875 [date unclear]. RLDS Church Archives.

Smith, John Henry. Diary, 1875–1911. Photocopy of holograph in George A. Smith Family Collection, Manuscripts Division, Special Collections, Marriott Library, University of Utah, Salt Lake City.

Smith, John Lyman. Journal, 1828–97. BYU Archives.

Smith, Joseph, Sr. Patriarchal Blessing Book, Vol. 1, 1935. LDS Church Archives.

———. Patriarchal blessing given to Elijah Abel, 1836. Minutes of the Council of the Twelve, June 4, 1879, Bennion Papers, BYU Archives. Courtesy of Lester E. Bush, Jr.

———. Patriarchal blessing given to Flora Jacobs, June 13, 1837. RLDS Church Archives.

———. Patriarchal blessing given to Stephen Post, March 26, 1836. LDS Church Archives.

———. Patriarchal blessing given to Amanda Rogers, August 11, 1837. BYU Archives.

———. Patriarchal blessing given to Lorenzo Snow, December 15, 1836. LDS Church Archives.

Smith, Joseph, III. Letter to John Smith, March 21, 1848. Joseph Smith, Sr., Family Collection, BYU Archives.

Smith, Joseph Fielding. Meeting of Patriarchs, October 11, 1958. Council of the Twelve Circular Letters, LDS Church Archives.

———. Memo, n.d. LDS Church Archives. Also appears as first item in Patriarchal Reference Book 18, March 18, 1933, LDS Church Archives.

Smith, Lucy Mack. Preliminary manuscript of Lucy Mack Smith's *History*, n.d. BYU Archives.

Smith, William. Address, August 17, 1845. LDS Church Archives.

———. Letter to Brother Little, August 20, 1845. Journal History, LDS Church Archives.

———. Letter to Brother [Lewis] Robbins, October 5, 1845. LDS Church Archives.

———. Letter to Lewis Robbins, St. Louis, November 7, 1845. LDS Church Archives.

———. Letter to Emma Smith, [month unclear] 21, 1845. LDS Church Archives.

———. Letter to Brigham Young, August 8, 1854. Brigham Young Collection, LDS Church Archives.

———. Letter to Brigham Young, August 24, 1844. Brigham Young Collection, LDS Church Archives.

———. Letter to Brigham Young, June 30, 1845. In William Clayton Diaries and in copy of John Taylor Journal, LDS Church Archives.

———. Patriarchal Blessing Book, June–September 1845. Theodore A. Schroeder Collection, State Historical Society of Wisconsin, Madison; copy in RLDS Church Archives.

Snow, Eliza R. Diary, 1846 (holograph). Huntington Library, San Marino, Calif.

Snow, Erastus. Journal, 1818–57. Holograph in LDS Church Archives; copy in Huntington Library, San Marino, Calif.

Stewart, Emily Smith. Collection. Special Collections, Marriott Library, University of Utah, Salt Lake City.

Suggestions to Patriarchs, May 25, 1943; 1970; 1975; 1978; 1981. HDC.

Talmage, James E. Journals, 1876–1933. 30 vols. BYU Archives.

Taylor, John. Journal, 1844–45. Copy of holograph in LDS Church Archives; copy in authors' possession; original in private collection.

———. Papers. Special Collections, Marriott Library, University of Utah, Salt Lake City.

Temple Lot Suit. Special Collections, Marriott Library, University of Utah, Salt Lake City.

Wallis, James H. Diaries, 1931–40. LDS Church Archives.

Woodruff, Wilford. Journal, 1833–98. 15 vols. LDS Church Archives; copy in Special Collections, Marriott Library, University of Utah, Salt Lake City.

———. Letter to John Smith, January 20, 1888. LDS Church Archives.

———. Letter to Brigham Young, October 9, 1844. Manuscript History of the Church, LDS Church Archives.

Young, Brigham. Journal, 1801–44; Diaries, 1832–63. LDS Church Archives.

———. Letter to Willard Richards, July 8, 1844. Journal History, LDS Church Archives.

———. Letter to William Smith, June 30, 1845. LDS Church Archives. Also quoted in Benjamin Johnson, Letter to George Gibbs, 1903 (typescript), Huntington Library, San Marino, Calif.; and in William Clayton Diary, July 4, 1845, LDS Church Archives; copied by John Taylor into his Journal, June 30, 1845.

———. Letter to William Smith, August 9 and 10, 1845. Brigham Young Collection, LDS Church Archives.

———. Letter to Wilford Woodruff, June 27, 1845. Wilford Woodruff Collection, LDS Church Archives.

Young, Brigham, Jr. Diaries, 1862–1903; February 1903–December 1903. 30 vols. in LDS Church Archives; Book 215 in New York Public Library.

Newspapers and Periodicals

Brigham Young University Studies, Provo, Utah

Church News, Salt Lake City, Utah

Deseret Evening News, Salt Lake City, Utah

Dialogue: A Journal of Mormon Thought, Salt Lake City, Utah

Ensign, Salt Lake City, Utah

Evening and Morning Star, Kirtland, Ohio

Improvement Era, Salt Lake City, Utah

Instructor, Salt Lake City, Utah

Millennial Star, London, U.K.

Nauvoo Expositor, June 7, 1844. Facsimile of the only issue of the *Expositor* at the Huntington Library, San Marino, Calif.

New York History

Review of Religious Research

Salt Lake Tribune

Sunstone, Salt Lake City, Utah

The Prophet, Newspaper Collection, New York Public Library Annex, New York

Times and Seasons, Nauvoo, Illinois

Utah Genealogical Magazine, Salt Lake City, Utah

Warsaw Signal, Nauvoo, Illinois

Books and Pamphlets

Alexander, Thomas G. *Things in Heaven and Earth: The Life and Times of Wilford Woodruff, a Mormon Prophet.* Salt Lake City: Signature Books, 1991.

Allen, James B., and Glen M. Leonard. *The Story of the Latter-day Saints.* Salt Lake City: Deseret Book, 1976.

Arrington, Leonard J., and Davis Bitton. *The Mormon Experience: A History of the Latter-day Saints.* New York: Alfred A. Knopf, 1979.

Barlow, Phillip. *Mormons and the Bible.* New York: Oxford University Press, 1991.

Bendix, Reinhard. *Max Weber: An Intellectual Portrait.* Berkeley: University of California Press, 1977.

Bennett, Richard E. *Mormons at the Missouri, 1846–1852: "And Should We Die. . . ."* Norman: University of Oklahoma Press, 1987.

A Book of Commandments for the Government of the Church of Christ. Zion [Independence, Mo.]: W. W. Phelps, 1833. Reprint. Independence, Mo.: Herald Publishing, 1971.

Brodie, Fawn M. *No Man Knows My History.* New York: Alfred A. Knopf, 1945.

Brooks, Juanita. *John D. Lee: Zealot-Pioneer Builder-Scapegoat.* Glendale, Calif.: Arthur Clark, 1973.

———, ed. *On the Mormon Frontier: The Diary of Hosea Stout.* 2 vols. Salt Lake City: University of Utah Press, 1964.

Brough, R. Clayton, and Thomas W. Grassley. *Understanding Patriarchal Patriarchal Blessings.* Bountiful, Utah: Horizon, 1984.

Bushman, Richard L., *Joseph Smith and the Beginnings of Mormonism.* Urbana: University of Illinois Press, 1984.

Cannon, Donald Q., and Lyndon W. Cook. *Far West Record: Minutes of the Church of Jesus Christ of Latter-day Saints, 1830–1844.* Salt Lake City: Deseret Book, 1983.

Cannon, Frank J. *Under the Prophet in Utah.* Boston: C. M. Clark, 1911.

Clark, James R., ed. *Messages of the First Presidency of the Church of Jesus Christ of Latter-day Saints, 1833–1964.* 6 vols. Salt Lake City: Bookcraft, 1965–75.

Collier, Fred C., ed. *The Teachings of President Brigham Young, 1852–1854.* 3 vols. Salt Lake City: Collier's, 1987.

Conference Reports of the Church of Jesus Christ of Latter-day Saints. Salt Lake City: Church of Jesus Christ of Latter-day Saints, 1900, 1901, 1912, 1927, 1942, 1944, 1946, 1947, 1960, 1979.

Corbett, H. Pearson. *Hyrum Smith, Patriarch.* Salt Lake City: Deseret Book, 1963.

Coser, Lewis A., and Bernard Rosenberg, eds. *Sociological Theory: A Book of Readings.* New York: Macmillan, 1957.

Davies, Douglas James. *Mormon Spirituality: Latter Day Saints in Wales and Zion.* Nottingham, England: Department of Theology, University of Nottingham, 1987. Distributed by Utah State University Press, Logan, Utah.

Deseret News 1989–1990 Church Almanac. Salt Lake City: Deseret News, 1988.

Doctrine and Covenants of the Church of Jesus Christ of Latter-day Saints. Salt Lake City: Deseret Book, 1955.

Doxey, Roy W., *The Latter-day Prophets and the Doctrine and Covenants.* 4 vols. Salt Lake City: Deseret Book, 1963–65.

Durham, Reed C., Jr., and Steven H. Heath. *Succession in the Church.* Salt Lake City: Bookcraft, 1970.

Durkheim, Émile. *The Elementary Forms of the Religious Life.* Translated by J. W. Swain. London: Allen and Unwin, 1915.

Foster, Lawrence. *Religion and Sexuality: Three American Communal Experiments of the Nineteenth Century.* New York: Oxford University Press, 1981.

———. *Women, Family, and Utopia: Communal Experiments of the Shakers, the Oneida Community, and the Mormons.* Syracuse, N.Y.: Syracuse University Press, 1991.

General Handbook of Instructions. Salt Lake City: Church of Jesus Christ of Latter-day Saints, 1960, 1968.

Graffam, Merle, ed. *Salt Lake School of the Prophets Minute Book, 1883.* Palm Desert, Calif.: ULC Press, 1981.

Hardy, B. Carmon. *Solemn Covenant: The Mormon Polygamous Passage.* Urbana: University of Illinois Press, 1992.

Hardy, John. *History of the Trials of Elder John Hardy.* Boston: Conway, 1844.

Hill, Donna. *Joseph Smith, the First Mormon.* Midvale, Utah.: Signature Books, 1977.

Hill, Marvin S. *Quest for Refuge: The Mormon Flight from American Pluralism.* Salt Lake City: Signature Books, 1989.

Howard, Richard P., ed. *The Memoirs of President Joseph Smith III, 1832–1914.* Independence, Mo.: Herald Publishing, 1979.

Hughes, Richard T., and C. Leonard Allen. *Illusions of Innocence: Protestant Primitivism in America, 1630–1875.* Chicago: University of Chicago Press, 1988.

Jensen, Andrew. *Latter-day Saints Biographical Encyclopedia.* 4 vols. Salt Lake City: Andrew Jensen Historical Co., 1901–36.

Jessee, Dean C., comp. and ed. *The Personal Writings of Joseph Smith.* Salt Lake City: Deseret Book, 1984.

Johnson, Benjamin F. *My Life's Review.* Independence, Mo.: Zion's Printing and Publishing, 1947.

Journal of Discourses by Brigham Young, President of the Church of Jesus Christ of Latter-day Saints, His Two Counsellors, the Twelve Apostles and Others. 26 vols. Liverpool, England: Latter-day Saints Books Depot, 1855–86.

Kenney, Scott G., ed. *Wilford Woodruff's Journal, 1833–1898.* 9 vols. Midvale, Utah: Signature Books, 1983–85.

Marquardt, H. Michael, comp. *Later Patriarchal Blessings of the Church of Jesus Christ of Latter-day Saints.* Salt Lake City: Smith-Pettit Foundation, 2012.

McConkie, Bruce R. *Mormon Doctrine.* Salt Lake City: Bookcraft, 1958.

Madsen, Truman G. *Defender of the Faith: The B. H. Roberts Story.* Salt Lake City: Bookcraft, 1980.

Marini, Stephen A. *Radical Sects of Revolutionary New England.* Cambridge, Mass.: Harvard University Press, 1982.

Melchizedek Priesthood Handbook. Salt Lake City: Church of Jesus Christ of Latter-day Saints, 1975.

Muir, Leo J. *A Century of Mormon Activities in California.* 2 vols. Salt Lake City: Deseret News Press, 1951–52.

Newell, Linda King, and Valeen Tippetts Avery. *Mormon Enigma: Emma Hale Smith, Prophet's Wife, "Elect Lady," Polygamy's Foe.* New York City: Doubleday, 1984.

O'Dea, Thomas. *The Mormons.* Chicago: University of Chicago Press, 1957.

Pusey, Merlo J. *Builders of the Kingdom: George A. Smith, John Henry Smith, George Albert Smith.* Provo, Utah: Brigham Young University Press, 1981.

Quinn, D. Michael. *Early Mormonism and the Magic World View.* Salt Lake City: Signature Books, 1987.

———. *J. Reuben Clark, Jr.: The Church Years.* Provo, Utah: Brigham Young University Press, 1983.

———. *The Mormon Hierarchy: Origins of Power.* Salt Lake City: Signature Books, 1994.

Richards, Franklin D., and James A. Little. *A Compendium of the Doctrines of the Gospel.* 1882. Reprint. Salt Lake City: Deseret News, 1925.

Roberts, B. H. *A Comprehensive History of the Church of Jesus Christ of Latter-day Saints: Century I.* 6 vols. Salt Lake City: Deseret News Press, 1930.

———. *Succession in the Presidency of the Church.* 1894. Reprint. Salt Lake City: Deseret News Publishing, 1900.

Rytting, Gloria. *James H. Wallis: Poet, Printer and Patriarch.* Salt Lake City: R. & R. Enterprises, 1989.

Sessions, Gene A. *Mormon Thunder: A Documentary History of Jedediah Morgan Grant.* Urbana: University of Illinois Press, 1982.

Shils, Edward. *Center and Periphery: Essays in Macrosociology.* Chicago: University of Chicago Press, 1975.

Shipps, Jan. *Mormonism: The Story of a New Religious Tradition.* Urbana: University of Illinois Press, 1985.

Smith, Jesse N. *The Journal of Jesse Nathaniel Smith, 1834–1906.* 1953. Reprint. Provo, Utah: Jesse N. Smith Family Association, 1970.

Smith, Joseph. *History of the Church of Jesus Christ of Latter-day Saints.* Edited by B. H. Roberts. 2d rev. ed., 7 vols. Salt Lake City: Deseret Book, 1978.

———. *The Pearl of Great Price: A Selection from the Revelations, Translations, and Narrations of Joseph Smith.* Salt Lake City: Church of Jesus Christ of Latter-day Saints, 1955.

Smith, Joseph, III, and Heman C. Smith. *History of the Reorganized Church of Jesus Christ of Latter Day Saints.* 7 vols. Lamoni, Iowa: Herald Publishing, 1896–1903.

Smith, Joseph Fielding. *Doctrines of Salvation.* 3 vols. Compiled by Bruce R. McConkie. Salt Lake City: Bookcraft, 1954–56.

———. *Essentials in Church History.* 1922. Reprint. Salt Lake City: Deseret Book, 1966.

———, comp. *Teachings of the Prophet Joseph Smith.* 1938. Reprint. Salt Lake City: Deseret Book, 1969.

Smith, Lucy Mack. *Biographical Sketches of Joseph Smith the Prophet and His Progenitors for Many Generations.* Liverpool, England: Published for Orson Pratt by S. W. Richards, 1853. Reprint. New York: Arno Press and New York Times, 1969.

———. *History of Joseph Smith by His Mother, Lucy Mack Smith.* Notes and comments by Preston Nibley. Salt Lake City: Bookcraft, 1958.

———. *History of the Prophet Joseph Smith.* Revised by George A. Smith and Elias Smith. Salt Lake City: Improvement Era, 1902.

Smith, Ruby K. *Mary Bailey.* Salt Lake City: Deseret Book, 1954.

Snow, Eliza R. *Biography of Lorenzo Snow.* Salt Lake City: Deseret News Press, 1884.

Tullidge, Edward W. *The Women of Mormondom.* New York: Tullidge and Crandall, 1877.

Van Wagoner, Richard S. *Mormon Polygamy: A History.* Salt Lake City: Signature Books, 1986.

Watson, Elden Jay, ed. *The Orson Pratt Journals.* Salt Lake City: E. J. Watson, 1975.

Weber, Max. *Economy and Society: An Outline of Interpretive Sociology.* 3 vols. Edited by Guenther Roth and Claus Wittich; translated by Ephraim Fischoff et al. Berkeley: University of California Press, 1978.

Widtsoe, John A. *Priesthood and Church Government in the Church of Jesus Christ of Latter-day Saints.* Compiled under the direction of the Council of the Twelve. 1939. Reprint. Salt Lake City: Deseret Book, 1954.

Wrong, Dennis, ed. *Max Weber.* Englewood Cliffs, N.J.: Prentice Hall, 1970.

Articles

Alexander, Thomas G. "The Reconstruction of Mormon Doctrine: From Joseph Smith to Progressive Theology." *Sunstone* 10 (May 1985): 8–18.

———. "The Word of Wisdom: From Principle to Requirement." *Dialogue: A Journal of Mormon Thought* 14 (Fall 1981): 78–88.

Allen, James B. "Emergence of a Fundamental: The Expanding Role of Joseph Smith's First Vision in Mormon Religious Thought." *Journal of Mormon History* 7 (1980): 43–61.

Allen, James B., and Leonard J. Arrington. "Mormon Origins in New York: An Introductory Analysis." *BYU Studies* 9 (Spring 1969): 241–74.

Bates, Irene M. "Patriarchal Blessings and the Routinization of Charisma." *Dialogue: A Journal of Mormon Thought* 26 (Fall 1993): 1–29.

———. "Uncle John Smith, 1781–1854: Patriarchal Bridge." *Dialogue: A Journal of Mormon Thought* 20 (Fall 1987): 79–89.

———. "William Smith, 1811–1893: Problematic Patriarch." *Dialogue: A Journal of Mormon Thought* 16 (Summer 1983): 11–23.

Bennion, Lowell L. "My Odyssey with Sociology." In *The Best of Lowell Bennion,* ed. Eugene England. Salt Lake City: Signature Books, 1988.

Bishop, M. Guy. "What Has Become of Our Fathers? Baptism for the Dead at Nauvoo." *Dialogue: A Journal of Mormon Thought* 23 (Summer 1990): 85–97.

Blakeslee, J. "For the Times and Seasons." *Times and Seasons* 2 (July 15, 1841): 484.

Blau, Peter. "Critical Remarks on Weber's Theory of Authority." In *Max Weber,* ed. Dennis Wrong. Englewood Cliffs, N.J.: Prentice Hall, 1970.

Buerger, David John. "The Fulness of the Priesthood: The Second Anointing in Latter-day Saint Theology and Practice." *Dialogue: A Journal of Mormon Thought* 16 (Spring 1983): 10–44.

Bush, Lester E., Jr. "Mormonism's Negro Doctrine: An Historical Overview." *Dialogue: A Journal of Mormon Thought* 8 (Spring 1973): 11–68.

———. "The Word of Wisdom in Early Nineteenth-Century Perspective." *Dialogue: A Journal of Mormon Thought* 14 (Fall 1981): 47–65.

Cornwall, Marie. "The Gender Question." *Sunstone* 13 (December 1989): 46–48.

Crawley, Peter. "The Passage of Mormon Primitivism." *Dialogue: A Journal of Mormon Thought* 13 (Winter 1980): 26–37.

Edwards, Paul M. "The Secular Smiths." *Journal of Mormon History* 4 (1977): 3–17.

———. "William B. Smith: The Persistent Pretender." *Dialogue: A Journal of Mormon Thought* 18 (Summer 1985): 128–39.

Faust, James L. "Patriarchal Blessings." In *Devotional Speeches.* Provo, Utah: Brigham Young University Press, 1981.

Hamilton, Marshall. "Thomas Sharp's Turning Point: Birth of an Anti-Mormon." *Sunstone* 13 (October 1989): 16–22.

Haven, Charlotte. "A Girl's Letters from Nauvoo." *Overland Monthly* 16 (December 16, 1890): 635.

Hefner, Loretta L. "From Apostle to Apostate: The Personal Struggle of Amasa Mason Lyman." *Dialogue: A Journal of Mormon Thought* 16 (Spring 1983): 90–104.

Hill, Marvin S. "A Note on Joseph Smith's First Vision and Its Import in the Shaping of Early Mormonism." *Dialogue: A Journal of Mormon Thought* 12 (Spring 1979): 90–99.

———. "The Shaping of the Mormon Mind in New England and New York." *BYU Studies* 9 (Spring 1969): 351–72.

Irving, Gordon. "The Mormons and the Bible in the 1830s." *BYU Studies* 13 (Summer 1973): 471–88.

Jessee, Dean C. "The Early Accounts of Joseph Smith's First Vision." *BYU Studies* 9 (Spring 1969): 275–94.

———. "Joseph Knight's Recollection of Early Mormon History." *BYU Studies* 17 (Autumn 1976): 29–39.

———. "Priceless Words and Fallible Memories: Joseph Smith as Seen in the Effort to Preserve His Discourses." *BYU Studies* 31 (Spring 1991): 19–40.

Kimball, James N. "More Words of Wisdom." *Sunstone* 10 (March 1985): 41.

Lambert, Neal E., and Richard H. Cracroft. "Literary Form and Historical Understanding: Joseph Smith's First Vision." *Journal of Mormon History* 7 (1980): 31–42.

McCue, Robert J. "Did the Word of Wisdom Become a Commandment in 1851?" *Dialogue: A Journal of Mormon Thought* 14 (Fall 1981): 66–77.

Matthews, Robert J. "Adam-ondi-Ahman." *BYU Studies* 13 (Autumn 1972): 27–35.

Paul, Robert E. "Joseph Smith and the Plurality of Worlds Idea." *Dialogue: A Journal of Mormon Thought* 19 (Summer 1986): 13–26.

Pratt, Parley P. "Correspondence of Parley P. Pratt, Jan. 21, 1843." *Millennial Star* 3 (April 1843): 206–8.

Quinn, D. Michael. "The Evolution of the Presiding Quorums of the Church." *Journal of Mormon History* 1 (1974): 21–38.

———. "Ezra Taft Benson and Mormon Political Conflicts." *Dialogue: A Journal of Mormon Thought* 26 (Summer 1993): 1–87.

———. "From Sacred Grove to Sacral Power Structure." *Dialogue: A Journal of Mormon Thought* 17 (Summer 1984): 9–34.

———. "The Mormon Succession Crisis of 1844." *BYU Studies* 16 (Winter 1976): 187–233.

———. "150 Years of Truth and Consequences about Mormon History." *Sunstone* 16 (February 1992): 12–14.

Richards, LeGrand. "A Chosen Vessel unto Me." *Instructor* 99 (December 1964): 466.

Russell, William Dean. "Defenders of the Faith: Varieties of RLDS Dissent." *Sunstone* 14 (June 1990): 14–19.

Shepherd, Gordon, and Gary Shepherd. "Mormonism in Secular Society: Changing Patterns in Official Ecclesiastical Rhetoric." *Review of Religious Research* 26 (September 1984): 28–42.

Smith, E. Gary. "The Office of Presiding Patriarch: The Primacy Problem." *Journal of Mormon History* 14 (1988): 35–47.

———. "The Patriarchal Crisis of 1845." *Dialogue: A Journal of Mormon Thought* 16 (Summer 1983): 24–35.

Smith, Eldred G. "What Is a Patriarchal Blessing?" *Instructor* (February 1962): 42–43.

Smith, Hyrum G. "Patriarchs and Patriarchal Blessings." *Improvement Era* 33 (May 1930): 465–66.

Smith, Joseph Fielding. "Presiding Patriarchs." *Improvement Era* 38 (April 1935): 216.

Smith, Timothy L. "The Book of Mormon in a Biblical Culture." *Journal of Mormon History* 7 (1980): 3–21.

Smith, William. "Communications [to] D. C. Smith, Plymouth, Dec. 1st, 1840." *Times and Seasons* 2 (December 15, 1840): 252–53.

———. "Minutes of a Conference Held at Walnut Grove, Knox Co., Ill., January 30th, 1841." *Times and Seasons* 2 (March 1, 1841): 338.

————. "Patriarchal." *Times and Seasons* 6 (May 15, 1845): 904.

Taylor, John. "From England." *Times and Seasons* 1 (June 1840): 121.

————. "Patriarchal." *Times and Seasons* 6 (June 1, 1845): 920–22.

Thompson, John E. "A Chronology of Danite Meetings in Adam-Ondi-Ahman, Missouri, July to September 1838." *Restoration* 4 (January 1985): 11–14.

Underwood, Grant R. "Millenarianism and the Early Mormon Mind." *Journal of Mormon History* 9 (1982): 41–51.

Wallis, James H. "Death of Patriarch Hyrum G. Smith." *Millennial Star* 94 (March 17, 1932): 168–69.

Weber, Max. "Some Consequences of Bureaucratization." In *Sociological Theory: A Book of Readings,* edited by Lewis A. Coser and Bernard Rosenberg. New York: Macmillan, 1957.

Widtsoe, John A. "What Is the Meaning of Patriarchal Blessings?" *Improvement Era* 45 (January 1942): 33, 61.

Wood, Gordon S. "Evangelical America and Early Mormonism." *New York History* 61 (October 1980): 359–86.

Young, Brigham. Letter to William Smith, September 28, 1844. In *The Prophet* (newspaper published in New York by the Church of Jesus Christ of Latter-day Saints), November 9, 1844, Newspaper Collection, New York Public Library.

Theses, Dissertations, and Unpublished Papers

Bachman, Danel W. "Mormon Plural Marriages before the Death of Joseph Smith." M.A. thesis, Purdue University, 1975.

Bates, Irene M. "Transformation of Charisma in the Mormon Church: A History of the Office of Presiding Patriarch, 1833–1979." Ph.D. diss., University of California, Los Angeles, 1991.

Ehat, Andrew F. "Joseph Smith's Introduction of Temple Ordinances and the 1844 Mormon Succession Question." M.A. thesis, Brigham Young University, 1982.

Maxwell, Margaret F. "They Also Served: Women and the Building of the Kingdom in Kirtland." Paper presented at the Mormon History Association annual meeting, Salt Lake City, May 2, 1986.

Morley, Robert Henrie. "The Life and Contributions of Isaac Morley." M.A. thesis, Brigham Young University, 1965.

Mouritsen, Dale C. "A Symbol of New Directions: George Franklin Richards and the Mormon Church, 1861–1950." Ph.D. diss., Brigham Young University, 1982.

Mouritsen, Glen. "The Office of Associate President of the Church of Jesus Christ of Latter-day Saints." M.A. thesis, Brigham Young University, 1972.

Ouellette, Richard D. "Authority and Ecclesiology in Primitive Christianity and Mormonism." Paper presented at the Sunstone Theological Symposium, Salt Lake City, August 24, 1990.

Peterson, Paul H. "An Historical Analysis of the Word of Wisdom." M.A. thesis, Brigham Young University, 1972.

Prince, Gregory A. "The Development of LDS Priesthood Authority and Organization, 1823–1844." Paper presented at the Mormon History Association annual meeting, St. George, Utah, May 3, 1992.

Quinn, D. Michael. "Comment on Patriarch Papers." Response to papers presented by E. Gary Smith and Irene M. Bates at the Mormon History Association annual meeting, Salt Lake City, May 2, 1986.

———. "The Mormon Hierarchy, 1832–1932: An American Elite." Ph.D. diss., Yale University, 1976.

Rudd, Calvin. "William Smith, Brother of the Prophet Joseph Smith." M.A. thesis, Brigham Young University, 1973.

Shipps, Jan. "The Prophet, His Mother, and Early Mormonism: Mother Smith's History as a Passageway to Understanding." Paper presented at the Mormon History Association annual meeting, Logan, Utah, May 6, 1979.

Skinner, Earnest M. "Joseph Smith, Sr., First Patriarch to the Church." M.S. thesis, Brigham Young University, 1958.

Smith, E. Gary. "Heber J. Grant and the Office of Presiding Patriarch: A Decade of Uncertainty, 1932–1942." Paper presented at the Mormon History Association annual meeting, Laie, Oahu, Hawaii, June 14, 1990.

Underwood, Grant R. "The Millenarian World of Early Mormonism." Ph.D. diss., University of California, Los Angeles, 1988.

Interviews

Boyer, Selvoy J. Conversations with E. Gary Smith. Winter 1958.

Secretary of Joseph F. Smith II. Interview by E. Gary Smith. October 5, 1991.

Smith, Eldred G. Unless a specific date is given in the notes, conversations between Eldred G. Smith and his son E. Gary Smith were of an informal and ongoing nature, flowing naturally from the relationship between the two, the exact dates of which cannot now be determined with accuracy.

Smith, Ralph. Interview by E. Gary Smith. June 17, 1981.

Smith, Ruth. Interview by E. Gary Smith. April 4, 1981.

Smith, Samuel S. Telephone conversation with E. Gary Smith. August 8, 1980.

Index

IRENE M. BATES received a Ph.D. in history from UCLA. She died in 2015.

E. GARY SMITH is the son of the last Presiding Patriarch and is retired after being senior partner at Smith & Smith in Santa Ana, California.

The University of Illinois Press
is a founding member of the
Association of American University Presses.

University of Illinois Press
1325 South Oak Street   Champaign, IL 61820-6903
www.press.uillinois.edu